QUANTITATIVE EASING

Finance Matters

Series Editors: Kathryn Lavelle, *Case Western Reserve University, Cleveland, Ohio* and Timothy J. Sinclair, *University of Warwick*

This series of books provides advanced introductions to the processes, relationships and institutions that make up the global financial system. Suitable for upper-level undergraduate and taught graduate courses in financial economics and the political economy of finance and banking, the series explores all aspects of the workings of the financial markets within the context of the broader global economy.

Published

Quantitative Easing
Jonathan Ashworth

QUANTITATIVE EASING
The Great Central Bank Experiment

JONATHAN ASHWORTH

agenda
publishing

First published in 2020 by Agenda Publishing

Agenda Publishing Limited
The Core
Bath Lane
Newcastle Helix
Newcastle upon Tyne
NE4 5TF
www.agendapub.com

ISBN 978-1-78821-221-2 (hardcover)
ISBN 978-1-78821-222-9 (paperback)

British Library Cataloguing-in-Publication Data
A catalogue record for this book is available from the British Library

Typeset by Newgen Publishing UK
Printed and bound in the UK by TJ International

CONTENTS

PREFACE

Amid impressive economic growth, rising asset prices and generally short and mild recessions in the decades before the Great Financial Crisis (GFC) of 2008–09, central banks began to believe that they had largely managed to tame the business cycle. However, the onset of the crisis firmly put paid to any such illusions. With the US and major western economies on the precipice of a repeat of the Great Depression, central bankers were forced to innovate rapidly and experiment with new policy tools in an attempt to stabilize collapsing financial markets and their economies. With little room to cut official interest rates further, the US Federal Reserve (Fed) and Bank of England (BoE) adopted a policy of quantitative easing (QE), which together with large government fiscal stimulus programmes, helped their economies avoid collapse and embark on economic recoveries. Over the following decade, QE and other unconventional monetary policies have become key parts of the toolkits of the major central banks as they have largely battled alone to stimulate their economies and raise inflation back to their target levels.

Before the crisis, few economists would have expected to see such momentous changes in monetary policy-making over their careers, if ever. Indeed, any contemporary economist recommending the use of QE in the western economies would have been considered dangerous by the rest of the profession given that some of its most notable recent uses in Weimar Germany and Zimbabwe had resulted in economic calamity amid runaway inflation. This explains why its introduction was greeted by newspaper cartoons showing central bankers distributing large amounts of banknotes to the general public either by throwing them into the air or shovelling them into sacks! At the same time, it was also generally thought that it was not technically possible for either official short-term or longer-term market interest rates to move into negative territory, owing to the ability of the general public and investors to switch into banknotes. At the time of writing, however, a not insignificant portion of developed market sovereign bonds do indeed have negative interest rates!

A key aim of this book is to provide a complement to the existing textbooks on monetary economics with a comprehensive analysis of the remarkable developments in unconventional monetary policy over the past decade, focusing on the key policy of QE. To set up the context for the events that follow, I begin, however, with an overview of historical developments in conventional monetary policy for those less well-versed in monetary economics and in order to help readers develop a framework to think about how monetary policy-making could change again in the future given prevailing economic conditions.

When discussing the story of and assessing QE, I have not confined myself to the domain of monetary economics, as its footprint has extended far beyond into a number of other important areas of the discipline. The political issues raised by the use of QE have been particularly salient and challenging. The Fed received significant domestic criticism when enacting later rounds of QE, while the European Central Bank (ECB) has consistently faced vociferous criticism and opposition to its actions from Germany and to a lesser extent other northern European countries. Moreover, a general ex-post criticism of QE has been that it has fuelled a further a rise in inequality and some have even suggested that it contributed to a rise in populism. On the international front, countries adopting QE have been accused of "beggar thy neighbour" policies through covertly depreciating their currencies. The US in particular has faced fierce criticism from emerging economies about its undesirable spillovers, some of which reflect long-running criticisms of the US dominated international monetary system. Meanwhile, among other things, I will also discuss why initial fears of soaring inflation have not come to pass and what this could potentially mean for the independence of central banks in the future and/or their willingness to try ever more experimental policies if another severe downturn were to occur.

The main conclusion of the book is that the initial rounds of QE during the GFC proved very powerful, helping to avert another Great Depression and contributing significantly to economic recoveries. However, subsequent rounds of QE, once the crisis had passed, while providing a positive boost for growth and financial markets, suffered from diminishing returns and were not able to drive robust economic recoveries and return inflation back to central bank targets. Hence, QE has not proved quite as powerful a tool as many may have thought. At the same time, while the most-feared negative externalities of QE have not transpired, the negative side effects have probably increased as interest rates have been pushed ever lower and into negative territory in some countries. At the time of writing, central banks do not have a great deal of scope to support their economies in the next downturn via QE and their other conventional and unconventional policies, particularly the Bank of Japan (BoJ) and the ECB. Fiscal policy will have to play a much more prominent role in helping economies to escape from the next major recession.

The book is set out as follows. Chapter 1 provides a summary of the major changes in monetary policy-making since the end of the Bretton Woods system of quasi-fixed exchange rates, culminating in the adoption of central bank independence and inflation targeting in the decades following the Great Inflation of the 1970s. It also provides an overview of the key elements of contemporary monetary policy-making by central banks, including the decision-making process, communication and the transmission mechanism of monetary policy changes. Chapter 2 discusses the major trend of sharply falling official central bank interest rates during the Great Moderation and several key monetary policy events such as the onset of the Zero-Lower Bound (ZLB) on Japanese interest rates, the adoption of QE by the BoJ in 2001 and the reduction of US interest rates to a then record low of just 1 per cent in 2003.

Chapter 3 gives a brief overview of the immediate build up to and events following the GFC, including the broad-based policy response from the leading economies. It then provides a timeline and discusses the use of QE by the major central banks. The Fed and BoE were the first movers during the crisis and then again over subsequent years as their recoveries began to lose steam as fiscal easing by their governments was replaced by significant fiscal tightening amid concerns about soaring levels of government debt. Japan had been less at the epicentre of the GFC and did not begin major asset purchases until the launch of its quantitative and qualitative easing (QQE) programme in 2013, which was an important part of new Prime Minister Abe's "Abenomics programme" to revitalize the Japanese economy and end decades of pernicious deflation. In the euro area, the ECB enacted major lending programmes during the crisis and some small-scale asset purchase programmes during the euro area sovereign debt crisis, which it ultimately brought to an end with the announcement of a programme to purchase government bonds in unlimited amounts, which it never actually had to enact. It finally embarked on large-scale QE in early 2015 as its recovery weakened and fears of deflation began to increase.

Chapter 4 discusses the main channels through which QE was expected to work when it was first announced, including supporting confidence, policy signalling, portfolio rebalancing, improving market functioning and boosting the money supply, and how the QE carried out by the Fed and BoE differed in important ways to that first carried out by Japan in its initial experiment with QE between 2001 and 2006. It also highlights some other channels of QE that have received increased prominence over time such as exchange rates, public finances and inflation expectations and discusses how QE may have differing impacts across countries and, importantly, why it is likely to experience diminishing returns over time.

Chapter 5 summarizes the main methods used in the academic literature to measure and assess the impact of QE and provides a detailed examination of its use by the Fed, BoE, BoJ and ECB. The initial rounds of QE had significant positive impacts on financial markets and economic activity by further reducing various longer-term interest rates, reducing elevated tail risks, improving liquidity in dysfunctional financial markets and boosting the confidence of investors and the general public. However, subsequent rounds of QE once the crisis had passed, while providing a positive boost for financial markets and growth, appeared to suffer from diminishing returns and were not able to drive strong economic recoveries and return inflation back to central bank targets. Japan's monetary experiment in particular, where the BoJ now owns almost half of all outstanding government bonds, appears to highlight the fact that despite extraordinary easing, it is not always easy for a central bank to create inflationary expectations and inflation, casting doubts on the views of some leading academics who previously suggested central banks could always create sufficient inflation.

Chapter 6 explores the international aspect of QE, amid significant criticism about its spillover effects on other countries. In its early programmes the Fed was accused of seeking a competitive advantage through covert currency depreciation and its QE2 and QE3 programmes were criticized for, among other things, fuelling massive capital flows into emerging markets. With a number of emerging economies already growing very strongly at this point, these latter QE programmes may have been on balance negative for these countries. However, given the huge benefits provided to the US and global economies and financial markets from the Fed's QE1 programme, US QE was still on balance likely to have been a net positive for the developing world. Meanwhile, amid diverging monetary policies over recent years as the Fed has unwound its post-crisis monetary easing, the BoJ and ECB have come under criticism from US President Trump, who suggested they were engaging in currency depreciation amid their ongoing QE programmes.

At different times, QE has received significant criticism on various fronts amid fears of its probable consequences. This is the subject of Chapter 7. The primary fear when first enacted – that it would fuel runaway inflation – has clearly not materialized, with insufficient inflation and fears of disinflation actually being a key post-crisis theme. Another major fear was that its ongoing use would create major financial stability risks, in a similar way as easy money had prior to the GFC. It is not clear at this stage that QE and other unconventional policies have created major asset price bubbles and significant risks to financial stability, although admittedly the jury is still out. Despite the far greater focus on financial stability by policy-makers since the crisis, the unexpected impact of the US housing slowdown on the global financial system highlights how significant and hard to identify vulnerabilities can develop. It may not be until the next global slowdown that any such vulnerabilities fully emerge. A major ex-post criticism of the latter QE programmes has been that they have fuelled large rises in inequality. Central banks have typically tried to play this down, although they could have been better served acknowledging some of these negative side-effects, as it may have placed greater onus on governments to be more supportive with fiscal and other policies. Meanwhile, amid the increased dissatisfaction and increasing politicization of central banks during the period of QE and other unconventional policies, debates have increased about whether they should remain independent in the future. With the current problem being too-low inflation, some leading economists have suggested that the initial arguments in favour of independence have been turned on their head.

Chapter 8 examines the process of exiting QE and the tools available for central banks to counter the next economic downturn. The Fed is the only central bank to have unwound its asset purchases due to QE and, despite some prior fears, the process did not have much of a negative impact on the economy or financial markets. Meanwhile, with economic recoveries in the developed economies in train for quite a significant period now, the next global downturn may not be too far away. Unfortunately, the major central banks no longer have much ammunition, either conventional or unconventional, with which to deal with it. Governments will probably have to step up to the plate with significant fiscal stimulus. But even then, there could be some limitations amid government debt around record levels as a share of peacetime GDP and deficits already high in some countries. In particular, political economy constraints against fiscal easing could increase again as was the case after the crisis. If the existing toolkit of monetary policies together with the available fiscal stimulus are unable to dig economies out of a future major downturn, central banks will likely come under significant pressure to enact increasingly aggressive and experimental policies such as the outright monetary financing of government deficits to fund tax cuts or increased government spending.

All in all, after the unprecedented changes in central banking and monetary policy over the past ten years, it seems likely that the next decade could be similarly eventful. I sincerely hope you enjoy the book and find it useful.

Acknowledgements

I owe great thanks to my friend and former colleague Charles Goodhart for his very helpful comments and suggestions on the book and for his kind contribution of the foreword. I similarly wish to thank my former colleagues Bill O'Neill and Michael Dicks and the two anonymous referees for their valuable comments and suggestions. Lastly, I would like to thank my publisher Alison Howson for her useful advice throughout the process of writing the book.

ABBREVIATIONS

%Y	percentage change year-on-year
AfD	Alternative für Deutschland
ARM	adjustable-rate mortgage
BoE	Bank of England
BoJ	Bank of Japan
bps	basis points
CBPP	Covered Bond Purchase Programme
CPI	Consumer Price Index
BIS	Bank for International Settlements
BLS	Bureau of Labour Statistics
DM	German Deutschmark
DSGE	dynamic stochastic general equilibrium
ECB	European Central Bank
ECJ	European Court of Justice
EMU	Economic and Monetary Union
ETFs	exchange trade funds
EU	European Union
FCIs	Financial Conditions Indices
Fed	Federal Reserve
FFR	federal funds rate
FOMC	Federal Open Market Committee
GDP	Gross Domestic Product
GFC	Great Financial Crisis
GSEs	government sponsored enterprises
JGBs	Japanese government bonds
LOLR	lender of last resort
LSAPs	large-scale asset purchases
LTRO	longer-term refinancing operation
MBS	mortgage-backed securities
MEP	maturity extension programme
MMT	Modern Monetary Theory

MRO	main refinancing operation
NAIRU	non-accelerating inflation rate of unemployment
OECD	Organization for Economic Cooperation and Development
OMT	Outright Monetary Transactions
PBoC	People's Bank of China
pp	percentage points
QE	quantitative easing
QQE	quantitative and qualitative easing
QT	quantitative tightening
RBNZ	Reserve Bank of New Zealand
REITs	real estate investment trusts
SMP	Securities Markets Programme
TARP	Troubled Asset Relief Program
TLTRO	targeted longer-term refinancing operation
UOCR	uncollateralized overnight call rate
VARs	vector autoregressive models
ZIRP	zero interest rate policy
ZLB	zero-lower bound

FOREWORD

C. A. E. Goodhart

A thorough and comprehensive analysis of the history and effects of quantitative easing (QE), a policy introduced by many of the world's leading central banks, notably the Fed, Bank of Japan, European Central Bank, and the Bank of England, in the aftermath of the Great Financial Crisis (GFC), 2007–09, is most welcome. This is exactly what my friend and colleague, Jonathan Ashworth, has now provided in this book. We worked together in the economic research section of Morgan Stanley in London for over half a decade and have jointly authored several published papers. Perhaps he will forgive me if I start by setting out some of my own idiosyncratic thoughts on our recent experience with QE.

Prior to the sluggish recovery from the GFC, the idea that central banks might struggle to raise inflation would have been laughed out of court, regarded as hare-brained. Consider the following syllogism:

> *Premise 1* Inflation is always, and everywhere, a monetary phenomenon;
>
> *Premise 2* The central bank can create (high-powered) money;
>
> *Conclusion* The central bank can raise inflation whenever it wants to do so.

In the exercise of QE the central banks involved did expand their assets and monetary liabilities by a large multiple of their initial starting point, often four or five times, in one case returning the central bank to its earlier nineteenth-century status as the largest bank in the country, i.e. in the UK. Moreover, with the non-banks' demand for currency growing slowly (another area of analysis where Jonathan and I have collaborated), the bulk of this ended up in commercial banks' deposits at the central bank, which at one point in the United States expanded by over 100 times their initial value.

So what went wrong? While a few braver souls are beginning to query Premise 1 above, the main blame is usually put on the inability of the central bank to guarantee a commensurate expansion of the broader money supply by raising the monetary base. The money multiplier has collapsed. The commercial banks appear to be in a liquidity trap, where they cannot expand their assets, either because the demand for (profitable) lending is not there, and/or they do not want to buy securities, since the meagre return (at low, or negative, interest rates and a flat yield curve) is insufficient to match the added risk and regulatory requirements. The balance between these various explanations remains underexplored, since most macroeconomic analysis ignores financial intermediation altogether, focusing solely on the direct links between central bank control/influence on interest rates and the real economy.

Another feature of much mainstream macroeconomic analysis is that it ignores, or assumes away, the possibility of default. Absent default, no one needs liquidity; indeed, the concept of liquidity (and money) then becomes meaningless. What the GFC did was to raise the spectre of default into a horrifying present menace and set off a panic scramble for liquidity, for cash. It was just this massive extra demand for liquidity that QE satisfied (alongside US dollar swaps from the Fed and the use of TARP funds to recapitalize US banks), and saved the day.

But once this surge in demand for liquidity had been satiated, and confidence returned to financial markets, the bulk of the beneficial work of QE was done. In my view, although read this book for an extended and much more balanced view, the direct effect on the real economy via interest rates, either actual or expected, and on portfolio balance, was of second-order importance. QE2, QE3 and QE Infinity are relatively toothless.

But my own idiosyncratic prejudices should indicate that the analysis of QE's effects on our economies remains controversial and important. You will get a much fuller and more rounded assessment of QE by reading on. Enjoy!

1
MONETARY POLICY-MAKING SINCE THE END OF BRETTON WOODS

The Bretton Woods system of quasi-fixed exchange rates that had been in place for much of the period since the end of the Second World War finally came to an end in early 1973. Under Bretton Woods, the value of the US dollar (USD) had been fixed against gold while other currencies such as the British Pound (GBP), German Deutschmark (DM), etc. were pegged against the USD, with only periodic adjustments permitted in order to help countries correct deficits in their balance of payments. Its demise led to the major industrialized countries allowing their currencies to float freely on global financial markets.[1] The move from fixed to flexible exchange rates allowed national policy-makers to shift from having to use economic policy to *help* maintain the economy's external balance (the balance of payments and the exchange rate peg),[2] to a *primary* focus on using it to better achieve the economy's internal balance (stimulating/ dampening aggregate demand, achieving full employment, etc.).[3]

The main tool used by policy-makers to manage aggregate demand and control inflation since the end of Bretton Woods has been monetary policy, particularly official short-term interest rates. This primarily reflects the fact that changes in interest rates are much easier to enact and typically impact the economy much faster than fiscal policy. Indeed, for obvious electoral reasons politicians are typically averse to raising taxes or cutting government spending to slow growth, while to avoid wasteful spending or what are commonly referred to as "white elephant" projects, it can often take considerable time to plan and start new infrastructure projects when activity needs stimulating. Tax cuts have remained a favourite recession fighting tool in the US, although a number of economists have questioned their effectiveness, suggesting that they are more likely to be saved (Rivlin 2015).[4] Meanwhile, countries where the power to enact fiscal stimulus does not lie solely with the executive branch of government, such as the US, may suffer resistance to and/or delays in passing timely legislation.

For much of the second half of the twentieth century, most central banks did not always have significant leeway to set monetary policy independently of their governments, often facing pressure to maintain interest rates lower than they may deem optimal to control inflation in order to support growth and/or limit the government's borrowing costs. Among the major central banks, only the German Bundesbank had a truly independent monetary policy (despite the exchange rate constraints until the end of Bretton Woods), which had been enshrined in law in 1957 (Issing 2005, 2018). The 1951 Fed-Treasury Accord had re-established a degree of independence for the US Federal Reserve (Fed), but its Chairmen still faced significant pressure from Presidents in the 1960s and 1970s to be more accommodating with policy (Thoma 2017). In the UK, the final decision on interest rates was made by the government with the Bank of England (BoE) acting in an advisory capacity (Goodhart 2010a). Following on from the work of Phillips (1958),[5] policy was typically set on the assumption of a downwards sloping "Phillips Curve" relationship, which posited a long-run inverse relationship between the unemployment rate and wage inflation (Jevcak 2014); a lower unemployment rate leads to rising wages and consequently higher inflation. Policy-makers typically utilized this relationship to decide on an acceptable trade-off in terms of the amount of additional inflation they were willing to tolerate in order to boost output and employment by a certain amount (Samuelson & Solow 1960).

A new framework for monetary policy: central bank independence and inflation targeting

The first decade after the end of Bretton Woods saw soaring inflation across the major economies in what is commonly referred to as the "Great Inflation" (see Figure 1.1). Inflation rose from under 4 per cent in the US in January 1973 to over 13 per cent by the end of the decade, with an eventual peak of almost 15 per cent in March 1980. In the UK, inflation rose from around 8 per cent in January 1973 and peaked at almost 27 per cent in August 1975. German inflation also rose, but by much less than elsewhere, rising from 6.3 per cent in January 1973 to a peak of almost 8 per cent in December 1973. Central banks attempted to tighten monetary policy in order to contain the rising inflationary pressures, which resulted in soaring official nominal interest rates. The US effective federal funds rate (FFR) and the BoE's Bank rate rose from 5.9 and 8.75 per cent in January 1973 before ultimately peaking at almost 20 per cent in the early 1980s. Official nominal interest rates peaked at a much lower level of almost 10 per cent in Germany, although given much lower inflation, German *real* interest rates were materially higher than in the US for much of the period[6] (European Central Bank (ECB) 2010) (see Figure 1.4).

The Great Inflation led to a breakdown in belief in the Phillips Curve as both inflation and unemployment had moved sharply higher in most countries in what was commonly dubbed "stagflation". It also fuelled significant debate and

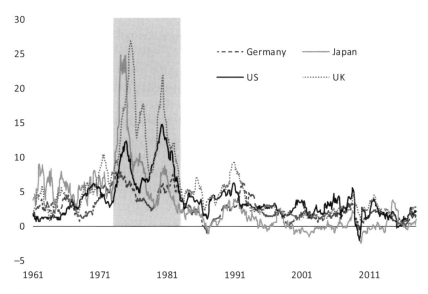

Figure 1.1. Developed market inflation (%Y)
Source: IMF.

research into why the major central banks, with the exception of Germany, were either unable or unwilling to keep inflationary pressures in check (Issing 2018). An in-depth discussion of the Great Inflation is beyond the scope of this book. For a superb exposition, see ECB (2010), where the authors critique conventional wisdom that "bad luck" amid the massive oil price shocks in 1973 and 1979 was the *predominant* driver. They stress instead the importance of policy mistakes in countries such as the US and highlight the far superior inflation performances in countries such as Germany and Switzerland, where the central banks placed a much greater emphasis on controlling inflation rather than supporting output. They highlight the introduction of monetary targets by the German Bundesbank as helping to anchor price and wage-setting expectations in the second half of the 1970s in contrast to most other countries, which lacked credible monetary anchors after the end of Bretton Woods. Jordan (2017) suggests the high degree of independence from political interference seems to have played an important role in the superior performance of the Bundesbank and the Swiss National Bank.[7]

The relative success of the independent German Bundesbank in containing inflation during the 1970s, important academic work and the success of the independently minded Fed Chairman Paul Volcker in culling US inflation in the early 1980s helped shift the institutional debate in favour of greater independence for central banks in setting monetary policy.[8]

Seminal academic work by Kydland and Prescott (1977) explored the time inconsistency problem in economic policy-making. They highlighted that because private sector agents anticipate the incentive of politicians to try and unexpectedly generate short-term inflation in order to reduce unemployment, they would always factor this into their wage- and price-setting behaviour. As a result, inflation would consequently be higher than desired without any resultant reduction in unemployment. Therefore, rather than setting monetary policy in such a discretionary manner they suggested that it is optimal for policy-makers to compel themselves by policy rules[9] or commitments to maintain low inflation in the beginning, which by tempering price and wage setting would help them in their task. Barro and Gordon (1983) and Rogoff (1985) expanded on this, with the former suggesting that it is possible that the reputation or credibility of policy-makers (or the potential loss of it) could support or possibly substitute for formal policy rules, while the latter suggested that countries could benefit from choosing an independent central banker that is more inflation averse than the society as a whole given the favourable impact this would have on the private sector's inflation expectations (although not one so inflation averse that negative supply shocks are primarily absorbed by lower employment). Moreover, important empirical work showed that greater independence for central banks resulted in lower inflation without any resultant reduction of output (Grilli *et al.* 1991 and Alesina & Summers 1993).[10]

Meanwhile, the appointment of Paul Volcker as the new Fed Chairman in August 1979 fuelled a major shift to more restrictive monetary policy in an attempt to tame runaway inflation. Bernanke (2005a) cites US President Jimmy Carter's appointment of the renowned "inflation hawk" Volcker as the inspiration for Rogoff's work on credibility. Under Volcker, the Fed placed greater emphasis on restraining money supply growth from October 1979. This fuelled soaring interest rates with the effective FFR peaking at over 19 per cent during 1981 (see Figure 1.2), pushing the US economy into a short recession in January 1980 and then a much deeper and longer recession from July 1981. But it ultimately resulted in inflation falling back under 4 per cent by the end of 1982 from over 12 per cent in October 1979 (Walsh 2004). Thoma (2017) suggests that "Volcker's success in bringing down the inflation rate cemented the idea that an independent Fed could do what elected officials could not. Thereafter, it became conventional wisdom that the Fed should run free". A number of other countries targeted the growth in their money supply as a means to control inflation in the 1970s and 1980s;[11] however, this practice fell out of favour amid the short-term instability of relationships between monetary growth, nominal incomes and inflation (Goodhart 2010a).

New Zealand was the source of the next major innovation in monetary policy-making. Goodhart and Lastra (2018) note that the introduction by the government in 1989 of a framework combining operational independence and an inflation target for the Reserve Bank of New Zealand (RBNZ) rapidly caught on over the next few years as best practice for central banks around the world. This (and close alternatives) continues to remain the framework used by most of

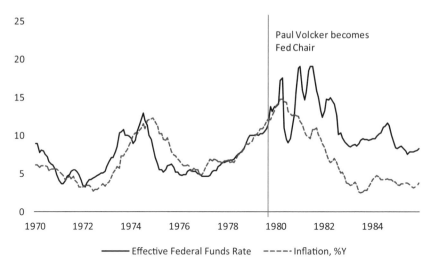

Figure 1.2. US Inflation and Effective Federal Funds Rate, %
Source: Board of Governors of the Federal Reserve System, IMF, Federal Reserve Bank of St. Louis (FRED).

the world's central banks. *Operational* independence (also referred to as instrument independence by Debelle & Fisher 1994) means that central banks typically have significant flexibility to choose which tools they want to use and can decide on the magnitude of any changes in the settings of those tools in order to hit the goal or objective set by their governments. In addition, their room for manoeuvre is not constrained by the compulsion to finance government borrowing (Balls *et al.* 2018). Prior to the Great Financial Crisis (GFC) they would typically decide by what amount to change interest rates (for example, raise/lower interest rates by 25 basis points (bps); a quarter of a percentage point), but post the GFC their toolkits have also included QE and forward guidance.

Most major central banks do not have *political* independence, however, which Balls *et al.* (2018) define as "the absence of the possibility for politicians to influence central bank goals or personnel". Indeed, Goodhart and Lastra (2018) stress the continued ability of governments to redesign existing monetary arrangements (except the ECB) including changing central bank mandates/targets, revoking independence, etc. and politicians' control of top appointments where a President/Prime Minister could purposefully choose a Chair/Governor whom it is widely known favours very easy monetary policy. For example, in the US the Fed's mandate or goal is set by the Congress and the Fed Chair, Vice Chairs and Governors are chosen by the President and confirmed by the Senate.[12] A notable recent example of significant political influence being exerted over an operationally independent central bank is Japan (see Chapter 3). Most studies find that, in developed economies, there is a negative statistically significant relationship between the degree of operational independence of central banks and inflation, but no relationship between measures of political independence and inflation (Debelle & Fisher 1994; De Haan & Kooi 1997; Balls *et al.* 2018).

Most countries have now adopted inflation targets. Of the major developed central banks, the Fed does not have an explicit inflation target as its primary goal; it has instead a "dual mandate" to achieve both maximum employment and stable prices. In 2012, it announced that an inflation rate of 2 per cent is most consistent over the long-run with the price stability part of its mandate. In Europe, the ECB has set interest rates independently since the launch of the euro in 1999 with its primary objective being to maintain price stability, which it clarified in 2003 as meaning inflation at "below, but close to, 2% over the medium-term". In the UK, the BoE was given operational independence from the government in 1997 and has a 2 per cent inflation target as its main remit, while the Bank of Japan (BoJ) was given operational independence in 1998 with price stability as its main objective, but it did not adopt an explicit inflation target of 2 per cent until 2013.[13] Krugman (2014) suggests the choice of 2 per cent as the inflation target by most central banks was not the result of a particularly scientific process. It was generally thought of as being low enough so that inflation was not a source of inefficiency and distortions in economic decision-making, but far enough away from zero to reduce the risk of falling into deflation and also allowing real interest rates to remain negative in the case where nominal interest rates had reached the zero-lower bound (ZLB).[14]

An inflation target acts as a clear and transparent goal or objective for policy-makers and helps provide a guide to and anchor for the inflation expectations of investors, the private sector in its wage and price setting and the broader general public. Bernanke and Mishkin (1997: 106) highlight its importance:

> Arguably, many of the costs of inflation arise from its uncertainty or variability more than from its level. Uncertain inflation complicates long-term saving and investment decisions, exacerbates relative price volatility, and increases the riskiness of nominal financial and wage contracts. Uncertainty about central bank intentions may also induce volatility in financial markets.

Despite the greater focus on inflation, central banks had not become "inflation nutters"

The primary focus on inflation for most central banks represented a shift from the greater focus on employment in the 1970s, although this does not mean that they must aim for inflation to be at target at all times with little regard for the consequences for economic growth and the labour market. Indeed, most goals or mandates stipulate that central banks must achieve their inflation targets over a medium-term time horizon of around two or three years. As former BoE Governor Mervyn King suggested, inflation targeting did not mean central bankers had to become "inflation nutters"; they had adopted a policy of "flexible inflation targeting" (King 1997). The benefits of this approach have been evident over recent decades, where central bankers have been able to "overlook" the short-term negative impact of oil price shocks. This typically meant that, provided various measures of inflation expectations did not show signs of becoming unanchored from inflation targets, central bankers would temporarily tolerate above target inflation and allow it to gradually fall back to its target over the medium-term forecast horizon. This eschewed the need to tighten monetary policy at a time when higher than expected inflation was already weighing on growth. That said, as I will discuss in Chapter 8, some of the drawbacks of the approach have become evident in recent years as persistent below target inflation raises the risk of inflation expectations becoming unanchored or permanently anchored below central bank targets (Clarida 2019).

Thus far, I have discussed the institutional evolution that led to the current best practice of operationally independent central banks with inflation targets. In the remainder of the chapter, I highlight and discuss the main features of contemporary monetary policy-making such as the decision-making process, communication, forecasting, the monetary policy transmission mechanism and methods to gauge the stance of monetary policy. This should provide a helpful foundation for our discussion of QE.

The monetary policy decision-making process and central bank communication

The greater transparency provided by inflation targeting also means that independent central banks are better able to be held accountable by politicians, investors and the general public for their decisions and performance (Debelle 2017), which is important given that they are not democratically elected but their policies can have major economic consequences. As Draghi (2018) notes:

> This framework offered the public a guarantee that independent central banks would not exercise power arbitrarily. Their discretion was limited to *how* they formulated monetary policy. They had no discretion over *whether* to pursue their goals, and *what* goal they had to achieve.[15]

Monetary policy decisions at the major central banks are made by committees. For example, the Federal Open Market Committee (FOMC), which sets monetary policy in the US, has twelve members, which includes seven members of the Washington DC-based Board of Governors of the Fed System (including the Chair and the Vice-Chair) and on a rotational basis five Presidents of the twelve regional Fed banks. The ECB's Governing Council consists of six Executive Board members based in Frankfurt and the Governors of the central banks of the nineteen countries in the euro area (although countries rotate in terms of voting). The BoE's Monetary Policy Committee has nine members based in London, of which four are appointed from outside the bank in order to reduce the risk of groupthink in decision-making. The committees typically have around eight policy meetings per year and in the event of major crises, emergency meetings are often called. Changes in monetary policy at the Fed, ECB, BoJ and BoE simply require a majority of the committee to be in favour and decisions can either be split or unanimous.

The volume, breadth and timeliness of information released by central banks on their decisions and thinking has increased significantly over recent decades. As then Fed Vice Chair Janet Yellen (2012a: 3) previously noted:

> In 1977, when I started my first job at the Federal Reserve Board as a staff economist in the Division of International Finance, it was an article of faith in central banking that secrecy about monetary policy decisions was the best policy: Central banks, as a rule, did not discuss these decisions, let alone their future policy intentions.

In contrast, monetary policy decisions are now clearly communicated at the end of the scheduled meetings and are typically accompanied by a summary statement which provides more detail on the decision such as the breakdown of the vote and a summary of the committee's view on the current economic backdrop and outlook and what that may mean for future policy in relation to the committee's main objectives. Some central banks also have a press conference after every meeting. The minutes of the meetings are typically published several weeks later and provide more colour on the decisions and the deliberations behind them. They often highlight key debates such as the amount of spare capacity in the economy, and can often give a sense about the likely trajectory for future policy and the imminence of any changes. Detailed transcripts of the meetings are also provided with a lag of a number of years. Central bank members also regularly communicate by speeches and through testimony to their national parliaments. For example, the US Fed Chair testifies through the Semi-Annual Monetary Policy Report to Congress.[16]

Each quarter, a pre-determined specific monthly meeting takes on additional importance as this is where central banks carry out a major update of their thinking and publish new forecasts for key variables such as real gross domestic product (GDP) growth, inflation and the unemployment rate. Some also provide forecasts on the most likely path for official central bank interest rates, which can be the median estimate of the individual members' own forecasts or the best collective judgement of the committee as a whole. Central banks typically also highlight the distribution of risks around their main forecasts. When attempting to forecast key variables such as GDP and inflation, central banks typically utilize a wide mixture of inputs: forecasts based on large-scale macroeconomic models such as general equilibrium models[17] or dynamic stochastic general equilibrium models (DSGE) and from a number of smaller-scale econometric models; their own surveys of businesses and financial institutions such as the US Beige Book and the Fed's Senior Loan Officer Opinion Survey on Bank Lending Practices; various economic statistics that are published by the central bank or other government agencies such as the Bureau of Labour Statistics (BLS) and Census Bureau in the US (such as employment changes, retail sales, factory orders, etc.); external private sector economic, financial market and survey data; their own judgement. These key quarterly meetings or forecasting rounds are typically more likely to lead to a decision to change policy than other meetings.

The implementation of monetary policy changes

Once the decisions have been made to change the target for official short-term interest rates, they are implemented by the main financial market trading desks at the central banks via what are called "open market operations". In the US, the New York Fed's Trading Desk will adjust the supply of funds or reserve balances in the banking system so that the overnight FFR at which commercial banks can borrow from and lend to each other is equal to the target FFR set by the FOMC. Reserves balances are the funds that commercial banks keep overnight in their own bank accounts at the central bank. For each bank, the reserve balance typically consists of their *required* reserves (set by the central bank) and any *excess* reserves (Bernanke 2009c). Before the GFC, the latter were typically extremely small reflecting the Fed's chosen operating regime for controlling short-term interest rates (Powell 2019b). Banks with excess reserves (which were unremunerated) would lend them overnight to their peers who needed to borrow in order to have sufficient required reserves.

When a central bank wants to raise market interest rates, the trading desk will sell a certain amount of its holdings of government bonds to reduce the supply of reserve balances in the system and hence push up the cost of funds for commercial banks wanting to borrow reserves overnight. In contrast, it will purchase bonds and inject reserve balances into the system when wanting to reduce market interest rates for commercial banks seeking to borrow reserves overnight. In addition to the outright buying or selling of government bonds, trading desks also use repurchase operations or "repos" in order to temporarily inject or drain reserve balances from the system.[18] Note that the traditional process for controlling short-term interest rates and implementing changes in the monetary policy stance changed after the GFC and the onset of QE; I will discuss this in Chapters 3 and 8.

How the transmission mechanism of monetary policy works

Changes in official short-term central bank interest rates impact the economy in four main ways. First, via their influence on other types of market-based interest rates such as mortgage rates, auto loan rates, business and consumer loan rates, etc., which affect the borrowing, saving and spending decisions of private sector agents. Second, via their impact on the value of assets such as stocks and housing, which changes the wealth of the private sector. Third, by influencing expectations about the future. Fourth, via their impact on exchange rates, whose level and movement influence the exports, imports and trade balance of a country. Moreover, as Yellen (2012a) notes, given that many spending decisions such as the financing of a home or capital expenditure depend on longer-term interest rates, private sector expectations of the future path of monetary policy are as important, perhaps more so, than the actual interest rate today. The same is true for asset prices. Figure 1.3 is a flow diagram of the transmission mechanism of official interest rate changes. The economic impacts of a change in interest rates can be instantaneous via stockmarkets and exchange rates, although central banks typically estimate that it takes up to two years for the full impact to feed through. The sensitivity to changes in interest rates is not fixed over time, however. It should vary with the level of indebtedness in the economy.

The impact of interest rate changes can differ across countries. For example, changes in short-term interest rates can have a larger impact on the housing market in countries such as the UK, where mortgage rates are tied to or more closely follow official short-term central bank interest rates compared with the US, where mortgage rates are more closely tied to longer-term interest rates such as 30-year yields. Likewise, the exchange rate impact of a US interest rate change will have less of a domestic economic impact given that the US is a largely closed economy compared say with a very small, open economy such as Sweden. Meanwhile, changes in US interest rates will typically have a much larger impact on global financial markets such as bond markets, stockmarkets, currency markets, etc. than those of other countries. This is because the US is the largest global economy when measured at market exchange rates and the USD is the global reserve currency amid the country's very broad and deep financial markets. Monetary policy changes by the ECB also have quite large global impacts and this has also increasingly become the case for the People's Bank of China (PBoC) in the post-GFC era, given that China is now the world's second largest economy.

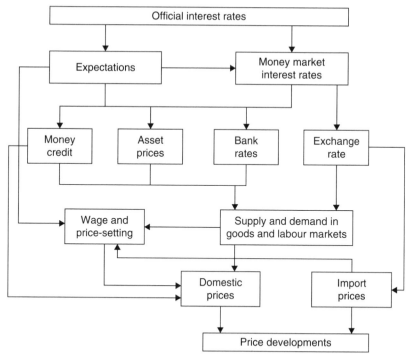

Figure 1.3. Flow diagram of interest rate effects
Source: European Central Bank www.ecb.europa.eu/mopo/intro/transmission/html/index. en.html. In addition to the diagram, there is also a very useful summary of the monetary policy transmission process.

Gauging the stance of monetary policy

As highlighted, there are a number of channels through which monetary policy works and in general its impact will depend on how well the monetary transmission mechanism is working. In the aftermath of banking or financial crises, the monetary transmission mechanism can become severely impaired and the impact of even very large interest rate cuts can be extremely modest. In contrast, in periods of market euphoria and heightened risk-taking, the monetary transmission mechanism can become significantly more powerful as commercial banks and financial market investors greatly relax their lending standards. Being able to gauge with a fair degree of precision the tightness or easiness of the monetary policy stance is extremely important for policy-makers, so that they do not overtighten and throw the economy into recession when they are trying to moderate growth and reduce inflation or on the other hand provide insufficient stimulus when the economy is slowing or in recession. Fortunately, policy-makers have several measures or benchmarks which can help them attempt to gauge how easy or tight monetary policy is:

(i)   The real official short-term interest rate compared with its level historic-ally. This can be measured on an "ex-ante" or "ex post" basis. The ex ante real official interest rate equals the nominal official short-term interest rate minus expected inflation (usually over the next twelve months). The ex-post real official interest rate equals the nominal official short-term interest rate minus the current rate of inflation. These provide a rough approximation of how easy or tight the policy setting may be by historical standards. It is more important to look at real rather than nominal interest rates when gauging the stance of monetary policy, as the former is key for borrowing and lending decisions. For example, if the nominal interest rate on a one-year consumer loan is 6 per cent, the relative attractiveness to a borrower would be far greater if expected inflation was 5 per cent instead of 2 per cent, with the former consistent with an ex-ante real interest rate of just 1 per cent and the latter of 4 per cent. The ex-post real FFR in the US has averaged around 1.3 per cent since the 1960s (see Figure 1.4), 1.8 per cent if you exclude the period since the onset of the GFC in 2008.

(ii) The "natural rate of interest" or "equilibrium real rate of interest" or "neu-tral rate of interest" or sometimes referred to as R*. Davies (2016) defines it as "the real short-term interest rate that would pertain when the economy is at equilibrium, meaning that unemployment is at the natural rate and inflation is at the 2% target".[19] If the real official short-term interest rate (as discussed in (i)) equals its equilibrium real rate then monetary policy is neutral on this metric, being neither stimulatory nor contractionary. If it is below (above) the equilibrium real interest rate, then monetary policy is stimulatory (contractionary). An economy's equilibrium real rate of interest is driven by a number of factors including the economy's trend rate of real GDP growth (equal to trend productivity growth plus labour force growth) and the savings and investment preferences of the private sector and governments both domestically and at a global level (Rachel & Smith 2015). An increase in desired savings relative to desired investment will reduce the equilibrium real interest rate and vice versa. Major shifts in the equilibrium real rate of interest such as after a major financial crisis, may mean that simple historical comparisons of the real official short-term interest rate (as in (i)) provide a misleading picture of the overall stance of monetary policy. Unfortunately, the equilibrium real interest rate is not observable and, hence, economists attempt to estimate it using various econometric techniques. Holston *et al.* (2016) acknowledge the imprecision surrounding any such estimates, however.[20]

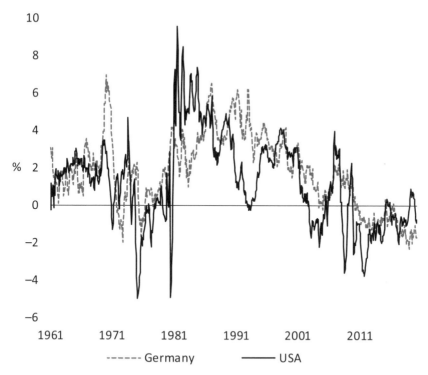

Figure 1.4. Real official central bank interest rates
Source: Board of Governors of the Federal Reserve System; OECD (2020), Inflation (CPI)
(indicator). doi: 10.1787/eee82e6e-en (accessed 1 April 2020); International Monetary Fund;
European Central Bank; Federal Reserve Bank of St. Louis (FRED). For Germany, ECB interest
rates since 1999.

(iii) Taylor Rule models, named after economist John Taylor (Taylor 1993),
which suggest that nominal official short-term interest rates should be set
as a function of the equilibrium real rate of interest (as discussed in (ii)),
the amount of spare capacity in the economy and the difference between
current inflation and its target rate (see Equation 1). The amount of spare
capacity is typically measured by the Output Gap, which is the difference
between the level of real GDP and its estimated potential level.[21] However,
material difficulties in measuring the latter and the tendency for the former
to be revised mean that a labour market version of spare capacity is often
used, the difference between the unemployment rate and its natural rate/
non-accelerating inflation rate of unemployment (NAIRU). Admittedly,
estimating the latter is not without difficulties either.[22] Some economists
also use Okun's Law to approximate the output gap (Yellen 2012a, 2012b).

Other variants of the model include *forecasts* of inflation and the output gap instead of current levels (Clarida *et al.* 2000; Orphanides 2001, 2002) and different coefficients on the difference between inflation and its target and spare capacity (Taylor 1999 uses a version of his model where the coefficient on the Output Gap is raised from 0.5 to 1). In general, the Taylor Rule suggests that if inflation is at its target and output is at its potential level, the real official interest rate should be set at its equilibrium real rate (similarly for their nominal counterparts). If real GDP is above its potential and/or inflation is above its target, then the real official interest rate should be above its equilibrium real rate and vice versa (similarly for their nominal counterparts). Taylor (1993) stresses that it is not practical for policy-makers to mechanically follow his rule and that it should serve as one of a number of factors in decision-making.

Equation 1: Original Taylor Rule

$$r = r^* + p + 0.5y + 0.5(p - p^*)$$

r = official nominal interest rate, r^* = equilibrium real interest rate, y = output gap, p = current inflation rate, p^* = inflation target (for simplicity purposes the ordering of the variables is slightly different to Taylor (1993) and r^* and p^* are not already filled in with their *assumed* actual values).

(iv) Financial Conditions Indices (FCIs) attempt to estimate how easy or tight overall financial conditions are in an economy. Given the large number of different financial-related indicators, it is very useful to aggregate these into a composite, easily understandable measure of financial conditions. They help gauge how well changes in monetary policy are feeding through into actual financial conditions and are particularly important to focus on during times of banking distress or financial crises. For example, as I discuss in Chapter 3, as the GFC intensified in 2008–09, actual financial conditions in the major economies were extraordinarily tight amid a seizing up of the financial system despite the fact that official nominal short-term interest rates were at or close to zero. In general, FCIs are watched very closely by central banks and economists.

Simple versions of FCIs often use basic econometric techniques to aggregate several financial variables together such as stock prices, sovereign bond yields, exchange rates, corporate bond yields, etc., while more complex versions such as the Chicago Fed National Financial Conditions Index use more advanced techniques and include around 100 different financial-related variables (Brave & Butters 2011). These more complex versions typically include a wide variety of market interest rates, measures of risk (such as the spread of corporate bond yields over sovereign bond yields – credit risk), house price indices and survey-based measures of banks' willingness to lend to households/businesses, etc. (for a useful literature review on FCIs see Nicoletti *et al.* 2014).

In this chapter, I have reviewed how monetary policy-making evolved as a consequence of the Great Inflation, resulting in the current practice of independent central banks with inflation targeting frameworks. Together with the summary of contemporary monetary policy-making it should provide a foundation for our discussion of QE, while also providing a framework to think about how central banking could change again in the future given the prevailing economic and political circumstances which I discuss later in the book. In Chapter 2, I highlight how, after peaking at very elevated levels in the early 1980s amid efforts to quell inflation, official nominal interest rates in the developed economies fell very sharply over subsequent decades, ultimately hitting the ZLB in Japan after the bursting of its asset price bubbles and coming very close in the US and some western economies in the decade before the GFC. I also discuss the BoJ's adoption of QE, the first by a developed central bank in modern times as it attempted to rid the economy of deflation.

2

KEY MONETARY POLICY TRENDS AND EVENTS IN THE DECADES BEFORE THE GREAT FINANCIAL CRISIS

After peaking at very elevated levels in the early 1980s as policy-makers attempted to end the Great Inflation, official central bank interest rates fell very sharply over subsequent decades, during a period commonly referred to as the "Great Moderation". During the latter, there were several key events or periods for monetary policy which I will also discuss: the reaching of the ZLB on official interest rates in Japan after the bursting of its asset bubbles in 1990/91 and the onset of deflation; the reduction in US official interest rates to a record low of 1 per cent after the bursting of its Information Technology (IT) stockmarket bubble in 2000/2001; the introduction of QE in Japan in 2001.

The events in Japan were particularly noteworthy as it became the first central bank in modern times to reach the ZLB on official interest rates and to experiment with QE as it attempted to battle the protracted fallout from the bursting of its massive asset price bubbles. Meanwhile, the period of ultra-loose US monetary policy in the years following the bursting of its IT bubble, as the Fed attempted to avoid falling into a Japanese-style deflationary scenario, proved particularly consequential as it helped "sow the seeds" of the enormous real estate bubble and the GFC once it finally burst. Admittedly, there were other major contributing factors which I briefly discuss. The experiences of the Japanese authorities with the ZLB, QE and other unconventional policies ultimately provided some lessons for the US authorities when their time came to enact such policies.

Sharply falling interest rates during the Great Moderation

After rising markedly during the 1970s and early 1980s amid the Great Inflation, inflation and official short-term central bank interest rates declined markedly in developed countries over subsequent decades (see Figures 1.1 and 2.1). The period from the mid-1980s up until the early rumblings of the GFC in the summer of

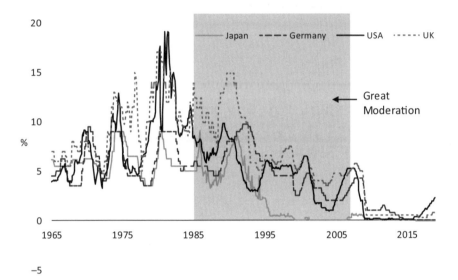

Figure 2.1. Developed market official short-term nominal interest rates
Source: National sources, ECB, IMF, Federal Reserve Bank of St. Louis (FRED). For Germany, ECB interest rates since 1999.

2007 is commonly referred to as the Great Moderation when industrial countries experienced significant reductions in the volatility of both their GDP growth and inflation and recessions were typically much shorter and shallower (Rivlin 2015). According to Blanchard and Simon (2001), the standard deviation of real GDP growth and inflation in the USA both fell by around two-thirds between the mid-1980s and the turn of the century (see Figure 2.2) with falls in volatility also evident in other major developed countries (except Japan), albeit with some differences in timing and magnitude.[1]

An in-depth discussion of the Great Moderation is beyond the scope of this book. The then Fed Governor Ben Bernanke (he became Chair in 2006), in a famous speech, highlighted the three main drivers typically cited in the literature as being behind it (Bernanke 2004)[2]:

(i)   structural changes in economies which better enable them to withstand shocks, of which he cites as possible explanations: better inventory management techniques; the increased depth and sophistication of financial markets; deregulation; the shift from manufacturing to services; and the globalization of trade and financial markets.

(ii) improved macroeconomic policies, particularly monetary policy since the 1980s (for example, the greater independence of central banks and the adoption of inflation targeting regimes as discussed in Chapter 1).

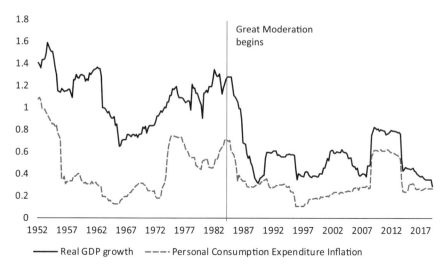

Figure 2.2. Standard Deviation* of US real GDP growth and inflation
* Quarterly five-year rolling standard deviation. Note, Blanchard and Simon (2001) use the GDP deflator when measuring the change in inflation volatility.
Source: Bureau of Economic Analysis, Federal Reserve Bank of St. Louis (FRED).

(iii) "good luck" as the shocks hitting the economy since the mid-1980s have been much smaller and rarer than previously (for example, economies were hit by massive oil price shocks in the 1970s).

There appears to be general agreement in the literature that the major changes to monetary policy-making were the main drivers of the reduction in inflation volatility, but there remains disagreement on the importance of the other factors in reducing output volatility. Giannone *et al.* (2008) conclude that a majority of academic studies favour the "good luck" explanation followed by structural changes. However, they argue that studies in favour of shocks typically rely on the use of small-scale econometric models using a limited number of explanatory variables and, hence, suffer from omitted variable bias (for example, what the models regard as exogenous shocks also include the impacts of variables not included in the models and the impacts of structural or policy changes). When using larger more detailed models they find a more limited role for shocks. Moreover, a number of authors (Bernanke 2004; Hakkio 2013) highlight the fact that there have been numerous major shocks since the mid-1980s[3] and, hence, it may be that structural changes and better macroeconomic policies have simply reduced the economy's vulnerability to such shocks (Hakkio 2013).

Bernanke (2004) suggests that "all of the above", namely structural changes, better macroeconomic policies and "good luck" likely explain the reduction in output volatility, although he thinks improved monetary policy practices played a more important role than often credited in the literature. He cites the close historical relationship between movements in inflation volatility and output volatility and the large reduction in the former amid the significant improvement in the conduct of monetary policy from the 1980s onwards. He also suggests that some of the benefits from improved monetary policy may be mistaken for positive structural changes or smaller shocks. For example, the benign inflationary environment and more firmly anchored inflation expectations as a result of improvements in monetary policy mean that a given change in commodity prices today will result in a smaller shock to inflation and output than previously.

As Figure 2.1 highlights, official central bank interest rates fell sharply from their peaks of 19 per cent, 17 per cent, 9.5 per cent and 9 per cent in the early 1980s in the US, UK, Germany and Japan and were down at 4.25 per cent, 5.5 per cent, 4 per cent and 0.5 per cent by the end of 2007 ahead of the GFC. Moreover, as Figure 2.3 highlights for the US, a typical feature of business cycles during this period has been both lower peaks and troughs for interest rates in the monetary tightening and easing cycles respectively. White (2016) suggests that this reflects the asymmetric approach of central banks, whose aggressive monetary easing was never matched by symmetric restraint when the economy was recovering, resulting in rising levels of public and private debt. He suggests that these monetary policies were made possible by the persistent downward pressure on inflation due to globalization and the entrance into the global economic system of

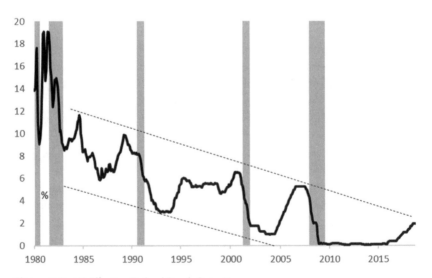

Figure 2.3. US Effective Federal Funds Rate, %
Source: Board of Governors of the Federal Reserve System. Shaded areas represent US recessions.

China and the former Eastern bloc countries. The ongoing rise in private sector debt levels also likely meant that the interest rate sensitive sectors needed stimulating yet more to revive the economy after each recession, with the increasing amounts of private sector debt accumulated as a result meaning that less monetary tightening was then subsequently needed to slow the economy in the tightening phase.

On the face of it, the secular decline in official central bank interest rates would suggest that monetary policy was becoming extraordinarily easy compared with the Great Inflation period. However, while monetary policy was undoubtedly very easy in certain periods during the Great Moderation, particularly the years following the bursting of the US IT bubble (see below), this was not necessarily the case throughout. Indeed, as previously noted, the declines in official central bank interest rates occurred against a backdrop of large declines in inflation amid the greater inflation-fighting credibility of central banks and the favourable global trends. As a result, after averaging 0 per cent during the 1970s, US ex-post *real* interest rates actually averaged over 4 per cent and around 2 per cent respectively throughout the 1980s and 1990s, a reflection of the greater emphasis on controlling inflation after Paul Volcker became Fed Chair.

The onset of the ZLB in Japan amid its "lost decade"

The Japanese economy boomed after the Second World War, aided initially by the rebuilding of the country's infrastructure and subsequently by a sharp rise in exports to the western economies, as the country rapidly moved closer to the technological frontier from focusing on products such as toys and textiles in the 1950s to cars and semiconductors in the 1980s (Ito 1997). Real GDP growth averaged 10.4 per cent, 5.2 per cent and 4.4 per cent in the 1960s, 1970s and 1980s respectively, far outstripping the OECD average (Hilpert 2003). Amid Japan's *apparent* rise, some commentators even speculated it would displace the US as the world's leading economic power (Vogel 1979). Alongside stellar growth came huge gains in domestic asset prices, which became particularly rapid during the second half of the 1980s as stock market and real estate prices tripled (IMF 2009).[4] Hayashi and Prescott (2002) suggest this "bubble" period, "when property prices soared, investment as a fraction of GDP was unusually high, and output grew faster than in any other years in the 1980's and 1990's" was owing to an expectation of faster productivity growth that never materialized. Shiratsuka (2005) suggests the "bubble was based on excessively optimistic expectations with respect to the future, which might be described as euphoria with the benefit of hindsight".

Indeed, the asset bubbles finally burst and the prices of real estate and the stock market began falling dramatically from the early 1990s (see Figure 2.4).[5] Against this backdrop, real GDP growth slowed sharply and the unemployment rate began to rise. According to Koo (2009), the massive falls in asset prices inflicted severe damage on the highly indebted corporate sector and resulted in a once in "every several decades" balance sheet recession, where companies, many of which had become technically insolvent, focused their efforts on paying down their debts as quickly as possible. He suggested that this dramatic change in behaviour, compared with before the bubble burst when companies were borrowing heavily to invest, led to a massive ongoing reduction in corporate sector demand between 1990 and 2003. Meanwhile, the banking system was also severely impaired by the collapsing asset prices,[6] moribund growth and the rise in non-performing loans, although the latter were masked for a considerable period by regulatory forbearance (IMF 2009). Hayashi and Prescott (2002) document a dramatic deceleration in underlying productivity growth in the 1990s, a key driver of trend growth in an advanced economy. Unfortunately, this all occurred at a time when demographics were becoming less favourable amid a peak in the size of the working-age population. Reflecting these dynamics, Kuroda (2017) suggests the potential growth rate declined from around 4 per cent in the early 1990s to around 1 per cent in the late 1990s and lower still in the 2000s.

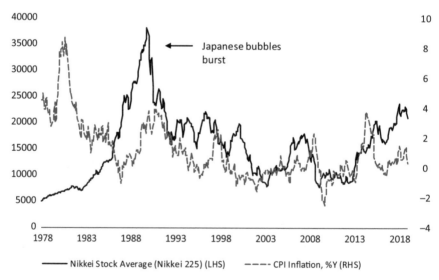

Figure 2.4. Japanese stock market and inflation
Source: IMF, Nikkei Industry Research Institute, Federal Reserve Bank of St. Louis (FRED). Nikkei 225 is owned by Nikkei Inc.

In an attempt to try to limit the economic fallout from the bursting bubbles, the authorities enacted a number of policies to boost growth. The government embarked on numerous fiscal stimulus programmes which resulted in general government gross debt increasing from 64 per cent of GDP in 1990 to over 130 per cent by the end of the decade. The BoJ reduced its main official interest rate from 6 per cent in 1991 to just 0.5 per cent by Autumn 1995 and rates were reduced to effectively zero after the introduction of a zero-interest rate policy (ZIRP) in February 1999 (IMF 2009). Japan had become the first major country to cut the official interest rate to zero in the post-Second World War era. Moreover, in the minutes of its April 1999 meeting, it introduced forward guidance, a form of unconventional monetary policy, suggesting that "it was important to maintain the current decisive easy stance of monetary policy, firmly underpinning economic activity until deflationary concerns were dispelled" (Kuttner 2014). Interest rates have remained close to zero ever since.

Despite aggressive easing, real GDP growth averaged just 0.8 per cent over the 1992–2001 period, resulting in what is commonly referred to as the "lost decade" and the economy entered into deflation in the mid-1990s as prices began to fall.[7] Japan was the first industrial country to experience deflation since the 1930s (Hilpert 2003). This was particularly problematic for an economy where the private sector was trying to reduce its debt levels as these increased in real terms, while deflation also meant that real interest rates became positive (despite the fact that official nominal interest rates were at the ZLB). Indeed, a key problem for Japan was that, on most estimates, the real equilibrium interest rate had fallen close to zero (Sudo *et al.* 2018) and hence, in order to provide significant stimulus, real official interest rates needed to be materially negative. Krugman (1998) characterized Japan as being in a "liquidity trap" which he defined "as a situation in which conventional monetary policies have become impotent". In Chapter 1, I discussed changes made by central banks to their monetary policy frameworks since the 1980s in an attempt to bolster their inflation-fighting credibility with the private sector and, hence, reduce inflation expectations. Krugman suggested that the BoJ now faced the inverse of this problem and needed to credibly convince the private sector that it will be irresponsible in the future and, hence, through raising inflation expectations it could reduce real interest rates.

The bursting of the IT bubble fuelled record low US rates

The US and a number of Western economies boomed in the second half of the 1990s with the global IT or Dot-Com boom amid a rapid increase in the use of the Internet, email and other technology products. Firms invested heavily in new IT equipment and the US experienced a significant acceleration in productivity growth, which helped contain underlying inflation despite robust real GDP growth. Amid this ebullient backdrop, global stock markets soared, led by huge gains for IT-related companies. Fears began to grow, however, that a major bubble may be building, and Fed Chairman Alan Greenspan warned about "irrational exuberance" in a speech in late 1996 (Greenspan 1996). However, he subsequently argued that central banks should not attempt to prick bubbles given the difficulty in identifying and/or successfully pre-empting them, but that they should stand ready to support the economy if a bubble burst (Greenspan 2002a). The Nasdaq Composite Index – which consists mainly of IT-related companies – increased by almost 600 per cent between the beginning of 1995 and its peak in March 2000 (see Figure 2.5) and the large wealth gains and boost to confidence helped fuel robust consumer spending. However, the huge gains in equity prices ultimately resulted in the valuations of many of these companies looking exorbitant.

The bubble finally burst in 2000 amid ongoing policy tightening by the Fed and surging oil prices (Meyer 2001). Stock prices fell dramatically and firms which had previously been large investors in IT equipment quickly switched to being net savers and the US economy fell into recession in March 2001, ending the longest economic expansion in its history.[8] With the Fed fearing the bursting of the bubble could fuel a major recession or perhaps even a Japanese-style deflationary scenario or Japanization[9] of the US economy, they cut interest rates

Figure 2.5. Nasdaq Composite Index
Source: NASDAQ OMX Group, Federal Reserve Bank of St. Louis (FRED).

sharply from 6.5 per cent at the end of 2000 to 3.5 per cent by summer 2001 and then to a record low of 1.75 per cent by year-end after the economy was hit by the massive shock of the September 2001 terrorist attacks. The Bush administration also supported growth with large tax cuts. Despite exiting recession in late 2001, growth remained sub-par amid a jobless recovery and the negative impact on sentiment from major corporate accounting scandals and geopolitical uncertainty ahead of the onset of war in Iraq in Spring 2003 (Greenspan 2002b). Inflation also remained very subdued, which increased fears that the US may be slipping into a Japanese style deflationary cycle (Bernanke 2002, 2003). As a result, the Fed cut rates further to a record low of 1 per cent in June 2003 and the committee subsequently introduced forward guidance suggesting that "policy accommodation can be maintained for a considerable period" (Jevcak 2014). In addition, the Bush administration enacted further major tax cuts.

Amid the massive policy stimulus and the end of major hostilities in Iraq, the US economy sprang back to life in the second half of 2003. The recovery, buoyed by a further strengthening in the housing market, helped drive a robust global economic recovery. Despite the strong rebound in growth, the Fed did not initiate its first interest rate hike until June 2004 and then subsequently enacted a gradual 25bps rate hike at every meeting over the next couple of years. However, given rising inflation, the real FFR did not actually become positive again until the middle of 2005 after being in negative territory since late 2002 (see Figure 1.4). Kuttner (2014) highlights the fact that the Fed was much more aggressive in easing monetary policy in the years following the bursting of its IT bubble than the BoJ had been with the bursting of its bubbles and Taylor (2007) notes that the FFR was much lower during this period than a Taylor Rule would proscribe. Moreover, in what Fed Chair Alan Greenspan termed a "conundrum" (Greenspan 2005), in contrast to the typical historical relationship, long-term US government bond yields actually fell during the Fed's interest rate hiking cycle, suggesting much less tightening in financial conditions than would typically be the case. A key factor behind this was what then Fed Governor Ben Bernanke characterized as the "Global Savings Glut" where China and other emerging economies invested their huge current account surpluses into US financial assets, helping to boost the prices and depress the yields on long-term US government bonds and mortgage-related securities (Bernanke 2005b).

Amid this prolonged period of extremely easy monetary policy, the housing market boomed, with US house prices rising at an average year-on-year rate of around 10 per cent between mid-2003 and mid-2006, with rates of gain often reaching around 30 per cent in Sun Belt states such as California, Florida, Arizona and Nevada. Moreover, new and existing home sales and housing construction surged to record levels. In addition to the easy policy settings, the long period of solid growth and low inflation during the Great Moderation helped to fuel a general sense of complacency about risks (Bernanke 2013). This contributed to a significant easing in lending standards by mortgage lenders and investors who, struggling to find adequate yields in government bonds, switched to investments such as mortgage-related securities on the assumption (later to be proved false) that they were largely risk-free like government bonds. Strikingly, at the peak of the housing boom, around one-third of new mortgages were being made to non-prime borrowers and between 2003 and 2007, 40–60 per cent of non-prime mortgage loans were made with little or no documentation and the initial down payments were typically zero or much lower than on prime mortgages (Bernanke 2013).[10]

While the housing market was booming, there were large positive knock-on effects to the economy and the stock market recovered most of its losses from the bursting of the IT bubble. However, continued monetary tightening by the Fed led to an eventual bursting of the housing market bubble and the fallout from this ultimately led to the GFC. I will discuss this further in Chapter 3.

An in-depth discussion of the causes of the GFC is beyond the scope of this book. With the benefit of hindsight, the Fed's misplaced fears of falling into a Japanese-style deflationary scenario does seem to have been a key factor behind it keeping policy too easy for too long after the IT bubble burst, resulting eventually in the far larger and more destructive real estate bubble. Admittedly, the Fed's ability to tighten policy and manage financial conditions was complicated by the huge global savings glut, whose investments into US assets fuelled a massive misallocation of resources. There were other important contributing factors, some related to the Fed and others that were less so. Amid an excessive focus on inflation control, the Fed (and other central banks) placed insufficient emphasis on their traditional roles of maintaining financial stability during the Great Moderation. Regulatory oversight was generally weak, although the Fed (and other central banks) were far from the only ones to blame for this. Unfortunately, this was at a time when it was arguably needed the most given that the US and other governments had previously enacted major deregulation of the financial industry and amid rapid financial innovation (much of which subsequently largely proved very ill advised and has received major criticism). Moreover, the long period of economic stability during the Great Moderation seemed to make key players in financial markets and the general public underestimate risks and encouraged many to engage in excessive risk taking. Fed policy likely exacerbated this somewhat. Whenever financial markets suffered material losses, the Fed typically intervened with monetary easing in what is commonly referred to as the "Greenspan Put", creating a general impression that downside risks were relatively limited. (For further reading on the build up to and causes of the GFC, see Bernanke 2013, 2015a; Blinder 2013; White 2016).

The Bank of Japan enacts "drastic" measures with QE

With the Japanese economy mired in deflation and at risk of another recession amid the bursting of the global IT bubble and sharp slowdown in the US, the BoJ concluded in the minutes of its March 2001 meeting that "the economic conditions warrant monetary easing as drastic as is unlikely to be taken under ordinary circumstances" and enacted a policy of QE.[11] Japan was the first modern developed central bank to enact such a policy and, hence, there was no established precedent for policy-makers to follow. The rationale for embarking on QE was to provide additional monetary stimulus to the economy given that official short-term nominal interest rates were constrained by the ZLB.[12] As part of the policy change, the BoJ also provided forward guidance again and made its commitment clearer than had previously been the case under ZIRP, suggesting that it would continue with QE "until the CPI [consumer price index] … registers stably a zero percent or an increase year on year" (Kuttner 2014).

As discussed previously, as with other central banks, when the BoJ sets a target for its official short-term nominal interest rate, it uses open market operations to adjust the amount of reserve balances held by financial institutions (called current account balances in Japan) so that the interest rate on overnight loans between financial institutions equals its target rate. However, under QE, the BoJ shifted from targeting the interest rate on overnight loans (the price of money), to the amount of outstanding current account balances in the financial system (the quantity of money). Its initial target of ¥5 trillion for current account balances represented an increase from previously and, hence, the BoJ expected its main uncollateralized overnight call rate (UOCR) to fall from slightly positive to around zero. Given its commitment that the policy would remain in place until inflation became zero, the BoJ also expected a decline in interest rates across the yield curve, through what is commonly referred to as the "commitment effect" or "policy duration effect" (Ugai 2006).[13] For example, previously a two-year Japanese Government bond (JGB) may have had a moderately positive interest rate such as 0.3 per cent, based on the assumption of investors that as the economy recovers the BoJ would ultimately end QE and begin raising interest rates. But with guidance that QE would not end until inflation becomes positive, even if growth has recovered, this interest rate may now have fallen close to zero as investors discount a later start to rate rises.[14]

The size of the target current account balances rose over time to a range of ¥30–35 trillion from January 2004, which was significantly in excess of required reserves of banks and also well beyond the amount necessary to keep overnight rates at zero, thus helping to boost liquidity in the banking system (Bowman *et al.* 2011). Reflecting the bank-centric nature of the Japanese financial system, the BoJ's efforts to increase current account balances and boost liquidity occurred primarily through the banks (Ueda 2012).[15] These included purchases of shorter-term Treasury Bills and JGBs and funds-supplying operations (loans through open market operations backed by collateral) (IMF 2009). JGB purchases were typically of medium-term maturities (two, four, five and six years) and ten years and, reflecting this, the maturity of the BoJ's bond portfolio actually declined from over five years in 2001 to under four years in 2005 (McCauley & Ueda 2009). The BoJ also purchased equities from banks which had been acquired previously amid the practice of cross-shareholdings, in an attempt to improve their capital positions and the functioning of the financial system. These purchases were relatively modest, but represented about 6 per cent of banks' total equity holdings (IMF 2010).[16] It also purchased small amounts of asset-backed securities in an attempt to try to support the development of this market in Japan (IMF 2012a).

Ugai (2006) provides an extensive summary of the numerous academic studies examining the impacts of this first bout of Japanese QE via the various transmission channels. Chapter 4 contains a more detailed discussion of the theoretical and practical transmission channels through which QE works. In general, he suggests the main positive impact of QE appears to have come through the "policy duration effect", where government bond yields at short and intermediate-term maturities declined. The main driver of this was the BoJ's commitment to continue with QE until inflation becomes positive on a sustainable basis. Ugai also finds evidence from the various studies that QE helped ease funding conditions for financial institutions and improved the financial environment. Overall, however, he notes that the various studies tended to find a rather limited impact of QE in boosting real GDP and inflation, with a number of authors suggesting that, in addition to the ZLB on interest rates, this was due to the impaired transmission mechanism amid the weakened banking system and ongoing corporate deleveraging. Indeed, Ugai highlights the fact that the surge in monetary base (current account balances + banknotes in circulation) due to QE led to relatively little change in the broader measures of money supply which include bank deposits of the general public (for example, M2 + CDs), reflecting a collapse in the money multiplier (I discuss this further in Chapter 5).

With the economy strengthening amid robust global growth, an improving financial system and inflation turning positive, the BoJ ended its policy of QE in March 2006. During QE, the size of its balance sheet had increased from 22 per cent to around 30 per cent of GDP, but it unwound its balance sheet quite quickly over subsequent months (IMF 2010). I will discuss central bank balance sheets further in Chapter 3 and their winding down in Chapter 8.

Despite the BoJ's unprecedented efforts, it became clear over subsequent years that it had not been successful in permanently ridding the economy of deflation. The reasons behind this remain a major source of debate. Ueda (2012) cites three reasons for the ineffectiveness of policy during this period: (i) the sheer magni-tude of the negative shock that hit the economy; (ii) as with bank recapitalizations and interest rate cuts, unconventional monetary policy measures should have been adopted earlier as their effectiveness may have been undermined by the emergence of deflationary expectations; (iii) the lack of well-developed capital markets in Japan, compared with say the US, which made it difficult for the BoJ to bypass the ailing banking system when trying to stimulate the economy. Kuttner (2014) notes that Japanese QE focused mainly on liquidity provision, eschewing the purchase of longer-dated government bonds[17] and private sector assets. He also suggests that communication around unconventional policies typically emphasized their risks rather than potential benefits and that policies were prematurely reversed. Greenwood (2017) notes that the BoJ policy of purchasing government bonds from commercial banks, rather than the non-bank private sector, meant that the mon-etary base increased but there was little impact on broad money growth given the banks' unwillingness to lend and the private sector's reluctance to borrow.

In this chapter, I have described how interest rates in Japan reached the ZLB in the 1990s after the bursting of its asset bubbles and how it subsequently became the first modern developed economy to adopt QE in an attempt to emerge from deflation. The balance of evidence suggests that while its impact was positive, the benefits were quite modest. Critics suggest that QE came too late, was too restrained and should have focused on longer-term government bonds. I have also highlighted how the US came very close to the ZLB in the pre-crisis decade after the bursting of its IT bubble and how excessively easy policy during this period contributed – along with a number of other factors – to the massive real estate bubble that eventually burst so spectacularly. In Chapter 3, I highlight and discuss how, faced with the ZLB after the bursting of the real estate bubble and the onset of the GFC, the Fed and BoE enacted massive QE programmes in order to prevent another Great Depression or potentially falling into deflation. I also discuss the beginning of major QE in Japan as part of the new Prime Minister's attempts to revitalize the economy and its eventual adoption in the euro area amid deflationary fears.

3

THE GREAT FINANCIAL CRISIS AND THE
ONSET OF QUANTITATIVE EASING

Continued interest rate increases by the Fed, which saw the target FFR reach 4.25 per cent by the end of 2005 and 5.25 per cent the following summer, helped cool the US housing market. As the cost of mortgage borrowing rose and the housing market slowed, particular pressure was felt by many sub-prime borrowers who had taken out adjustable-rate mortgages (ARMs) on low initial rates and were struggling to afford their payments once they had reverted to the higher prevailing interest rates (Bernanke 2007, 2013, 2015a). In states that experienced the largest booms such as California, Florida, Arizona and Nevada, house prices peaked in 2006 and then began to fall. Previously, when prices increased rapidly, this created significant equity for homeowners, allowing many sub-prime borrowers to remortgage their properties at more attractive interest rates or extract equity from their properties to help with rising mortgage payments. However, the slowdown and eventual decline in house prices meant that many had little or no equity in their properties (Bernanke 2013).

The national housing market began to weaken significantly in 2007 (see Figure 3.1) amid a surge in mortgage delinquencies and a sharp rise in the number of homeowners suffering negative equity (Bernanke 2013). This created a vicious cycle. Surging delinquencies and foreclosures significantly added to the supply of houses for sale, while at the same time demand weakened as mortgage lenders tightened their lending standards. The tightening became particularly severe in the sub-prime space as investors, suffering significant losses on their sub-prime mortgage assets, effectively withdrew from the market. The result was more rapid declines in house prices and volatility began to rise quite sharply in global financial markets as fears increased about potentially massive losses on the housing investments of US and European financial institutions.

The August announcement by the large French bank BNP Paribas that it was suspending customer withdrawals from some of its investment funds that invested in US sub-prime mortgages, because it could no longer value such assets,

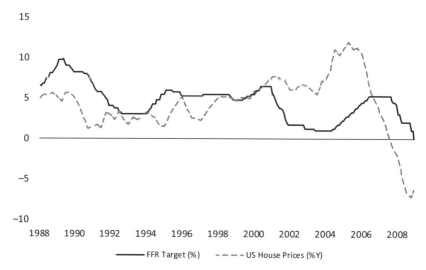

Figure 3.1. US house prices and the Federal Funds Rate
Source: US Federal Housing Finance Agency, Board of Governors of the Federal Reserve System, Federal Reserve Bank of St. Louis (FRED). House prices are the Federal Housing Finance Agency's All-Transactions House Price Index. The series are quarterly, but I have used linear interpolation to present the data in monthly form.

shocked global financial markets and is generally said to be when the global financial panic began in earnest (Irwin 2013). Financial institutions became increasingly wary about lending to each other amid fears they may not be paid back if their counterparties were to fail. Problems for investors were greatly exacerbated by prior changes in US mortgage lending practices[1] and the complex and opaque nature of many of the financial instruments created to facilitate greater investment in sub-prime mortgages. This resulted in widespread uncertainty about the institutions most exposed to future losses (Bernanke 2013).[2] In the euro area, where borrowing difficulties for financial institutions were initially most acute, the ECB responded aggressively by offering to provide an unlimited amount of funding to financial institutions, while the Fed also injected increased funds into the financial system (Irwin 2013; Geithner 2014). In September, UK bank Northern Rock (whose business model particularly exposed it to the problems in mortgage and bank lending markets), was experiencing significant difficulties and became the first UK bank to experience a bank run since 1866; Northern Rock was ultimately nationalized by the government (Irwin 2013). Over subsequent months, major global financial institutions would unveil record losses on the value of their holdings of US mortgage-related assets (Geithner 2014).

Amid the deteriorating backdrop, the Fed began cutting interest rates in September 2007 and by January 2008 the FFR had been reduced from 5.25 per cent to 3 per cent (see Figure 3.1). In an attempt to help calm financial markets, the Fed and other developed central banks expanded their traditional roles as "lenders of last resort" (LOLR), typically lending greater amounts to financial institutions, for longer periods, at lower interest rates and against a wider array of collateral than was normally the case. The Fed also began lending USDs to other major central banks, which would lend these to their own domestic financial institutions who were now finding it difficult to borrow USDs from their American counterparts[3] (Irwin 2013). Amid mounting fears of a recession, the Bush administration enacted a fiscal stimulus package in February 2008 consisting of tax cuts for individuals and incentives to encourage business investment (Wilson 2008).

Despite the policy easing by the US authorities, with housing market weakness intensifying, consumer and business confidence depressed and the stock market falling, the economy had actually entered recession in December 2007.[4] Amid mounting economic weakness, massive ripple effects began to be felt increasingly across global financial markets. US investment bank Bear Stearns was on the verge of failure in March 2008 and was taken over by one of the largest US commercial banks (JP Morgan) with some financial support provided by the Fed. It was feared that allowing it to go bankrupt would have caused a massive financial panic given its size and interconnectedness with the rest of the global financial system (Bernanke 2013). The Fed cut interest rates yet further, to just 2 per cent, in April. However, the continued surge in oil prices to a record level over the summer acted as an additional major economic headwind.

Massive financial panic after the collapse of Lehman Brothers

A dramatic intensification of the financial crisis occurred with the collapse of major US investment bank Lehman Brothers in September. It had made massive losses and despite the significant efforts of policy-makers, a buyer was unable to be found and it subsequently filed for bankruptcy, which Geithner (2014) notes was by far the largest in US history.[5] This triggered a huge global financial panic. Stock markets fell dramatically and the usual sources of funding for financial institutions and non-financial corporations largely evaporated (Bernanke 2013). Indeed, financial institutions were unwilling to lend to anybody amid fears that their counterparties could be the next to go bankrupt. They also wanted to conserve their own funds to meet any redemptions they may have faced from their own clients and many financial institutions had to engage in fire sales of their own assets in order to generate such funds. This dramatically exacerbated the vicious cycle that had been set in train. It was feared that the US and global economies stood on the precipice of a rerun of the Great Depression of 1929–33.

In order to try to quell the panic, the Fed and other central banks massively expanded their LOLR schemes, widening the eligibility of both the type of institutions able to participate and the pool of collateral able to be used to borrow. They also dramatically expanded both the amount of funds available and the duration over which they were willing to lend them. The Fed significantly increased its lending of USDs to other major central banks, with Irwin (2013) suggesting: "In late 2008, Ben Bernanke's Fed became the lender of last resort to much of the world".

Meanwhile, the Bush administration enacted a major package of support to the financial system called the Troubled Asset Relief Program (TARP), which ultimately resulted in significant amounts of capital being injected into the major financial institutions and a small number of non-financial companies.[6] Similar support packages were implemented in other affected countries. To suggest that these packages were hugely unpopular with the general public and politicians alike is a major understatement, as they were quite correctly seen as a "bailout" of the very financial institutions whose excessive risk-taking and perceived "greed" had actually created the crisis. This was at a time when households were experiencing enormous job losses, spiralling mortgage foreclosures (particularly in the US) and a dramatic collapse in the value of their wealth amid tanking stock markets and house prices. In the US, it took two attempts to pass TARP in the House of Representatives, despite the fact that it was widely seen by almost all economists and financial market experts as being absolutely crucial in preventing a complete collapse of the financial system and global economy. In fairness, the finance ministers and central bank governors responsible for devising the various rescue packages were keenly aware of how unfair and deeply unpopular they would be. But they were simply caught "between a rock and a hard place", in the knowledge these institutions were simply "too big to fail" (Bernanke 2013).

Recognizing the importance of a coordinated response to what had rapidly become a global financial crisis, the major global central banks announced an unprecedented coordinated cut in interest rates on 8 October (Irwin 2013) which saw the FFR decline to 1.5 per cent. Moreover, at the meeting of G7 finance ministers and central bank governors on 10 October, officials suggested they would, among other things, use all available tools to prevent the failure of any more systemically important financial institutions and at the November G20 meeting leaders suggested they would "Use fiscal measures to stimulate domestic demand to rapid effect, as appropriate". Governments also expanded their commercial bank deposit insurance schemes and guaranteed against default new debt issued by their financial institutions. Bernanke (2013) suggests that the 10 October announcement was very effective resulting within days in a reduction in funding pressures in the banking system.

Central bank interest rates hit record lows

By the end of 2008, the US FFR had been cut to just 0–0.25 per cent, the BoE base rate was at 2 per cent and the ECB had reduced its main refinancing rate to 2.5 per cent. The Fed rate was the lowest on record and in March 2009 the BoE cut its rate to 0.5 per cent, which was the lowest in over 300 years. By May 2009, the ECB's main interest rate had fallen to a record low of just 1 per cent. Meanwhile, in February 2009, the new Obama administration enacted a major fiscal stimulus package in order to help generate a US recovery. The package was equivalent to around 5.5 per cent of GDP and consisted primarily of tax cuts, infrastructure spending and support for the states, low income individuals and the unemployed (*Guardian* 2009). Geithner (2014) notes that in today's prices, the programme was larger than President Roosevelt's entire New Deal programme to help the US economy recover from the Great Depression. Despite the large size, a number of prominent US economists suggested that it was unlikely to be sufficient given the massive headwinds facing the economy, with the boost to growth due to fall off rapidly from its peak in mid-2010 (Krugman 2012). Fiscal stimulus was enacted in the other advanced economies and China implemented an enormous policy stimulus equivalent to over 10 per cent of GDP (*The Economist* 2008). With its closed capital account, the Chinese financial system had been relatively immune to the GFC.[7] However, the economy was heavily dependent on exports to the developed world and, hence, the economy was at risk of a sharp slowdown given that these economies were in freefall.[8]

The US and UK begin large-scale QE

With the US and UK economies contracting sharply after the collapse of Lehman Brothers, financial markets still in freefall and fears of a major deflationary spiral increasing, central bank policy rule models such as Taylor Rules, were indicating that significant additional monetary easing was necessary i.e. in theory highly negative interest rates were needed (see Figure 3.2). But with central bank policy rates already at what was (at the time) assumed to be their effective lower bounds, the authorities needed to urgently consider more unconventional monetary policies in order to reduce borrowing costs further and boost aggregate demand (or at the very least stabilize it) (Ashworth 2013). Indeed, despite record low interest rates, financial conditions had become extraordinarily tight by historical standards (see Figure 3.3). This reflected the fact that the monetary transmission mechanism had become severely impaired as financial markets and the banking system were no longer functioning properly – banks were no longer lending to each other (or only on strict terms for very short periods) and bank lending standards on loans to the private sector had dramatically tightened. Meanwhile,

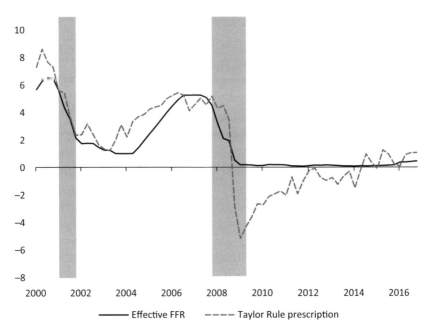

Figure 3.2. Taylor Rule prescriptions for the US Federal Funds Rate (%)
Note: The Taylor Rule used has a coefficient of 1 on the output gap as in Taylor (1999) and it uses Holston, Laubach and Williams one-sided real time estimates of the natural rate of interest and the US Survey of Professional Forecasters expected four-quarter PCE inflation three-quarters hence.
Source: Federal Reserve Bank of Atlanta.

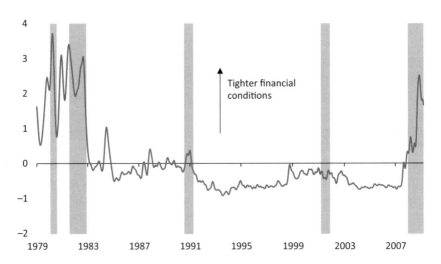

Figure 3.3. Chicago Federal Reserve National Financial Conditions Index*
* Positive values indicate that financial conditions are tighter than on average, while negative values suggest they are looser than on average.
Source: Federal Reserve Bank of Chicago.

as highlighted in Chapter 2, a key criticism of the Japanese authorities after the bursting of its asset bubbles was that they took far too long to enact drastic measures, by which time deflation and other negative dynamics had already become entrenched. The Fed did not want to repeat such mistakes.

The Fed launched QE in November 2008, dubbed large-scale asset purchases (LSAPs), with the announcement that it would buy the debt (agency debt) issued by the housing-related government sponsored enterprises (GSEs)[9] – Fannie Mae and Freddie Mac, and the mortgage-backed securities (MBS) guaranteed by them (agency MBS). This included $100 billion of agency debt and $500 billion of agency MBS. In March 2009, it announced its intention to purchase an additional $100 billion of agency debt, $750 billion of agency MBS and $300 billion of longer-term government bonds in a package "designed to get markets' attention" (Bernanke 2015a). Indeed, the initial programmes were large, with Gagnon *et al.* (2011) noting that the purchases represented almost a quarter of the stock of longer-term agency debt, agency MBS and Treasury securities outstanding at the beginning of purchases. The main aim of the purchases was to support the housing market by reducing the cost and increasing the availability of mortgage credit and to improve conditions in financial markets more broadly. I will discuss the transmission mechanism of QE in Chapter 4 and how the Fed's QE differed to that first carried out by Japan. Existing laws already permitted the Fed to purchase these types of assets, although it did not have the authority to buy private sector bonds such as corporate bonds or MBS not guaranteed by the GSEs (Bernanke 2015a). Despite concerns from some commentators about the inflationary consequences, initial public and political opposition to QE was relatively modest. This probably reflected the fact that the public's ire was more squarely focused on TARP, which was widely seen as a "Wall Street" bailout. The ongoing urgency to stop the continued collapse in the economy and financial markets also probably helped to quell opposition to the Fed's experimentation with these new unconventional policies.

The Fed also adopted another form of unconventional monetary policy called "forward guidance", through which central bankers use communication about the expected path of the official nominal short-term interest rate to influence longer-term interest rates (see Box 1). As discussed in Chapter 2, it had used guidance previously after the bursting of the IT bubble. After cutting the FFR to zero at its December 2008 meeting, it suggested "the Committee anticipates that weak economic conditions are likely to warrant exceptionally low levels of the federal funds rate for some time" and at its March 2009 meeting it strengthened this guidance somewhat suggesting that it "anticipates that economic conditions are likely to warrant exceptionally low levels of the federal funds rate for an extended period" (Bernanke 2015a). Kuttner (2018) characterizes these early forward guidance statements as being "qualitative and vague".

BOX 1: UNDERSTANDING LONGER-TERM INTEREST RATES

Longer term interest rates (for example, the yield on 5-year and 10-year US Treasury bonds) reflect the average expected official short-term interest rate (for example, US FFR) over the said period plus what is commonly referred to as the "term premium". The latter is the compensation that investors require for bearing the risk that short-term interest rates do not evolve as they expected (Adrian *et al.* 2014). In particular, Yu (2016) notes that if an investor needed to sell a 10-year government bond before it matures, they could make losses if short-term interest rates had risen in the interim (as the price of bonds moves inversely to their yield). He highlights the fact that given longer-maturity bonds experience larger price changes for the same change in short-term interest rates, investors demand more compensation (term premium) for holding longer-term bonds. Our discussion of the Great Inflation in Chapter 1 provides an example of this risk. At the end of 1977, a 10-year US government bond yielded around 8 per cent. New Fed Chair Paul Volcker tightened policy aggressively, resulting in yields rising above 15 per cent in 1981. As a result, an investor needing to sell bonds purchased at the end of 1977 during this period would likely have made large losses. The losses would be greater the longer the maturity of the bond (for example, losses on 30-year government bonds would be greater than those on the 10-year). Note, the term premium cannot be directly observed, but rather must be estimated from data on short- and long-term interest rates (Bernanke 2015b). I will discuss this further in the next chapter. Typically, the average expected short-term interest rate accounts for the vast majority of the longer-term interest rate.

In terms of forward guidance, it works by influencing expectations about the future average official short-term interest rate. In an extreme case, if the Fed were to credibly commit to keep the FFR at zero for the next five years, then the rate of the 5-year government bond should fall close to zero, while the rate on the 10-year should also fall sharply given that interest rates would be expected to be zero in the first half of the period.

In the UK, the Chancellor of the Exchequer authorized the creation of the Asset Purchase Facility by the BoE, which it could use to buy government bonds and certain private sector assets using central bank created electronic money if it so chose. The BoE began QE with £75 billion of purchases of longer-term government bonds in March 2009. It hoped the sellers would use the funds to buy other assets such as corporate bonds and equities, thus boosting wealth and improving the availability of corporate financing. It also bought very small quantities of commercial paper and corporate bonds with the main aim being to provide liquidity in those markets and help restore their normal functioning (Fisher 2010). By the end of QE1, the BoE had purchased around £200 billion of government bonds, which Joyce *et al.* (2011a) note represented around 30 per cent of the outstanding stock held by the private sector. Initial opposition to QE in the UK was also quite muted, probably reflecting similar reasons as in the US.

The euro area did not initially enact QE

The ECB did not initially embark on QE, but instituted several major lending programmes to financial institutions termed "Enhanced Credit Support" which were "taken to enhance the flow of credit above and beyond what could be achieved through policy interest rate reductions alone" (Trichet 2009a). It announced that financial institutions could borrow unlimited funds for seven days from its weekly main refinancing operation (MRO) at the specified interest rate and on a similar basis expanded its lending for periods of up to twelve months through longer-term refinancing operations (LTROs). It also significantly expanded the eligible collateral that could be used to borrow money. The LTROs guaranteed the availability of liquidity over longer periods for financial institutions and were expected to encourage greater lending to the private sector (Trichet 2009a). Borrowing under the LTROs was significant, with Trichet (2009a) noting that it equalled around 5 per cent of GDP in the first operation.

The ECB did directly purchase some assets via its Covered Bond Purchase Programme (CBPP)[10] in June 2009 and its Securities Markets Programme (SMP) introduced in May 2010. In the SMP, it purchased in secondary markets the government bonds of the peripheral euro area countries Greece, Ireland, Portugal, Spain and Italy in an attempt to reduce their yields which had soared amid stresses in their banking systems and rising investor concerns about the sustainability of their public finances. However, Giannone *et al.* (2012) note that these purchase operations were relatively small when compared with the size of the ECB's balance sheet and their main aim was to support an improvement in functioning in what had become dysfunctional asset markets. Moreover, unlike QE in the US and UK, they were not intended to expand the amount of liquidity in the financial system, since any increases were to be offset by special liquidity absorbing operations, although these were more presentational than real (Ashworth 2013).[11]

There were likely several reasons the ECB did not initially enact large-scale QE programmes like the Fed and BoE. First, the different structure of financial markets in the various regions (Antolin-Diaz 2013). Similar to Japan, bank-based financing of households and non-financial corporates is much more important in the euro area, whereas in the US, financial market-based financing such as corporate bonds, commercial paper, equity, etc. and securitization are much more prevalent. For example, at the end of 2007, the stock of outstanding bank loans to the private sector equalled around 145 per cent of GDP in the euro area compared with just 63 per cent in the US, with around 70 per cent of firms' external financing coming from banks in the former compared with around 20 per cent in the latter (Trichet 2009a, 2009b). Second, the Fed and the BoE were able to undertake purchases of a single riskless asset, namely bonds of their own sovereign government, while the existence of a large number of countries in the eurozone provides complications for broad-based operations in government bond markets (Antolin-Diaz 2013) (as we will see, this perceived constraint was later overcome). Lastly, it was also initially feared that large-scale asset purchases could breach the Treaty on the Functioning of the European Union, particularly the prohibition of monetary financing by the central bank. Germany, the eurozone's largest economy, which had emerged from the GFC in a relatively strong position, was particularly sensitive about this, given its experience after the First World War when the printing of money by its central bank to pay war reparations led to hyperinflation and the collapse of its currency.

The ECB nevertheless still received significant German criticism after the introduction of its SMP programme and its subsequent expansion in August 2011. Bundesbank President Axel Weber criticized the programme as "blurring the different responsibilities between fiscal and monetary policy" (Weber 2010) and resigned as a consequence in early 2011 (Brunnermeier *et al.* 2016). His compatriot, ECB Executive Board member Jurgen Stark, opposed the SMP's expansion and also resigned over his objections in September 2011 (Irwin 2013). Brunnermeier *et al.* (2016) suggest that Germans saw the shadow of indirect monetary financing in the SMP and note that "these asset purchase decisions were not just a question of personalities: this was a moment in which a substantial part of conservative opinion in Germany turned against the ECB and the monetary union".

Amid an intensification of the eurozone sovereign debt and banking crisis in 2011–12, a large number of additional programmes and policy initiatives were enacted by the authorities – both country-specific rescues and at the regional level – in an attempt to try and calm financial markets and prevent a potential break-up of the euro area. A useful summary of these is contained in Brunnermeier *et al.* (2016). On the monetary policy front, in late 2011 and early 2012, the ECB enacted massive new lending programmes (LTROs) to financial institutions for periods of up to three years, dramatically longer even than its lending programmes in the aftermath of the GFC. Brunnermeier *et al.* (2016) note that there was unanimous agreement on the ECB's Governing Council to implement the new LTROs. They suggest the Bundesbank's agreement was surprising given that it was widely expected that financial institutions in peripheral countries would use some of the borrowed money to purchase their own government's bonds and, hence, the ECB was encouraging a form of indirect monetary financing of governments. Cour-Thimann and Winkler (2012) suggest the take-up of loans was significant at around €500 billion on net (5 per cent of GDP) and it guaranteed funds for banks over the medium-term so they did not need to reduce lending in order to raise funds to meet redemption payments on their own bonds. The ECB also reduced interest rates further with the official deposit interest rate reaching zero in the summer of 2012.

Draghi's strong words end the euro area crisis

Key in quelling the euro area crisis, however, was ECB President Mario Draghi's famous "the ECB is ready to do whatever it takes to preserve the euro" speech in July 2012 and the subsequent unveiling of the Outright Monetary Transactions (OMT) programme. A key driver of soaring sovereign bond yields in the peripheral countries was "redenomination risk", amid investor fears that these countries may ultimately be forced to exit the euro and their bond holdings would be redenominated into national currencies such as the Spanish Peseta, which would subsequently depreciate sharply against the euro, leading them to renege on their bonds. From the ECB's perspective, the euro was irreversible and, hence, these fears were irrational and the elevated sovereign yields were impairing the transmission of its monetary policy (Draghi 2012). Under OMT, the ECB promised to buy shorter-dated sovereign bonds in unlimited quantities to reduce the elevated yields of peripheral countries subject to certain conditions, namely the countries must be in a financial rescue programme and committed to reforms. Cour-Thimann and Winkler (2012) note that the design of the OMT was aimed at addressing prior concerns with the SMP programme, which it replaced.[12] As with the SMP programme, any liquidity created through OMT would be sterilized. Crucially, the ECB never actually had to use OMT: its willingness to use this potentially very powerful tool was enough to calm financial markets. Brunnermeier *et al.* (2016) suggest this illustrated the ECB's power and unique ability to shape events. They note that, unlike with the ECB, the financial markets never found credible repeated assurances by political leaders that they would do whatever it takes to save the euro.

There was significant opposition once again in Germany to the ECB's actions, although this was not uniform among policy-makers. The Bundesbank and Weber's replacement as President, Jens Weidmann, were staunchly against the programme and a group which included politicians and academics challenged its constitutionality at the German Constitutional Court, which asked the European Court of Justice (ECJ) for an opinion.[13] Despite the backlash, German Chancellor Angela Merkel broke with the Bundesbank and supported the plan, provided that it was done under strict conditions (Brunnermeier *et al.* 2016).[14]

The Bank of Japan's response to the financial crisis was modest

As discussed in Chapter 2, the Japanese banking system had been severely impaired by the bursting of its asset price bubbles in the early 1990s and the subsequent process of recovery was extremely slow. However, a flip side of this was that Japanese banks had become extremely risk-averse and largely eschewed investments in risky US mortgage-related assets in the run up to the GFC. As a result, the Japanese banking system was relatively modestly impacted by the GFC, despite negative spillovers to its financial markets and a massive appreciation of the JPY. The BoJ cut interest rates back to effectively zero again, provided increased liquidity support to the financial system and implemented a number of measures to support the corporate bond and commercial paper markets which were becoming dysfunctional (Shirikawa 2009). The increase in the size of the BoJ's balance sheet was much smaller than occurred elsewhere, however (see Box 2 and Figure 3.4). That said, amid the slowing domestic and international recovery from the GFC (see below), it announced a programme of "Comprehensive Monetary Easing" in October 2010. This included purchases of JGB's, corporate bonds, commercial paper, equity exchange traded funds (ETFs) and Japanese real estate investment trusts (J-REITs). Kuttner (2014) suggested that at first-glance it had looked like a bold move from the BoJ, but the size of the purchases were "miniscule".

BOX 2: CENTRAL BANK BALANCE SHEETS

Similar to traditional commercial banks and non-financial corporations, central banks have balance sheets made up of both their assets and matching liabilities. When they make a purchase or a loan, the value of their assets will rise and this will be matched by an equal increase in liabilities. Before the GFC, the balance sheets of the major central banks were typically quite small both in absolute terms and as a share of GDP. Their main assets typically included government bonds and shorter-term Treasury bills (Bernanke 2009b) which were purchased to inject funds into the economy and may also include other items such as foreign exchange reserves (Bernanke 2009c). Their main liabilities were banknotes in circulation primarily held by the general public (Bernanke 2009b), and, to a lesser extent, the reserve balances commercial banks held in their own accounts at the central bank overnight. Prior to the GFC, the latter were typically modest, close to the minimum required reserves set by the central banks (see Figure 3.6).[15]

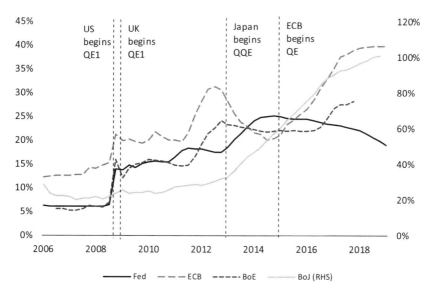

Figure 3.4. Central Bank Balance Sheets, per cent of GDP
Source: National central banks, national sources, Federal Reserve Bank of St. Louis (FRED).

Since the start of the GFC, the size of central bank balance sheets have increased enormously (see Figure 3.4). Initially, this was primarily owing to the expansion of their roles as LOLR during the panic phase, but subsequently it was a result of their asset purchases amid QE. The matching rise on the liability side has primarily occurred through a massive increase in the reserve balances held by commercial banks at the central bank, which are now dramatically in excess of required reserves (excess reserves). This happens because, to purchase new assets or make loans, central banks electronically create new money by crediting the bank accounts of the sellers of the assets or people receiving the loans and their commercial banks would then hold this money as reserve balances in their own accounts overnight at the central bank.

The sum of central bank liabilities, notes in circulation and reserve balances, equals the monetary base which is often also referred to as high-powered money, narrow money or central bank money. Hence, the massive rise in reserve balances fuelled a dramatic increase in the monetary base. This is why some feared that QE and the LOLR programmes would fuel runaway inflation, as they suggested the policies were akin to printing money (Bernanke 2009a). However, much more important for economic growth and inflation are the dynamics in broader measures of money (such as M2, M3 and M4) which include, among other things, the deposits held by households and firms at commercial banks (which could potentially be used to increase spending). These barely increased

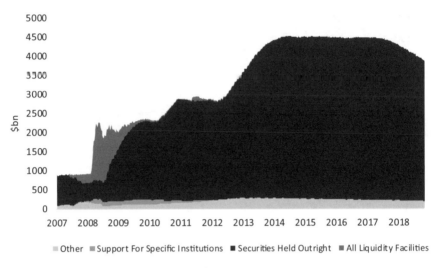

Figure 3.5. Federal Reserve balance sheet – assets
Source: Board of Governors of the Federal Reserve System.

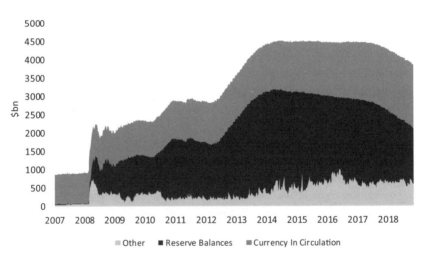

Figure 3.6. Federal Reserve balance sheet – liabilities
Source: Board of Governors of the Federal Reserve System.

amid the impaired banking system and tepid demand from borrowers for new loans. I will discuss this in more detail in Chapters 4 and 5. Figures 3.5 and 3.6 show the assets and liabilities sides of the Fed's balance sheet. As the financial crisis began to abate, the size of the LOLR programmes began to decline rapidly (see "All Liquidity Facilities" in Figure 3.5) and the growth in assets was driven by the QE programmes (see "Securities Held Outright" in Figure 3.5).

QE ends in the US and UK, but then restarts as recoveries slow

After a major improvement in financial markets and something of a recovery in economic growth over the second half of 2009 and the first half of 2010, partly as a result of QE1, the central banks in both the USA and the UK ended their asset purchases in 1Q 2010. By this time, their balance sheets had risen to over 15 per cent of GDP from a little over 5 per cent before the crisis (see Figure 3.4). However, after some initial optimism that a self-sustaining economic recovery was likely to occur across the developed economies, growth began to moderate in the second half of 2010 as the boost from the traditional inventory replenishment cycle and fiscal stimulus packages began to fade and amid the intensification of the euro area crisis (Ashworth 2013).

There was little appetite though on behalf of governments for new fiscal stimulus programmes. Indeed, there was rising public anger in a number of countries, which was particularly vociferous in the US, about record government deficits and surging government debt (see Figure 3.7). At the same time, the euro area sovereign debt crisis was putting governments under severe pressure to enact policies to repair their damaged public finances. There were also fears that the crisis could spread to other countries with weak public finances, with the famous PIMCO bond fund manager Bill Gross writing in February 2010 that UK government bonds "are resting on a bed of nitroglycerine" (Gross 2010). Amid such concerns, the Conservative party won the May 2010 UK general election on a platform of aggressive fiscal austerity, aiming to largely eliminate the fiscal deficit (which was an enormous 10 per cent of GDP in 2009) over the next five years. Against this backdrop of rising political and market pressure against deficits and rising government debt, it was difficult for governments to step in and support growth and, indeed, most were actually about to embark on a material fiscal tightening which would provide new headwinds to growth. As Figure 3.8 highlights, structural budget deficits began declining quickly (becoming less negative) as governments cut spending and/or raised taxes. As a result, central banks had become, in the words of former PIMCO CEO Mohammed El-Erian, "the only game in town" (El-Erian 2017).

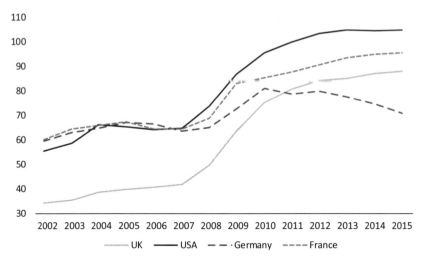

Figure 3.7. Government debt as a per cent of GDP surges amid the GFC
Source: IMF.

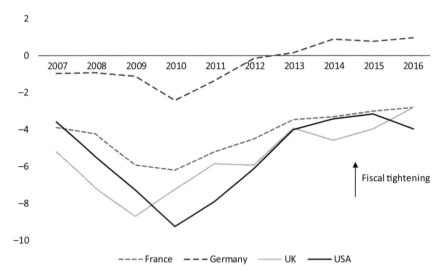

Figure 3.8. Fiscal tightening (structural government budget balance, per cent of GDP)
Source: IMF.

With US growth modest, the unemployment rate almost 10 per cent and weak inflation beginning to stoke some concerns about the risks of deflation (Dudley 2010), the Fed unleashed a second round of LSAPs (QE2) in November 2010, which consisted of $600 billion of government bond purchases through mid-2011. The decision was not supported by all Fed members, however, with some suggesting that the new purchases would only have a limited economic impact and risked an "undesirably large increase in inflation". One voted against the move suggesting it risked a further misallocation of resources and future imbalances and that it could jeopardize the Fed's independence and cause inflation expectations to rise (Board of Governors of the Federal Reserve System 2010).The new round of QE came at a time when the opposition Republican party had made massive electoral gains in Congressional elections, buoyed by the "Tea Party" movement, which mobilized public anger against the so-called Wall Street "bailouts", bankers' bonuses, the Obama administration's new healthcare programme and soaring government debt. Against this backdrop, the Fed received significant criticism from Conservative politicians, with the Republican leadership in Congress writing to Chair Ben Bernanke to express deep concerns about the new round of QE (Bernanke 2015a). They argued that "such a measure introduces significant uncertainty regarding the future strength of the dollar and could result both in hard-to-control, long-term inflation and potentially generate artificial asset bubbles that could cause further economic disruptions". They also highlighted criticism of the Fed's actions by foreign central banks and governments, suggesting that "any action taken by our nation or foreign nations that impairs U.S. trade relations at a time when we should be fighting global trade protection measures will only further harm the global economy and could delay recovery in the United States" (Business Insider 2010). Thoma (2017) suggests that Republican criticisms of the Fed partly reflected genuine fears about the inflationary consequences of QE and partly were a partisan inclination to attack an institution that was seen to be allied with the Obama administration.

I will discuss the international spillovers and criticisms of QE in Chapter 6 and its negative externalities in Chapter 7. Amid the significant political criticism both domestically and overseas, President Obama defended the Fed's actions suggesting that its mandate was to grow the economy and that a stronger US recovery would help to boost the global economy (Reuters 2010).

Kuttner (2018) notes that in 2011 the Fed's forward guidance on interest rates began to involve calendar-based statements and explicit time horizons (for example, at its August 2011 meeting, the Fed suggested it expected low rates "at least through mid-2013"), but suggests that the horizons were repeatedly pushed out given the softness in the economy. He notes that forward guidance subsequently became more explicit, with the FOMC suggesting that interest rates would remain low as long as the unemployment rate remained above 6.5 per cent and the FOMC's inflation forecast was below 2.5 per cent.

The Fed did not announce a further round of asset purchases when QE2 ended, but with slow growth, problems in euro area sovereign debt markets beginning to spill over to the global economy and political gridlock in Washington raising the risk of significant fiscal tightening, it announced a maturity extension programme (MEP) at its September 2011 meeting, whereby the Fed would sell some of its holdings of shorter-term government bonds and use the proceeds to purchase $400 billion of longer-term government bonds until mid-2012. This was similar to the policy carried out by the Kennedy Administration and the Fed in 1961 which was called "Operation Twist" (Alon & Swanson 2011; Swanson 2011). The rationale for the policy is that changes in longer-term interest rates are typically estimated to have much larger impacts on the US economy than shorter-term rates (Rudebusch 2010) given the much greater sensitivity of important sectors such as housing to longer-term rates. In contrast to QE, however, the MEP would not increase the size of the Fed's balance sheet and the level of reserve balances. This could help insulate the Fed somewhat from the growing criticism in Conservative circles that it was "money printing" and "debasing the US dollar" (Ashworth 2013). Nevertheless, three Fed members still voted against the action. The Fed announced an extension of its MEP programme in June 2012 until year-end.

Meanwhile, with the unemployment rate still elevated and concerns that growth would not be strong enough to generate a sustained improvement in the labour market, the Fed announced its final round of QE (QE3) in September 2012 with $40 billion per month in agency MBS purchases. This was expanded to $85 billion in December, with an additional $45 billion per month of government bond purchases. The Fed committed to continue with the programme on an open-ended basis until a substantial improvement in the labour market occurred (which led to the programme being dubbed "QE Infinity"). The announcement of a monthly "flow" of asset purchases marked a change from QE1 and QE2 where the Fed had announced an overall "stock" of purchases (Gagnon & Sack 2018) and there were a number of reasons for making the purchases open-ended. First, it would send a signal that the Fed was committed to doing whatever was necessary to fuel a sustainable recovery. Second, a number of FOMC members felt that an ongoing programme, whose size could be adjusted in response to the economic data, was preferable to previous rounds of QE which involved rather abrupt withdrawals of stimulus as the programmes ended, only to be followed by renewed purchases once growth began to moderate (Ashworth 2013). Ahead of November's presidential election, the Fed's actions once again received criticism from the opposition Republicans. The Romney electoral campaign also suggested the Fed's need to restart QE was further evidence that the incumbent

Obama administration's economic policies were not working (*Guardian* 2012). However, cynics may suggest Republican criticisms simply reflected fears that renewed QE would boost the stock market and economy and help President Obama win re-election.[16]

The Fed tapered off its asset purchases over 2014 and, when its programme ended in October, its balance sheet had reached approximately 25 per cent of GDP (see Figure 3.4). With the economic recovery accelerating in 2017, the Fed began to reduce the size of its balance sheet in a process typically referred to as balance sheet normalization or quantitative tightening (QT). I will discuss this in Chapter 8.

In the UK, with the economy on the verge of another recession in the autumn of 2011 amid fiscal tightening and the ongoing euro area crisis, the Monetary Policy Committee (MPC) launched QE2 announcing £75 billion of government bond purchases in October, with a further £50 billion unveiled in February 2012. After a brief pause, the MPC sanctioned an additional £50 billion of purchases at its July meeting. This took the size of its stock of asset purchases to £375 billion or approximately 25 per cent of GDP (see Figure 3.4). The MPC's final round of QE (QE3) came in August 2016, as the authorities attempted to support the economy in the aftermath of the public's surprise referendum vote to leave the European Union (EU). In addition to cutting interest rates from 0.5 per cent to 0.25 per cent and introducing a new long-term lending programme for banks (the Term Funding Scheme), the government increased QE by £70 billion – £60 billion and £10 billion of government and corporate bond purchases respectively.

From a political standpoint, the incumbent Conservative-Liberal Democrat coalition government was generally supportive of QE2 and other monetary easing by the BoE as it provided an important offset to the large negative economic impacts from its aggressive attempts to repair the public finances via fiscal austerity (which included VAT rate hikes and spending cuts). Moreover, the main initial focus of policy criticism from the opposition Labour party was centred on the government's fiscal austerity measures which it claimed were impoverishing people and damaging vital public services. The main criticisms of QE in the media were about the negative impact it was having on the value of people's pension income.[17] Over time, however, as the economy has recovered, QE has received criticism from both political sides for increasing inequality amid the sharp rise in house prices (see Chapter 7).

Japan unleashes a huge new QE programme amid "Abenomics"

With the economy remaining sluggish and still mired in deflation, Shinzo Abe of the Liberal Democratic Party (LDP) won the December 2012 Japanese general election on an aggressive economic platform dubbed "Abenomics", which aimed to propel the country out of its two-decade-long economic torpor since the bursting of its asset bubbles. One of the "three arrows" of Abenomics was very aggressive monetary easing, alongside fiscal stimulus and structural reforms.

Under significant pressure from the new government (which threatened to revise the law which granted its independence), the BoJ adopted a higher 2 per cent inflation target (Hausman & Wieland 2014) and a new Governor, Haruhiko Kuroda, known to favour very aggressive monetary easing, was appointed. This was a classic example of how an "independent" central bank and its policies can still be subject to significant political influence. At his first meeting in April 2013, Kuroda dramatically ratcheted up the pace of monetary easing with a new pro-gramme called "quantitative and qualitative easing" (QQE). This contained two main features: first, a strong and clear commitment to achieve the inflation target "at the earliest possible time, with a time horizon of about two years"; second, a massive monetary easing to underpin this commitment (Kuroda 2013a, 2013b).

As part of this easing, the target for monetary policy was changed from the main UOCR to the quantity of monetary base and there was an enormous increase in the purchases of JGBs, an increase in the maturity of the bonds bought and increased purchases of equity ETFs and J-REITs. Kuroda described QQE as being "a new phase of monetary easing" and an "unprecedented policy", which was clearly underlined by the sheer scale of the asset purchases involved, with both the size of the monetary base and the BoJ's holdings of JGBs set to double in the space of just two years! Meanwhile, the "qualitative" aspect of the policy also emphasized the importance given to the types of assets purchased. For example, purchasing longer-dated JGBs and/or equity ETFs/J-REITs is likely to have a significantly more powerful impact than purchasing in equal quan-tities Treasury bills and shorter-dated JGBs. As discussed in Chapter 2, a key criticism of Japan's initial experiment with QE between 2001–06 was that the BoJ's purchases were predominantly shorter-dated government bonds which are close substitutes for cash. I will discuss this further in Chapters 4 and 5 when discussing the efficacy of QE.

Overall, a key aim of what many observers described as a "regime change", was to shock the inflationary expectations of the general public, businesses and investors and, hence, permanently end the damaging deflationary mindset that had been so prevalent over recent decades. As a result, it was hoped that rising inflation, together with lower longer-term interest rates from the bond purchases, would help reduce real interest rates and boost economic growth.

Amid a large drag on the economy from a rise in the consumption tax rate and the depressing effect on inflation expectations from a sharp fall in oil prices (Shirai 2018b), the BoJ further significantly ramped up the scale of its easing in

October 2014, raising the annual increase in its holdings of JGBs from purchases from ¥50 trillion to ¥80 trillion, extending again the average maturity of JGB purchases and tripling the purchase of equity ETFs and J-REITs. Moreover, with inflation and inflation expectations struggling to rise to the BoJ's 2 per cent target despite a labour market approaching "full employment", further monetary easing was enacted, including two notable policy changes with the introduction of "QQE with a Negative Interest Rate" and "QQE with Yield Curve Control" in January and October 2016 respectively.[18] In the former, a modestly negative interest rate of –0.1 per cent was placed on a small portion of current account balances (reserve balances) held by commercial banks at the BoJ.[19] In the latter, instead of targeting a specific quantity of JGBs in its asset purchases, it switched to targeting specific interest rates for the short-term interest rate and the 10-year JGB, initially targeting a short rate of –0.1 per cent and a 10-year JGB yield of 0 per cent. In this framework, the quantity of JGBs purchased would thus be endogenous to achieving this target rate for the 10-year JGB.[20] Shirai (2018b) suggests that one of the reasons for adopting yield curve control (which was consistent with a slightly higher 10-year JGB yield and hence, a steeper yield curve) was criticism about the harmful impact that the adoption of negative interest rates was having on financial institutions, amid a squeeze on banking sector profitability and as an "excessive" decline in longer-term JGB yields made it difficult for pension funds and insurance companies to earn sufficient returns on such assets.

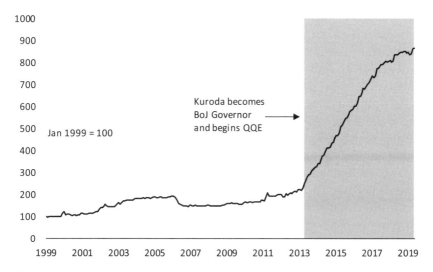

Figure 3.9. Japanese monetary base surges
Source: Bank of Japan, Federal Reserve Bank of St. Louis (FRED).

From the onset of QQE in April 2013, the size of the BoJ's balance sheet has increased from around 33 per cent of GDP at the beginning of 2013 to over 100 per cent at present (see Figure 3.4) and it now holds over 40 per cent of all outstanding government bonds. The monetary base has more than tripled (see Figure 3.9) and the massive increase in current account balances held by financial institutions at the BoJ account for almost all of the increase in the BoJ's liabilities. Political criticism of QE has been relatively muted in Japan. This may reflect a perceived acknowledgement on behalf of the general public and media that extraordinary measures needed to be taken to try to finally rid the economy of deflation or it could perhaps also to some extent reflect the weakness of opposition parties during this period. As noted above, the BoJ has received criticism that its policies have been harming the functioning and profitability of the banking sector.

Europe finally begins QE

Despite the easing of the region's sovereign debt crisis after Draghi's "whatever it takes" speech and the subsequent emergence from the "double-dip" recession in 2013, the region's economic recovery remained extremely tepid amid a severely weakened banking system, high unemployment and continued aggressive fiscal tightening as countries tried to repair their damaged public finances. The lack-lustre recovery came despite further monetary easing by the ECB. This included the introduction of forward guidance on interest rates from the summer of 2013 where it suggested that it "expects the key ECB interest rates to remain at present or lower levels for an extended period of time", a reduction of the official deposit interest rate into negative territory from the summer of 2014 and new large longer-term lending programmes called targeted longer-term refinancing operations (TLTROs) (Dell' Ariccia *et al.* 2018, Praet 2018). The latter provided loans for up to four years, with the amount that financial institutions could borrow linked to the size of their lending to businesses and consumers.

Against such a subdued economic backdrop – and with most measures of inflation extremely low and fears of deflation risks increasing – a programme of QE was finally announced in January 2015, with asset purchases of €60 billion per month beginning in March and to continue until the end of September 2016. Altavilla *et al.* (2016) note that the initial intended size was comparable as a share of GDP to that of US QE1. The ECB also provided an open-ended element to the purchases suggesting that they "will in any case be conducted until we see a sustained adjustment in the path of inflation which is consistent with our aim of achieving inflation rates below, but close to, 2 per cent over the medium term" (ECB 2015). The purchases consisted of both government bonds and private sector bonds such as covered bonds and asset-backed securities, although government bonds constituted the bulk of the purchases.[21]

The programme was specifically designed to help allay fears in Germany and some other northern European countries that it was not central bank financing of government deficits and disguised fiscal redistribution from the richer and fiscally sounder states to their poorer peers in the periphery. In particular, government bond purchases were made in *secondary* markets rather than directly from governments and in proportion to each country's share in the euro area's GDP and population rather than their share of government debt outstanding. Moreover, the ECB was not allowed to own more than one-third of a country's outstanding government debt and the national central banks such as Bank of Italy, Bank of Spain, etc., were responsible for four-fifths of both the purchases and any losses made rather than the ECB. [22]

Despite this, the vote in favour of QE was not unanimous, with Bundesbank President Jens Weidmann once again opposed (Reuters 2015), and there was firm opposition within Germany with "What happens to my money now? ECB takes billions of debt off ailing euro states" being the headline on the website of popular German newspaper *Bild* (*Financial Times* 2015a). Unlike with the OMT, the German government was not supportive of QE (*Financial Times* 2015b) and finance minister Wolfgang Schauble later suggested the ECB's easy monetary policy was helping to fuel the rise of populist parties. Brunnermeier *et al.* (2016) suggest that German opposition to QE was articulated in the public debate along several lines. From an economics standpoint, it was argued that low inflation was not necessarily a bad thing, given it was owing to falling oil prices, and that it was not clear that QE would be particularly effective in the euro area. On the programme itself, it was said to represent an inappropriate mixing of fiscal and monetary policy given that it would help recapitalize peripheral banks through the gains in value on their existing government bond holdings and there were worries about the credit risks from the ECB buying bonds from fiscally weaker countries and also that it may reduce the incentives of such countries to reduce their deficits and debts. Meanwhile, despite the agreement of all ECB Governing Council members that its QE as configured was legal (ECB 2015), the ECB's right to do it was once again challenged in the German Constitutional Court. The latter referred the case to the ECJ, which again ruled in favour of the ECB in late 2018, suggesting that "It does not exceed the ECB's mandate and does not contravene the prohibition of monetary financing" (Bloomberg 2018).

Amid continued depressed inflation and weaker than expected growth, the size of the ECB's monthly purchases rose to €80 billion per month in March 2016 and purchases of corporate bonds were included. They were expected to continue until March 2017, but retained an open-ended optionality. The governing council also used forward guidance to suggest that it "expects the key

ECB interest rates to remain at present or lower levels for an extended period of time, and well past the horizon of our net asset purchases" (ECB 2016). Asset purchases were eventually reduced back down to €60 billion from April 2017 as the economic recovery gained momentum and were further tapered before finally ending in December 2018. However, amid renewed economic weakness, the ECB restarted its QE programme in September 2019, purchasing €20 billion of government bonds per month. It also cut interest rates further to −0.5 per cent. There was significant internal dissent amongst ECB members from the northern European countries at the decision to resume QE and German ECB Executive Board member Sabine Lautenschlager announced her intention to resign over the issue (Reuters 2019).

Since the beginning of QE, the size of the ECB's balance sheet has increased from around 20 per cent of GDP to 40 per cent at present (see Figure 3.4) and the national central banks (which carried out the purchases) now own around one-fifth of outstanding government bonds in France, Germany, Italy and Spain (Bruegel database of sovereign bond holdings developed in Merler and Pisani-Ferry 2012).

After beginning with a brief overview of the GFC, in this chapter I have provided a timeline and detailed description of the QE programmes of the major central banks. This included discussing the economic rationale behind them, the types of assets bought and the huge resultant increase in the size of their balance sheets. I also highlighted the significant political economy issues that were encountered. The BoJ faced massive political pressure to be more aggressive with its monetary easing, while the Fed and ECB faced significant criticism against further easing from certain quarters. In the next chapter, I will discuss the main theoretical and practical channels in which QE was expected to work and why it is likely to have diminishing returns over time.

4

HOW QUANTITATIVE EASING WORKS

The initial rounds of QE in the major Western economies gained significant attention well beyond just the financial press, likely reflecting its reputation as such a "nuclear" policy option and given that some observers were suggesting that central banks were engaged in "money printing" which would ultimately fuel runaway inflation as in Weimar Germany or Zimbabwe. Indeed, various newspaper cartoons depicted central bankers distributing large amounts of banknotes to the general public either by throwing them into the air or shovelling them into sacks (see Figure 4.1). There has even been a Barry White-style themed song made about QE and a highly critical cartoon around the time of US QE2 has gained over six million views (the cartoon's creator has subsequently acknowledged that most of his criticisms have proved incorrect!).[1]

It must be acknowledged that any economist recommending QE's use in western economies prior to the GFC would have been considered rather dangerous, but with hindsight many of the well-publicized fears surrounding QE now appear overblown (although, as I discuss later, it is still too early to make a definitive judgement on whether they may ultimately transpire). At the same time, while it was undoubtedly crucial in helping to end the downward spiral in economies during the GFC and supporting growth subsequently, it has not proved quite as powerful an economic tool as many had initially expected. Summarizing his opinion on the experimentation with unconventional monetary policies at a 2015 IMF conference, Nobel Laureate Paul Krugman suggested "the bad stuff unpersuasive, the good stuff maybe, but not really compelling, this has just not turned out to be the game changing policy tool that people had expected".

In this chapter, I examine the practical and theoretical channels through which QE works. In Chapter 5, I examine the actual financial and economic impacts in the major countries in which it was deployed and, in Chapter 6, I analyze the international spillovers. In Chapter 7, I discuss the feared side-effects and other potential negative externalities.

Figure 4.1. Early newspaper depictions of QE
Source: Kipper Williams, *The Guardian*, 6 March 2009.

Main channels through which QE works

The main transmission channels through which QE was initially expected to boost growth and inflation around the time of the GFC were: (i) confidence; (ii) policy signalling; (iii) portfolio rebalancing; (iv) market liquidity; and (v) money (see Figure 4.2 below from the BoE's 3Q 2011 Quarterly Bulletin and Box 3 for a simple visualization of how some of these channels may work in practice). Of course, these channels are not mutually exclusive (IMF 2013a).

Confidence: By unleashing this new and potentially very powerful tool in an aggressive manner, policy-makers could increase expectations among investors, firms and households of a recovery in asset prices, economic growth and inflation. This could help end the vicious cycle and potentially create the underpinnings

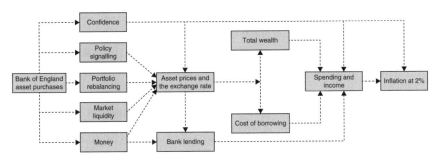

Figure 4.2. QE transmission channels
Source: Bank of England Quarterly Bulletin Q3 2011.

of a new virtuous one. Policy-makers were in effect trying to boost (or arrest the decline in) what Keynes famously referred to as the "animal spirits" of the private sector (Keynes 1936). Important in this regard, central banks were not just trying to shift expectations of the *modal* scenario, but limit perceived probabilities of far worse tail-risk outcomes such as another Great Depression or deflation.

Policy signalling: Asset purchases are likely to lead investors to expect short-term official interest rates to remain lower for longer than previously expected. First, the initial decision to begin asset purchases is likely to provide new information to investors about the committee's current assessment of the economic outlook and its policy bias (for example, growth is weak and policy needs to be eased in order for inflation to reach the central bank's target). Second, as previously discussed, another form of unconventional monetary policy that has been used is forward guidance on the future path of interest rates. Its efficacy, however, depends on the credibility of the central bank's commitment. Investors and the general public may fear that the central bank will renege on prior commitments to keep interest rates low as soon as the economy starts to recover. Given that QE is a policy that central banks are only likely to resort to at the ZLB when additional stimulus is deemed necessary, investors are likely to expect that short-term interest rates will not rise for at least the duration of the asset purchase programme (Bernanke 2020). Moreover, Clouse *et al.* (2000) suggest that asset purchases might be a way of signalling a commitment to keep short-term policy rates low in the future, as the increase in the size of the central bank's long-term bond holdings through QE would leave it vulnerable to capital losses in the event that it was to raise policy rates sooner or much more aggressively than financial markets expected.

For economists of the New Keynesian School, policy signalling is likely to be the most powerful channel of QE in boosting the economy (Woodford 2012). The combination of delayed expectations of the timing of future tightening in short-term interest rates and increased inflationary expectations should ensure that the projected path of real short-term interest rates is lower than before the onset of QE. This should encourage the private sector to bring forward future spending and also boost asset prices.

Portfolio rebalancing: This was a key transmission mechanism highlighted by both the Fed and BoE in QE1. The central bank buys a longer-dated bond from an investor such as a 10-year government bond in exchange for new electronically created money it deposits into the seller's account. In this first stage of portfolio rebalancing, this should reduce the interest rate on the longer-dated bonds purchased.

Fed Chair Ben Bernanke famously quipped after the fact that "the problem with QE is it works in practice, but it doesn't work in theory" (Bernanke 2014). He was in part referring to the fact that in a strict theoretical sense, as discussed in Chapter 3, the interest rate or yield on a longer-term government bond should primarily reflect the expected path of the short-term policy rate over the period in question (influenced somewhat by the policy signalling channel) plus a term premium. As a consequence, this should mean that if central bank purchases of longer-term bonds boosted their price and reduced their yield compared with shorter-term bonds and what is expected by investors based on the economic fundamentals, arbitragers would then sell these longer-term bonds and buy shorter-term bonds negating the impact of the Fed's actions (see Yu 2016 for an excellent and more in-depth exposition).

Yu (2016) highlights two key channels through which this mechanism may operate in practice. First, markets for certain types of bonds may be segregated with investors having what is called a "preferred habitat" (for example, life insurance companies like to hold longer-term bonds as they match the longer-term nature of their liabilities). Consequently, if the central bank reduces the available supply of these bonds through its purchases, it will boost their price and reduce their interest rate. For example, even if central bank purchases significantly pushed up the price of 10-year or 20-year government bonds beyond what may be deemed justified based on expected interest rates over the period and an appropriate term premium (see Chapter 3), life insurance companies may still prefer to continue to purchase the relatively expensive longer-term bonds than their shorter-term peers which they consider to be imperfect substitutes. In this case, asset prices partly reflect the valuations of these *segmented* investors (IMF 2013a). This is also commonly referred to in the literature as the "local supply" channel (Bhattarai & Neely 2016). Yu (2016) also highlights a number of reasons why in reality arbitragers face a number of impediments (such as the availability of financing), which are likely to increase during a financial crisis.

Second, as previously highlighted, the term premium is the compensation that investors require for the risks associated with investing in longer-term bonds.

This risk is often referred to as duration risk and increases with the maturity of the bond. Yu (2016) suggests that by reducing the amounts of these riskier longer-term bonds held by private investors (for example, government bonds and US agency MBS), central bank purchases will make the portfolios of investors safer and may result in them requiring less compensation to bear this duration risk, resulting in higher prices for longer-term bonds and lower interest rates.[2] The IMF (2013a) suggests that safer portfolios amid the lower exposure to interest rate risk should result in lower yields on bonds of all maturities, not just on the ones purchased. Similarly, Gagnon *et al.* (2011) highlight the additional specific risks inherent in mortgage-backed securities (for example, prepayment risk). By reducing the amount of these held by private investors, they note that central banks can similarly reduce the compensation investors require for bearing this risk and the interest rate on them should fall.

In the final part of portfolio rebalancing, given that the sellers of the bonds to the central bank are unlikely to view the new central bank money they hold as a perfect substitute for the asset they sold (the Fed and BoE eschewed buying shorter-dated government bonds like Japan in 2001–06, as these are close substitutes for cash at the ZLB), they are typically likely to want to use it to rebalance their portfolios by purchasing assets that are closer substitutes to the assets they sold such as corporate bonds and equities (Brunner & Meltzer 1973; Friedman & Schwartz 1982). This will boost the prices of these assets and reduce their yields, increasing wealth across the economy and reducing the costs for corporates of raising external financing via the corporate debt and equity markets.

Market liquidity: When financial markets have become dysfunctional, as they did in the GFC, asset purchases by central banks can improve market functioning and liquidity. By purchasing massive amounts of assets central banks can create huge amounts of excess reserves at commercial banks and hence, help satiate their liquidity needs and contribute to an improvement in bank funding markets.

Moreover, Gagnon *et al.* (2011) suggest that by providing an ongoing source of demand for longer-term assets, asset purchases may have allowed dealers and other investors to take larger positions in these securities or to make markets in them more actively, knowing that they could sell the assets, if necessary, to the central bank. This is where the central bank adopts the role of market maker of last resort (Buiter & Sibert 2007). Asset prices thus increase as investors demand a lower risk premium for liquidity.[3] During the crisis, the Fed's purchases of agency MBS and agency debt and the BoE's purchases of commercial paper and corporate bonds were important in this regard (see Chapter 5).

Central banks can also indirectly influence this channel in important ways. First, the reduction of major economic tail risks (such as another Great Depression or deflation) as a result of QE is also likely to improve market functioning and increase liquidity by renewing investor interest and participation in certain riskier asset classes which they may otherwise have eschewed. Second, by boosting asset prices, Bhattarai & Neely (2016) suggest QE is likely to improve the balance sheets of financial intermediaries and, hence, their willingness and capacity to bear risk. They note that according to "intermediary asset-pricing" theories, the balance sheets of financial intermediaries play a critical role in the pricing of corporate bonds, because such intermediaries are the marginal investors in the market. Given the severely impaired banking systems during the GFC, restoring financial intermediation through the financial markets was particularly crucial. Of course, the various LOLR programmes developed by central banks were also very important in this regard.

Money: Goodhart (2010b) notes:

> that the standard approach in monetary economics to explaining the supply of money, and the provision of bank credit to the private sector, has been the money multiplier approach, whereby the central bank sets the high-powered monetary base (H), and then the stock of money (M) is a multiple of that [see Equation 1].

By purchasing assets from the non-bank private sector via newly created electronic money, the central bank injects monetary base into the financial system and these funds should end up in deposits at the commercial banks. The extra liquidity at banks should help to fuel an increase in bank lending and a rise in the broader measures of money supply. This should help to boost nominal spending and inflation. This is a key channel through which the Monetarist School of economic thought would typically expect QE to work.[4] The BoE initially emphasized this as one of the main channels of QE, admittedly at times with a degree of caution. The Fed appeared less confident of this channel given the damaged banking system and perhaps reflecting the experience of Japan in its initial experiment with QE.[5]

Equation 1:

$$M = H \bullet \frac{(1 + \frac{C}{D})}{(\frac{R}{D} + \frac{C}{D})} \leftarrow \text{Money Multiplier}$$

M = broad money supply (for example, M2, M3, M4, etc.), H = monetary base, C/D = currency/deposits ratio, R/D = bank reserves/deposits ratio.[6]

BOX 3: HOW QE WOULD IMPACT BOND YIELDS DURING THE GFC

A very simple highly stylized diagram (see Figure 4.3) showing the interest rate on the same hypothetical 10-year US *corporate* bond both before and during the GFC can help visualize some of the channels through which QE was expected to work. As discussed previously, the yield on a 10-year US *government* bond has two components: the expected FFR over the 10-year period plus the term premium. Added to this for a 10-year *corporate* bond, there is what is called a liquidity premium and a credit risk premium. The former reflects an extra yield investors receive to compensate for the fact that market liquidity is lower for corporate bonds than government bonds (for example, it may be harder to sell the bond at the time you want for the price you desire), while the latter compensates for the risk that the company issuing the bond could go bankrupt in the future and default on the bond.[7]

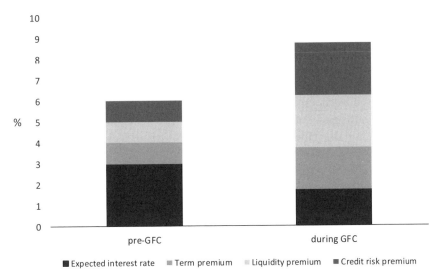

Figure 4.3. Stylized 10-year corporate bond yields
Source: Ashworth (2020).

As Figure 4.3 highlights, despite a much lower expected FFR during the GFC period given that the Fed had cut the FFR to the ZLB and amid the much weaker economic outlook, the overall corporate bond yield has actually significantly increased amid higher term, liquidity and credit risk premiums. The asset purchases can help significantly reduce the corporate bond yield by: (i) further reducing the expected path of the FFR over the next several years via the policy signalling channel; (ii) reducing the term premium through the portfolio rebalancing channel; (iii) reducing the liquidity and credit risk premiums by significantly calming and helping to restore the functioning of financial markets, reducing tail risks and contributing to a stabilization and subsequent recovery in growth. This would occur via the market liquidity and portfolio rebalancing channels and also via the confidence channel which will impact all the other channels to varying degrees. (For a useful summary of the various risks inherent in different types of bonds, see Bhattarai & Neely 2016: 45 and Table 1.)

US and UK QE differed from the initial Japanese experiment

Fed officials emphasized early on the significant differences between their own asset purchase programme and the policy of QE first pioneered by Japan in 2001 (Bernanke 2009a; Yellen 2009) with Fed Chair Bernanke initially often referring to the Fed's programmes as "credit easing" rather than QE and the Fed has since typically referred to them as "large-scale asset purchases" (Bhattarai & Neely 2016). Amid the financial market chaos in 2008–09, the key focus of the Fed and BoE was purchasing assets in order to boost their prices and lower their yields via the channels discussed previously. Hence, their focus was on the asset side of their balance sheets and the consequent increase in their liabilities (primarily reserve balances) were entirely a side effect of the purchases. The Fed and BoE also focused their purchases on the non-bank private sector (such as pension funds, mutual funds, insurance companies), in order to try to bypass the impaired banking system.

In contrast, as discussed in Chapter 2, when Japan first carried out QE, the BoJ was firmly focused on the liability side of its balance sheet, setting targets for the size of increase in its reserve balances (called current account balances in Japan) in order to boost liquidity in the banking system in the hope it would encourage banks to start lending. It did not pay much attention to the asset side of its balance sheet, injecting the funds by primarily buying short-dated government securities from the banks (with interest rates close to zero, these were very close substitutes for cash). Bernanke (2009a) suggests the respective strategies reflected their differing situations, where, in contrast to the US, the Japanese were no longer facing a financial crisis (for example, elevated credit spreads, dysfunctional asset markets, etc.) by the time they started QE in 2001.

Other channels in which QE is beneficial

There are some other channels through which QE is likely to be beneficial which appear to have gained more attention from some central banks over time.

Exchange rates: By reducing interest rates across the yield curve during QE, this should reduce the relative attractiveness of domestic assets for both domestic and foreign investors and hence, weaken the domestic currency. This should increase the country's international trade competitiveness and improve its net trade position. In the initial stages of the GFC, central banks did not go out of their way to emphasize this channel, probably reflecting fears of being accused of engaging in competitive devaluation which could stoke a deterioration in international trade relations and a rise in global protectionism. The latter was said to be an important factor in exacerbating the negative impacts of the Great Depression. The lack of early emphasis probably also reflected the fact that during the midst of the financial crisis this was probably seen as being a less important channel of QE. This is particularly the case for the largely closed US economy, while the UK had already experienced a massive currency depreciation over 2007 and 2008. The Bank for International Settlements (BIS) (2016) highlights the more frequent references made to exchange rates in monetary policy statements and press conferences by developed market central banks in recent years (see Figure 4.4), which they ascribe to the waning effectiveness of the domestic channels for unconventional monetary policy. Rajan (2014) suggests that "some advanced economy central bankers have privately expressed their worry to me that QE 'works' primarily by altering exchange rates".

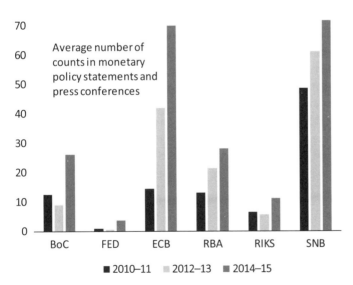

Figure 4.4. Increased references to exchange rates by central banks
Source: BIS (2016); M. Ferrari, J. Kearns and A. Schrimpf, "Monetary policy and the exchange rate", BIS mimeo, 2016; national data; BIS calculations. BoC = Bank of Canada, RBA = Reserve Bank of Australia, RIKS = Sveriges Riksbank, SNB = Swiss National Bank.

Improving the public finances: By purchasing medium and longer-term government bonds in the initial rounds of QE, central banks significantly reduced the interest rates that their governments had to pay on bond issuance, which was increasing substantially amid soaring fiscal deficits. In addition, in the process of QE, the Fed and the BoE accumulated bonds that were yielding low (single-digit) interest rates in exchange for providing investors with reserve balances which were yielding practically zero at the time. This spread represented a significant additional gain, which the central banks would send (the accrued payments on) back to their governments. Initially, the central banks did not really emphasize the benefits to the public finances, probably reflecting the fact that it was not one of the most important channels during the crisis. They may have also feared accusations that they were helping to monetize government deficits. Over time, however, the Fed and BoE have highlighted the benefits of QE to the government finances, often in the context of criticism from some quarters that their purchases could ultimately lead to capital losses and pose a risk to the public finances. Perhaps unsurprisingly, the ECB has typically stayed clear of mentioning the fiscal benefits for fear of the German reaction, if they appeared to be engaging in monetary financing of government deficits.

Raising inflation expectations: During QE1, the Fed and the BoE were quite explicit in their views that, by boosting growth and reducing economic slack, their asset purchases aimed to prevent inflation falling persistently below target (thereby risking inflation expectations permanently moving downwards, even raising the risk of deflation). That said, they were relatively measured in their language when discussing inflation expectations, perhaps reflecting the fact that they were in unknown territory, and amid some fears that the talk of "money printing" by certain commentators could lead to a jump in inflation expectations on behalf of investors and the general public (whether or not this was indeed justified or rational). In contrast, QQE in Japan has had a very clear focus on raising inflation and shocking long dormant inflation expectations upwards (towards the 2 per cent inflation target). An important explicit aim of the ECB's QE since 2015 has also been to boost flagging inflation expectations as low inflation has raised concerns about deflation setting in.

QE may have some differing impacts across countries

Some channels of QE are likely to be more efficacious for some economies than others. The boost provided to financial markets from QE through portfolio rebalancing and other channels could make a larger positive contribution to growth in a more market-based financial system such as the US compared with more bank-based systems such as the euro area and Japan. In the US, quite a significant proportion of the population own stocks (either directly or indirectly in their pensions) and, as highlighted previously, the bulk of external financing for US corporates comes from financial markets. Meanwhile, QE was likely more important for the US mortgage and housing markets than in the UK. This is because UK mortgages are predominantly based on shorter-term interest rates of less than five years, whereas US mortgages are based on longer-term interest rates and the Fed was also able to buy mortgage-related securities directly; these represented over 60 per cent of the purchases in US QE1 and QE2. Finally, the exchange rate channel may provide less of a boost to growth and inflation for a very large and relatively closed economy such as the US compared with a medium-sized open economy such as the UK or a small very open economy such as Sweden. That being said, it is still likely to have been quite an important channel in boosting the recoveries in the large, but relatively export dependent economies such as Japan and the euro area.

QE has increasingly involved the purchase of riskier assets

The initial rounds of QE in the US and UK during and following the GFC were almost entirely focused on the purchase of government bonds and, in the case of the former, bonds issued or guaranteed by the GSEs, namely agency debt and agency MBS, which, after the GSEs were taken under de facto government control, were widely seen as having the full-backing of the US government. More recent rounds of QE by central banks have seen them purchase larger amounts of riskier private sector assets. In Japan, around 6 per cent of the massive increase in assets since 2013 has been accounted for by the purchase of equities, which now account for almost 5 per cent of the BoJ's total assets. In the euro area, since the beginning of QE in 2015, around 7 per cent and 10 per cent of the increase in the ECB's assets has been accounted for by corporate and covered bonds respectively (Baltensperger & Call 2018). Moreover, £10 billion of the £75 billion of asset purchases by the BoE in QE3 beginning in 2016 were in corporate bonds. The purchase of private sector assets is often referred to in the literature as "credit policy" and results in central banks taking on credit risk (Borio & Zabai 2016). In some countries such as the UK the government has indemnified the central bank against any losses (including credit) from asset purchases.

QE is likely to have diminishing returns over time

There are a number of practical and theoretical reasons why the power of QE was likely to be at its greatest during the GFC and is likely to have suffered diminishing returns over time. ECB President Mario Draghi (2019a) recently acknowledged that unconventional monetary policy may suffer from decreasing returns, while suggesting that this would not prevent the ECB from doing more.

QE is no longer a new tool: Broadbent (2018) notes, "One thing that may have amplified QE when it was first used was its sheer novelty value. Once markets discover the policy is feasible, perhaps the premium for holding longer-term bonds is permanently lowered, if only to a small extent".[8] Its novelty value when first unveiled as this drastic new policy tool also probably meant that its initial use had powerful positive impacts on the expectations of investors, firms and the general public. While it no doubt played an important part in driving economic recoveries in countries such as the US and UK, the fact that these recoveries remained weak by historical standards and began to lose momentum in the second half of 2010 probably meant that its subsequent use may have influenced expectations somewhat less. Indeed, reflecting this and its widespread use, many economists now view QE as just another conventional monetary policy tool. In addition to the confidence channel, if investors become less confident that the use of QE will generate a robust economic recovery, this may weaken the portfolio rebalancing channel, as they are likely to be less willing to switch out of government bonds into riskier assets such as corporate bonds and equities.

Improved market functioning: As markets had become highly dysfunctional during the GFC, QE helped to improve liquidity and market functioning. In more normal times, this important channel will have no impact though.

Reduced tail risks: An important contribution of QE during the GFC was to reduce the probability investors, economists, firms and households placed on worst-case economic scenarios or deflation occurring (IMF 2013a). Once again, in more normal times, this important channel will have no impact.

Yields curves are significantly flatter now and are even in negative territory in some countries: Government bond yields across short-, medium- and long-term maturities are now significantly lower than during the GFC, meaning that there is much less scope for either the signalling or portfolio rebalancing channels to have an impact (see Figure 4.5). Bernanke (2017a) described the situation of Japan, where both short-term and long-term interest rates are at or near their effective lower bounds, as a "sort of 'super liquidity trap'". Since then, government bond yields have moved yet lower with those on 10-year and 30-year Japanese and German government bonds in or close to negative territory. When central banks purchase bonds with yields so low that the cash the seller receives is effectively a substitute for the sold bond, they are much less likely to rebalance their portfolios into riskier assets such as corporate bonds or equities (IMF 2013a). Moreover, as Turner (2019) notes, the policy signalling channel is

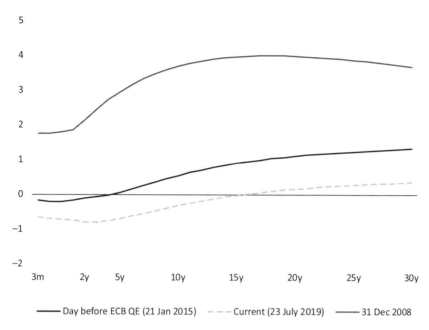

Figure 4.5. Government bond yields are now barely positive in the euro area
Source: ECB.

also likely to be increasingly ineffective: "When German bond yields show that investors expect negative ECB rates for a decade, promising they will not rise until 2021 cannot have more than trivial impact". Meanwhile, there will be a limit on how far into negative territory central banks can push market interest rates through official policy rate cuts and asset purchases. In addition to various negative externalities, at some point investors would probably prefer to hold banknotes than suffer negative returns from government securities.[9]

Negative externalities are likely to increase: When pursuing QE in more normal times, when financial markets are not stressed, the negative externalities are likely to increase. Asset purchases may fuel excessive risk-taking and push asset prices significantly out of line with fundamentals creating financial stability risks and the benefits from a further flattening of the yield curve could be offset by the negative impact it has on banking sector profits (BIS 2016). Indeed, Brunnermeier and Koby (2019) suggest there may be a "reversal interest rate" – a level of rates at which accommodative monetary policy reverses and becomes contractionary for lending, with QE increasing this reversal rate. Meanwhile, the increased purchases of riskier private assets (such as corporate bonds and equities) by central banks could create major political economy issues. This is because they are likely to have greater distributional consequences and expose central banks to greater credit risks. I will discuss negative externalities further in Chapter 7.

In this chapter, I have discussed the main channels through which QE was expected to work when it was first enacted during the GFC by the US and UK, with portfolio rebalancing, policy signalling, market liquidity and confidence expected to be very important. I have also highlighted some other channels that have gained increased attention over time such as exchange rates and the benefits to the public finances. I also argued that the efficacy of QE likely peaked during the GFC and is likely to have experienced diminishing returns over time, while the negative externalities are also likely to have increased. In Chapter 5, I examine in detail how QE has actually worked in practice in the different countries.

5
MEASURING THE EFFECTIVENESS AND IMPACT OF QUANTITATIVE EASING

Methods of estimating QE's impact

Since the 1950s, government statistical organizations in the major developed countries have collected quarterly data on key economic statistics such as GDP, household consumption, gross fixed capital formation, government consumption, exports and imports. They have also collected monthly data on other important series such as inflation, industrial production and retail sales. This wealth of historical data, together with the large number of monetary policy easing and tightening cycles, has allowed economists to make reasonably accurate estimates of the likely impact of changes in interest rates on real GDP and inflation and the time frame over which they are likely to occur. Initial estimations used simple statistical methods, but over time, more advanced econometric modelling techniques have been employed (for example, vector autoregressive models (VARs)) and central banks and public policy institutions have increasingly used large macroeconomic models such as general equilibrium and DSGE models. Given that QE had only ever been used before in Japan, there were few historical precedents to inform policy-makers about its probable impact and, in any case, many may have questioned how transferable the findings would be given the many seemingly unique characteristics of the Japanese economy since the bursting of its asset bubbles.

Numerous studies have now attempted to quantify QE's impact on asset prices, GDP growth (and other measures of economic activity) and inflation. The most common are "event study" analyses which attempt to estimate its effect by measuring the impact of central bank QE-related announcements on financial markets over very short time periods, such as the movement in US 10-year government bond yields over one- or two-day windows after important QE-related announcements from the Fed (see, for example, Gagnon *et al.* 2011; Krishnamurthy & Vissing-Jorgensen 2011; Neely 2011).[1] They then sum up the impact of all the relevant announcements. Table 5.1 based on analysis by Gagnon *et al.* (2011) provides an example of an event study for US QE1. The studies work on the premise that investors immediately factor into asset prices the news of central bank purchases at the time of announcement rather than in the future when the purchases actually occur. This is consistent with the Efficient Markets Hypothesis whereby in efficient, forward-looking financial markets the short-term impact on asset prices is expected to approximate its longer-term impact (Bhattarai & Neely 2016). Of course, some caution is warranted with this approach given that financial markets were not functioning very well during the initial QE announcements and given that the expectations of investors regarding the efficacy of these new instruments could change over time (Fratzscher *et al.* 2013). The focus on very short time windows represents an effort to clearly isolate the impact of the policy change. For example, in the extreme, if one tried to estimate the impact of US QE1 by observing the change in the stock market between the start of QE1 and when it ended, you would also capture the impact of many other factors such as the boost from the large government fiscal stimulus programme, the impact of various LOLR programmes and major economic and political developments overseas.

Subsequent to the announcements of the initial rounds of QE (which were something of a surprise to investors), robust event study analyses could no longer simply rely on just the central bank QE-related announcements to measure the impact of future rounds of asset purchases. This is because it was no longer a new policy tool and financial markets began to factor into asset prices its potential future use after weak economic data releases (Gagnon 2016) or a dovish speech by a policy-maker. For example, in their event study analysis of UK QE2, Goodhart and Ashworth (2012) included the release of the minutes of the September 2011 BoE monetary policy committee meeting, the dovish tone of which had suggested that QE was very likely to restart again at the October meeting, and they also suggested possibly including surveys of business confidence released at the beginning of September. Hence, in addition to some caution when using event studies due to uncertainty over the correct window size to choose, there is a risk that in the later rounds of QE some important events could inadvertently be excluded.

To arrive at a final estimate of the actual impact of QE on the economy, the sum of the estimated movements in the asset prices over the event windows, typically government bond yields, are then plugged into various macroeconomic models which quantify the impact on variables such as GDP and inflation. For example, to estimate the impact of US QE1 using the results from Table 5.1, we would plug the total 91bps decline in US 10-year Treasury yields into the models. Some caution must once again be taken, however, as there is a significant risk that in times of economic and financial stress the transmission

Table 5.1. Event Study of US QE1

Date	Event	Change in 10-year US Treasury yield (bps)
25/11/2008	**Initial LSAP Announcement***	**-22**
01/12/2008	Chairman Speech	-19
16/12/2008	FOMC Statement	-26
28/01/2009	FOMC Statement	14
18/03/2009	**FOMC Statement****	**-47**
12/08/2009	FOMC Statement	5
23/09/2009	FOMC Statement	-3
04/11/2009	FOMC Statement	6
	Total	**-91**

Source: Gagnon *et al.* (2011). This table is created from the authors' larger table and highlights their 'baseline' event set. The event study shows the one-day change in the 10-year US Treasury yield on key announcement dates selected by the authors. * Purchases of $100bn agency debt and $500bn agency MBS were announced. ** Purchases of $100bn agency debt, $750bn agency MBS and $300bn Treasury securities were announced.

mechanism from government bond yields and other asset price changes to economic activity will differ from more normal times under which the models were originally estimated (because of the impaired transmission mechanisms highlighted previously).

Another method to estimate the impact of QE uses time-series regression models. The dependent variable will typically be the 10-year government bond yield or the term premium, and the explanatory variables will include measures of the "net supply of government bonds" in the hands of private investors and other relevant macroeconomic variables (Gagnon *et al.* 2011: section 4.3; D'Amico *et al.* 2012). Historically, an important driver of government bond yields, in addition to monetary policy and the prospects for inflation, is the health of the public finances (for example, the size of the fiscal deficit and, hence, the amount of new bonds the government needs to issue each year in order to finance the excess of its spending over its receipts). As the fiscal deficit and magnitude of bond issuance by the government increases, this will increase the supply of bonds in the hands of private investors, reducing their price and raising their yield. By purchasing government bonds in QE and reducing this supply in the hands of private investors, central banks push up their price and lower their interest rates. The regression coefficient on the net supply of government bonds variable allows an estimation of the impact on government bond yields based on the size of the central bank purchases. As with event studies, one can then plug this number into macroeconomic models to estimate the impacts on real GDP and inflation.

Bhattarai and Neely (2016) highlight a number of problems with using regression analysis, not least the problem of endogeneity of the net supply of government bonds variable (for example, governments may issue more bonds when yields are low). They conclude that:

> Event studies have several advantages over research using lower frequency data. Specifically, the forward-looking nature of financial markets simultaneously makes event studies the appropriate tool for determining the long-run impact of policies while rendering regression studies with lower frequency data much less trustworthy.

Borio and Zabai (2016) also suggest that "Event analysis is probably the more reliable approach, as it better identifies the source of the market reaction".[2]

In the rest of the chapter, I examine the main asset purchase programmes of the major central banks since the GFC: (i) US and UK QE1 during the GFC; (ii) subsequent rounds of QE in the US and UK; (iii) QE in Japan since 2013; (iv) the ECB's OMT programme in 2012 and its QE programme since 2015.

(i) QE1 helped the US and UK economies avoid a worst-case scenario and begin to recover

There have been a large number of studies of QE1 in the US and UK which have typically found that it had large positive effects both on financial markets and the economy. While there is a significant degree of variation in the results, studies suggest that QE1 may have reduced the key 10-year US government bond yield by up to somewhere in the region of 100bps. Falls in the yields on agency debt and agency MBS were typically larger, while the declines in interest rates on corporate bonds, albeit significant, were smaller (see Figure 5.1). Two of the earliest and most frequently cited studies by Gagnon *et al.* (2011) and Krishnamurthy and Vissing-Jorgensen (2011) suggest that US QE1 reduced 10-year government bond yields by 91bps and 107bps respectively, with the majority of this estimated to have come through the portfolio rebalancing channel[3] and to a lesser extent the policy signalling channel. Some subsequent studies have argued, however, that the share of the boost from the policy signalling channel relative to portfolio rebalancing may have been underestimated and that it could account for around half or even up to three-quarters of the reduction in US yields from QE1 (Bauer & Rudebusch 2013; Bauer & Neely 2013; Christensen & Rudebusch 2013). The IMF suggests the evidence for the portfolio rebalancing and signalling channels for US QE1 is balanced (IMF 2013a).[4] Krishnamurthy and Vissing-Jorgensen (2011) find that US QE1 also significantly boosted the inflation expectations of investors, with 10-year expected inflation rising by between 100bps to 150bps, meaning

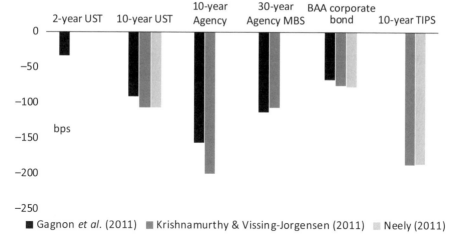

Figure 5.1. Event study analysis of US QE1 by various authors
Source: Estimates from Gagnon *et al.* (2011), Krishnamurthy and Vissing-Jorgensen (2011) and Neely (2011). UST = US Treasury bond, TIPS = Treasury Inflation Protected Security, whose yield in this case measures the 10-year real government bond yield after adjusting for inflation, BAA Corporate bond is an investment grade rated corporate bond whose credit rating is closest to the Speculative/Sub-Investment grade category.

that *real* 10-year interest rates or yields actually fell by up to 200bps for borrowers.[5]

The Fed's purchases also provided a boost through the market functioning and liquidity channel. At the most basic level, the massive increase in excess reserves at commercial banks helped satiate their liquidity needs and contributed to an improvement in bank funding markets. Meanwhile, Gagnon *et al.* (2011) note that spreads of the yields of agency debt and agency MBS over government bonds were well above historical norms at the start of QE1 (amid the dysfunctional markets) and that the Fed's purchases appeared to have improved liquidity in the market with spreads subsequently narrowing. Hancock and Passmore (2011) argue "this return to normal pricing occurred because the Federal Reserve's announcement signaled a strong and credible government backing for mortgage markets in particular and for the financial system more generally". Gagnon *et al.* (2011) also suggest that there was illiquidity in the Treasury market for some older Treasury bonds which improved after the Fed's asset purchases began.

The large overall falls in yields on agency debt and agency MBS from the Fed's purchases resulted in significant declines in mortgage rates for home purchases. Hancock and Passmore (2011) estimate that QE1 lowered mortgage rates by approximately 100bps to 150bps, with most of this occurring after the initial announcement of the programme but before any actual purchases occurred. They highlight the fact that the sharp initial falls in mortgage rates fuelled a surge in mortgage refinancing activity by homeowners. Then San Francisco Fed President John Williams suggested that the Fed's purchase of agency MBS provides the "biggest bang for the buck on private borrowing rates in the economy" (Reuters 2013).

Another way in which QE had a very significant positive impact was in materially reducing the perceived probability among the general public, firms and investors that worst-case tail-risk scenarios such as another Great Depression or deflation were likely to materialize. This worked through most of the major channels, particularly Confidence, Market Liquidity and Portfolio rebalancing. For example, by reducing concerns about another Great Depression, this likely moderated the extent to which households and firms reduced their spending and persuaded investors not to exit and/or to re-enter certain riskier asset classes which they otherwise would have eschewed, hence, supporting asset prices. The IMF (2013a) finds evidence to support the view that QE significantly reduced tail risks. First, the probabilities attributed to large depreciations in the USD and GBP in foreign exchange markets significantly decreased following the announcements of asset purchases, with earlier announcements appearing to have the largest effects. Second, the skewness of inflation forecast distributions based on forecasts from individual economists decreased noticeably after the initial announcements of asset purchases, suggesting that the tail risks of deflation or very low inflation were reduced.

Meanwhile, in his event study, Neely (2011) finds that the US stock market (S&P 500) increased by 3.4 per cent and the USD fell by between 3.6 per cent and 10.8 per cent against various currency pairs and 6.5 per cent on average, with the smallest fall against sterling, which may reflect the fact that the UK was also engaged in large-scale QE[6] (I will discuss exchange rates further in Chapter 6). Simple event study analysis likely significantly underestimates the impact that US QE had on the stock market. Strikingly, amid the significant economic improvement which QE helped to facilitate alongside fiscal stimulus, since its post-GFC trough on 9 March 2009, the US stock market had increased by around 75 per cent by the time QE1 ended in March 2010 (see Figure 5.2).[7] It may have been that the Fed's actual asset purchases helped to restore market functioning and liquidity by facilitating some portfolio rebalancing into equities (and other riskier assets) and that investors adjusted their expectations over time regarding the efficacy of QE (and the other policy measures) in strengthening the US and global economies (Fratzscher et al. 2013). Indeed, note that the IMF's forecast of US and global economic growth in 2010 rose from 0 per cent and 1.9 per cent in April 2009 to 3.1 per cent and 4.2 per cent by April 2010 after the end of QE1.

Studies also suggest that UK QE1 had similarly large positive effects on financial markets. Using event study analysis, Joyce et al. (2011b) suggest it reduced yields on medium- to long-term government bonds by around 100bps with the

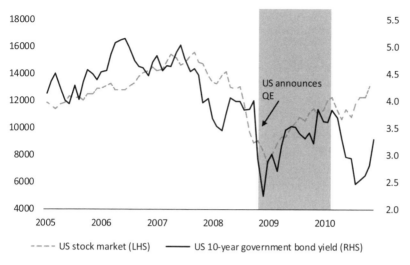

Figure 5.2. The US stock market and bond yields rose amid economic recovery
Source: Wilshire Associates, Board of Governors of the Federal Reserve System, Federal Reserve Bank of St. Louis (FRED). US stock market index is Wilshire 5000 price index. Shaded area represents US QE1 period.

overwhelming driver being the portfolio rebalancing channel. In terms of the latter, Daines *et al*. (2012) find evidence of both preferred habitat/local supply and duration risk effects. Joyce *et al*. (2011b) also recorded declines in yields on investment grade and sub-investment grade corporate bonds of 70bps and 150bps respectively and a depreciation of 4 per cent in the sterling effective exchange rate index. Perhaps surprisingly, the FTSE All-Share stock market index actually *fell* by 3 per cent on QE announcement dates. This may reflect the fact that the index is impacted more by global developments rather than with those in the UK economy and monetary policy, which may have been the case particularly during the GFC.[8] The authors also highlight that net equity and corporate bond issuance by non-financial corporations strengthened in 2009 compared with the 2003–08 period, suggesting that the improvement in financial markets in part owing to UK QE may have encouraged firms to use the capital markets to raise external funds. Christensen and Rudebusch (2012) estimate that QE1 reduced UK 10-year government bond yields by almost 50bps, but acknowledge the impact would be larger if they used two-day windows in their event study like Joyce *et al*. (2011b) rather than one-day windows. They also suggest portfolio rebalancing was key.

A key debate among academic economists and financial market participants was whether the "Stock" or "Flow" element of central bank asset purchases was key in boosting asset prices and reducing interest rates. Stock effects are a persistent change in the price and yields of government bonds in response to permanent changes in the supply of bonds available to be purchased by private investors (with expectations of future changes in supply being discounted into prices and yields as soon as the QE programmes are announced), while flow effects reflect changes in prices and yields in response to the actual ongoing *purchases* of government bonds (D'Amico & King 2011). This was an important initial consideration, because if the stock effect was key then significant stimulus would remain in place even after QE ended but this would not be the case if the flow effect was predominant. The large decline in government bond yields recorded by event studies in response to Fed and BoE announcements of QE1 supported the view that the stock effect was key and that has been the general consensus of opinion. D'Amico and King (2011), in their study of the Fed's government bond purchases in QE1, estimate the stock effect is a multiple of around eight of the flow effect while Daines *et al.* (2012) find that during UK QE1 there was only a very minor flow effect.

Another area where QE had a positive impact on both countries was in reducing the magnitude of the deterioration in the public finances. This occurred through several channels. First, by lowering government bond yields it reduced debt issuance costs for governments. Second, by helping to generate an economic recovery it helped boost government tax receipts and reduce fiscal expenditures compared with the counterfactual and reduced debt burdens compared with the size of the overall economy. Finally, by purchasing longer-dated government bonds in exchange for central bank reserves (whose interest rates were close to zero during QE), the central banks recorded a significant rise in their net interest income which they transferred to their governments. Based on estimates from Goodhart and Ashworth (2012), the latter effect alone would have been consistent with lowering the UK fiscal deficit by around 0.5 per cent of GDP in 2010, while in the US, the Fed's annual transfers to the Treasury rose from around 0.2 per cent of GDP in the pre-crisis decade to over 0.5 per cent of GDP by 2010 (Faria-e-Castro 2018).

Commonly used rules of thumb suggest that QE1 in the US and UK was equivalent to significant reductions in official short-term interest rates. A 10bps reduction in the US 10-year government bond yield is equivalent to a cut in the FFR of around 25bps (Bernanke 2017a), suggesting QE1 was broadly equal to a cut in the FFR of up to 250bps, while the BoE suggested that QE1 was equivalent to a cut in the bank rate of between 150bps to 300bps (Joyce *et al.* 2011a). Studies attempting to quantify the impact of QE on economic variables have produced quite a wide range of estimates, which should be treated with some caution. Overall, when normalized on an assumption that QE reduced long-term sovereign bond yields by around 100bps in the US and UK, the median estimate from various studies analyzed by the IMF is that it boosted GDP by around 2.5 percentage points (pp) in both countries at its peak, with the range of estimates extremely wide at 0.1 per cent to 6.7 per cent in the US and 0.5 per

cent to 8 per cent in the UK. The median estimate for the peak boost to inflation is 1.5 per cent in both countries, with ranges of 0 per cent to 1.7 per cent in
the US and 1.1 per cent to 1.8 per cent in the UK (IMF 2013c). Given that the
100bps fall in government bond yields may be closer to the upper bound of the
various estimates in both countries, it is probably fairer to say that US and UK
QE1 likely boosted real GDP by up to 2 per cent at its peak.[9] Admittedly, much
depends on your choice of counterfactual (IMF 2013c). If one were to make the
not unrealistic assumption that the GFC could have resulted in something closer
to the Great Depression in the absence of QE, then its estimated impact would
clearly be much larger.

Some observers were sceptical about the impact of QE1

Gagnon *et al.* (2011) note that some observers have suggested that QE1 did not
have a lasting effect, pointing to the fact that US 10-year government bond yields
actually rose over the period between the start of the Fed's asset purchases and
their ending in March 2010 (see Figure 5.2). The authors quite correctly point
out, however, that the ultimate recovery and rise in government bond yields
over the period was most likely driven by other factors, including the significant
economic rebound and the large increase in expected future fiscal deficits, rather
than the reversal of the effects of the QE announcements.

   Some QE sceptics pointed to the fact that the recoveries from the GFC were
very weak by historical standards in support of the view that QE1 was ineffective.
While the slow recoveries indeed suggested that QE may not have been quite as
powerful as some may have expected *a priori*, it is not fair to use this as conclusive proof that it was ineffective. Indeed, such criticism ignores the fact that QE,
alongside other policies such as fiscal stimulus, was working to offset enormous
headwinds weighing on economies in the aftermath of the GFC. Without QE,
the recoveries would have been much slower. As Bernanke (2013) notes, the
US stock market and industrial production troughed less than 18 months after
their peaks before the GFC, while during the Great Depression (which is probably the most apt comparator) these indicators fell much more and took around
three years to trough. Many observers have also highlighted the fact that the US
and UK – which both adopted QE soon after the financial crisis erupted – had
stronger recoveries than the euro area and Japan, which did not adopt it initially
(see Figure 5.3).[10]

   One channel where QE1 was not very effective in the US and UK was in its
ability to drive a recovery in broader measures of money supply and bank lending
to the private sector (Goodhart & Ashworth 2012; Goodhart *et al.* 2016). Indeed,
despite the massive increase in monetary base, the rise in broader measures of

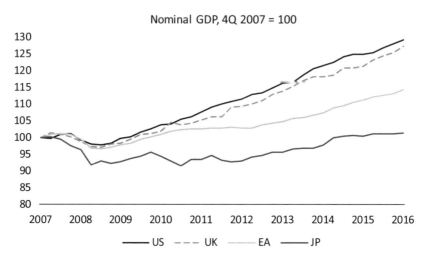

Figure 5.3. Recoveries from the GFC were much stronger in the US and UK
Source: National sources, Federal Reserve Bank of St. Louis (FRED).

Table 5.2. Despite the surge in monetary base, gains in broader money were modest

	Monetary base *(per cent change)*	Broad money *(per cent change)*	Bank credit to private non-financial sector *(per cent change)*
US QE1	44	6	-8
UK QE1	126	11	-3
Japan QE (March 2001–2006)	66	11	-15

Source: Ashworth (2020), national sources, Federal Reserve Bank of St. Louis (FRED). This is an updated version of the tables from Goodhart *et al.* (2016) and Goodhart (2010b).

money and bank lending to the private sector were very modest (see Table 5.2), reflecting a collapse in the money multiplier (see Chapter 4, Equation 1) as commercial banks opted to hold their new deposits as reserves at the central bank rather than risk lending them out to households or non-financial corporations or purchasing assets. As Figure 5.4 highlights, the US reserves-to-deposits ratio absolutely soared amid the onset of the GFC. Given the scale of the economic crisis and the fact that the financial and banking systems were at the epicenter of it, it is perhaps not surprising that lending to the private sector took time to recover. Many western banks had to be recapitalized and it took some time before they gained reasonable clarity on the magnitude of their likely losses as a result of the GFC. Moreover, demand for loans was also very weak given the

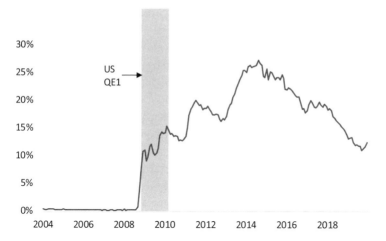

Figure 5.4. Commercial bank's holdings of reserves at the Fed soared (US reserves-to-deposits ratio)
Source: Board of Governors of the Federal Reserve System, Federal Reserve Bank of St. Louis (FRED).

prevailing economic circumstances and large increases in private sector indebtedness prior to the GFC. Overall, the experience of the US and UK in this regard appeared to follow the pattern of Japan in its initial QE experiment between 2001 and 2006 (see Table 5.2), although, as noted in Chapter 2, the BoJ did not begin QE until around a decade after the bursting of the Japanese asset bubbles.

(ii) Additional rounds of US and UK QE eased financial conditions further, with signs of diminishing returns

Results from event studies of additional rounds of QE in the US and UK typically show that it continued to have beneficial effects on both financial conditions and the economy. Krishnamurthy and Vissing-Jorgensen (2011) find that 10-year US government bond yields dropped by around 20bps on QE2-related announcements with real yields falling by around 25bps amid a modest rise in investors' inflation expectations. They also report declines in yields on corporate bonds and 30-year agency MBS of around 10bps. They suggest the policy signalling channel was an important driver behind the overall decline in yields. For the MEP, they find falls in yields on 10-year government bonds of around 10bps and of around 20bps for corporate bonds and 30-year agency MBS, while for QE3 they find a modest fall in government bond yields and a decline in 30-year agency MBS yields of around 15bps (Krishnamurthy & Vissing-Jorgensen 2013). Bauer and

Neely (2013) estimate the fall in 10-year government bond yields in QE2 at 23bps and 14bps in QE3 with around two-thirds of the impact via the policy signalling channel. Bowman *et al.* (2014) find that 10-year US government bond yields fell by around 35bps in QE2, 40bps during the MEP and by almost 10bps in QE3.

For the UK, using event study analysis of QE2, Goodhart and Ashworth (2012) do not find a major positive impact on financial conditions. Medium-to-long-term government bond yields actually rose slightly, the stock market (FTSE 100) declined by around 5 per cent and sterling was unchanged, although the authors acknowledge that slightly expanding their study to include a couple of potentially relevant events may lead to an overall fall in government bond yields of around 20bps.[11] Churm *et al.* (2015), using a slightly wider event set, find that 10-year government bond yields fell by around 50bps, while acknowledging that it was a less proportionate impact than for QE1. Banerjee *et al.* (2012) estimate that the portfolio rebalancing channel, particularly preferred habitat/local supply effects, continued to be an important driver of declines in government bond yields in UK QE2, while the IMF (2013b) suggest the duration risk channel of portfolio rebalancing was key.

As discussed earlier, making accurate inferences from event study analysis became more difficult with the additional rounds of QE, given that they were no longer a (complete) surprise to investors. Hence, the results need to be treated with additional caution. Some observers have at times used the results from event studies of the latter rounds of US and UK QE to make somewhat exaggerated claims about the extent of the diminishing returns of the programmes (sometimes not even adjusting for the differing sizes of the programmes in their analyses). Nevertheless, event study analysis, adjusting for the differing size of the various programmes, does tend to provide some support to the increasingly accepted view that the "bang for the buck" of the various rounds of asset purchases probably declined over time (see Figure 5.5 for the US; BIS 2016 also provides similar evidence for Japan and the euro area). Of course, this is not surprising since QE was no longer a new tool and given that some of the key channels through which it works are likely to be much more powerful during financial crises or periods of significant market disruption.

Some of the economic modelling of the actual impacts on GDP and inflation of asset purchases also supports the view that its efficacy may have waned since it was first used during the financial crisis. Haldane *et al.* (2016) estimate that the impact of QE in the US is greater when financial market stresses are high, with the boost to GDP around twice that of normal times. They suggest the results are consistent with the portfolio rebalancing and liquidity channels being more powerful when stresses exist in financial markets and conclude that the impact of US QE can differ over time. Their results are less conclusive for the UK. Similarly, Hesse *et al.* (2017) find that the boost to GDP from US and UK QE waned over time, although they acknowledge this may partly reflect previously discussed measurement issues with

Impact per 100 billion units of local currency*

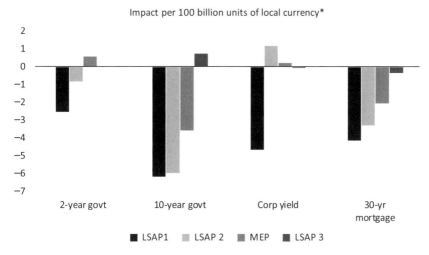

Figure 5.5. Asset purchases appear to have experienced diminishing returns*
* For each programme, the cumulative two-day change in basis points around the announcement dates, divided by the total size of each programme in local currency. For open-ended programmes, divided by the estimated size of the programme assuming an unchanged pace of purchases until December 2017. For terminated programmes, the total amount of purchases at the time of termination.
Source: BIS (2016); Bank of America Merrill Lynch; Bloomberg; national data; BIS calculations.

the latter programmes. Churm *et al.* (2015) estimate that QE2 boosted UK GDP by around 0.6pp and provided a peak boost to inflation of 0.6pp, which contrasts with estimates of QE1 by Kapetanios *et al.* (2012) (which included two of the authors of Churm *et al.* 2015) that suggest it boosted GDP by around 1.5pp and inflation by around 1.25pp.[12] Not all the literature points to diminishing returns from QE, however. Panizza and Wyplosz (2016) suggest the evidence is mixed when modelling the effects of QE on GDP and inflation in the US, UK, Japan and the eurozone. As Bean (2009) suggests, this is likely to be a major area of study for academic economists and their PhD students for years to come!

An area of general disappointment with the latter rounds of QE and US monetary policy in general was its inability to drive a sufficiently robust economic recovery and return inflation sustainably back up to the Fed's 2 per cent target (see Figure 5.6). Growth over much of the 2011–14 period was lacklustre and, despite a steady decline in the unemployment rate from a very elevated level, broader measures of unemployment remained high and wage growth subdued. Moreover, inflation has been beneath its target around 90 per cent of the time since the recession trough and start of the recovery in June 2009. Some cite this as an additional sign of QE losing its potency, although others cite in mitigation the fact that QE2, MEP and QE3 had to work to offset a number of major headwinds

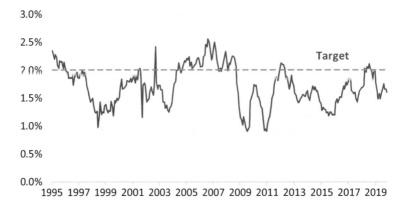

Figure 5.6. The Fed has struggled to raise inflation to its target*
* US Core PCE inflation. Note, the Fed's main target for inflation is actually the headline PCE measure, which includes food and energy items. However, given that the Fed is unable to influence food and energy prices with its policy, the main focus is typically on the Core PCE. *Source*: US Bureau of Economic Analysis, Federal Reserve Bank of St. Louis (FRED).

hitting the economy – prominent among these being the aggressive multi-year fiscal tightening that began in 2011 after the opposition Republican party took control of Congress on a platform against rising government deficits and debt.

Some observers criticized the Fed for not being more aggressive in its use of QE and other monetary policy tools in order to boost the recovery (Krugman 2012), which ironically was a criticism previously aimed at Japanese policy-makers by Fed Chair Ben Bernanke when he was an academic economist (Bernanke 1999). Krugman (2012) suggested political economy constraints likely precluded Bernanke and the Fed from taking more aggressive action: first, the significant criticism highlighted in Chapter 3 that the Fed received from various Conservative-leaning politicians since the unveiling of QE2; second, the desire to protect the Fed as an institution by not attempting new policy innovations for which it would be blamed if they failed. In response, Bernanke (2012) suggested that the Fed's policies were consistent with those he previously espoused and that a crucial difference was that, unlike Japan, the US economy was not stuck in deflation with inflation close to the Fed's objective. Nevertheless, in a 2017 speech "Some Reflections on Japanese Monetary Policy", Bernanke acknowledged that:

> in earlier writings I was too optimistic and too certain about the ease with which a determined central bank could conquer deflation, and I had little patience with the alternative view ... But when I found myself in the role of Fed chairman, confronted by the heavy responsibilities

and uncertainties that came with that office, I regretted the tone of some of my earlier comments.   (Bernanke 2017a: 3)

At a 2015 IMF conference on Unconventional Monetary Policies, Paul Krugman and Adam Posen suggested that there was a general level of distrust and fear regarding the use of QE and other unconventional policies beyond what the evidence would justify, resulting in political economy constraints with their use.[13] As Krugman (2015) noted:

> The argument why would you be talking about this [unconventional monetary policy] as our answer as opposed to fiscal policy. The answer has usually been, well there are political economy constraints to fiscal policy. Indeed, but it turns out that there are political economy constraints to unconventional monetary policy as well.

The UK economy ultimately embarked on an unexpected and surprisingly strong economic recovery beginning in 2013. However, economists generally believed that ECB President Mario Draghi's famous promise to do "whatever it takes" to save the euro in July 2012 was a more important driver of the acceleration in UK growth than the BoE's QE2 programme. The euro area is by far the UK's largest export market and their banking and financial systems are very closely intertwined. By substantially reducing the risk of a break-up of the European Monetary Union (EMU) and helping to bring an end to the multi-year euro-area financial crisis, Draghi's speech and the subsequent unveiling of the OMT programme helped to fuel a massive improvement in bank funding markets and business and consumer confidence in the UK. I will discuss the impact of the OMT further below.

(iii) Japan's new QE experiment has had some success, but is struggling to generate sufficient inflation

Shinzo Abe won the December 2012 Japanese general election on an aggressive economic revival platform dubbed "Abenomics", with significant monetary easing a key plank. Under pressure from the new government, the BoJ adopted a higher 2 per cent inflation target (Hausman & Wieland 2014) and a new Governor, Haruhiko Kuroda, known to favour very aggressive monetary easing, was appointed. He unveiled the programme of QQE at his first meeting in April 2013 and subsequently ratcheted up the pace of purchases and made some modifications (including QQE with a Negative Interest Rate and QQE with Yield Curve Control, as discussed in Chapter 3). The sheer scale of the programme is highlighted by the tripling of the monetary base in under four years[14] and the fact that, owing to its purchases of government bonds and equity ETFs, the BoJ now owns over 40 per cent of outstanding government debt and around 5 per cent of the total stock market capitalization (*Financial Times* 2019a, 2019b). The QQE policies appear to have had some success, although they have been less successful thus far in other areas.

Financial conditions eased markedly even before the launch of QQE (see Figure 5.7) reflecting the fact that future aggressive monetary easing was a key feature of Abe's election campaign. Hausman and Wieland (2014) highlight that in November 2012 "then-candidate Abe argued that the Bank of Japan should increase its inflation target and engage in 'unlimited easing'". The combination of expectations of a dramatic monetary easing and QQE itself resulted in a very significant easing in financial conditions. The JPY fell sharply and the Nikkei 225 stock market more than doubled between the end of October 2012 and the end of 2015 (see Figure 5.7), significantly outperforming its developed market peers. It has been the best performing of the major stock markets since October 2012, closely followed by the US, but dramatically outperforming the German and UK markets. The yield on 10-year government bonds has fallen by around 100bps from around 0.8 per cent to −0.1 per cent at the time of writing and interest rates have fallen sharply across the yield curve (yields had fallen materially before the introduction of a negative short-term interest rate in January 2016 and subsequently fell much further). Surveys suggest that lending attitudes of financial institutions are at their easiest since the late 1980s and lending growth has improved somewhat (Bank of Japan 2019). Residential property prices also appear to be consistently firming for the first time since the bursting of the asset

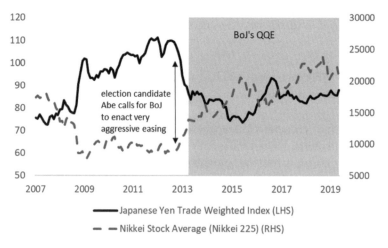

Figure 5.7. JPY and the Nikkei 225
Source: Bank of Japan, Nikkei Industry Research Association, Federal Reserve Bank of St. Louis (FRED). Nikkei 225 is owned by Nikkei Inc.

bubbles in the early 1990s, with prices up by over 10 per cent since the end of 2012.

The easing in financial conditions has fuelled some genuine economic improvements. Corporate profits surged to record levels, aided by the depreciation of the currency (Kuroda 2016c) and the unemployment rate has fallen from 4.3 per cent in December 2012 to around 2.5 per cent at present. This is close to its lowest since 1993, consistent with full employment and has driven some modest improvements in pay growth. The economic expansion that began in late 2012 is one of the longest in the postwar period (*Nikkei Asian Review* 2018) and nominal or money GDP has begun to rise again in a relatively material way for the first time since the 1990s. Attempting to quantify the impact of QQE on the economy is undoubtedly challenging though (Dell' Ariccia *et al.* 2018). As noted, financial conditions eased significantly before its launch reflecting expectations of future easing. Moreover, QQE was initially carried out alongside fiscal stimulus. Hausman and Wieland (2014) estimate that the initial programme of QQE boosted Japanese real GDP growth by up to 1pp in 2013 and based on different hypothetical scenarios Kan *et al.* (2016) estimate that QQE boosted real GDP by between 0.6 per cent and 4.2 per cent by the end of 2015, with mean and median estimates of around 2 per cent.

Where QQE has been notably less successful is in raising inflation expectations and inflation up to the BoJ's 2 per cent inflation target (Shirai 2018a, 2018b). Shirai (2018b) notes that Governor Kuroda initially expected to achieve the target in around two years, but the BoJ have repeatedly had to significantly reduce their inflation forecasts and have given up expressing the expected timing of reaching the target. Admittedly, some progress appears to have been made.[15] Consumer price indices, excluding volatile measures such as food and energy, have moved from clearly deflationary territory to being modestly positive; the GDP deflator troughed in early 2013 after many years of decline and has since moved gradually higher (see Figure 5.8). Kan *et al.* (2016) note that in three of their four hypothetical scenarios underlying inflation would have remained negative or close to zero in the absence of QQE.

Nevertheless, inflation expectations and pay growth still remain very subdued and without a much more meaningful and sustainable rise it seems very unlikely that the BoJ will be able to raise inflation consistently to its 2 per cent target. Indeed, the economy's continued external dependence means that any material slowdown in the global economy and/or a significant exogenous appreciation in the JPY (which can occur, as in the GFC, because of its role as a safe haven currency) could well put paid to the BoJ's efforts at reflation. The BoJ would then not be left with many easy options given its current monetary easing is seemingly approaching its limits and some negative spillovers are becoming more prevalent (Shirai 2018b). Shirai highlights the negative impact on the profitability of financial institutions

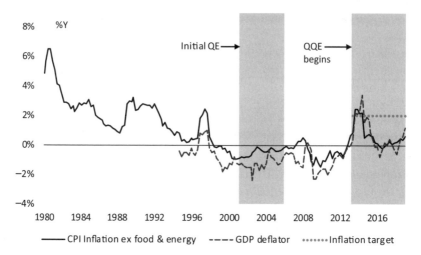

Figure 5.8. The BoJ has struggled to raise inflation and inflation expectations to its target
Source: Cabinet Office of Japan, OECD (2020), Inflation (CPI) (indicator). doi: 10.1787/
eee82e6e-en (accessed 30 March 2020).

due to negative interest rates and the flat yield curve. She also highlights the decline in the liquidity and functioning of the JGB market due to the massive asset purchases under QQE which she suggests is a concern given its disproportionately large size in the Japanese debt securities market and important role in providing a benchmark for the pricing of corporate bonds and loans. She also cites growing concerns about the functioning of the stock market due to reduced downside risk, overvaluation of some small-cap stocks, and the potential impact on corporate governance because of the growing presence of the BoJ as a large silent investor without actively exercising voting rights. I will discuss the negative externalities of QE and other unconventional monetary policies further in Chapter 7.

Japan's latest major monetary experiment clearly highlights the fact that, despite extraordinary monetary easing, it is not always easy for a central bank to create inflationary expectations and inflation. This cast doubts on the views of some academics who previously criticized the BoJ for being too timid in the 1990s, suggesting central banks could always create inflation (Bernanke 1999).

(iv) ECB's OMT programme a major success, QE not quite so much

As discussed in Chapter 3, ECB President Draghi's famous speech in the summer of 2012 – suggesting that the ECB would do "whatever it takes" to save the euro – and the subsequent unveiling of its OMT programme, represented the turning point in the region's sovereign debt and banking crisis (see Figure 5.9). It fuelled a

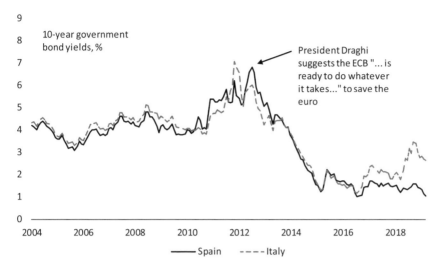

Figure 5.9. Draghi's strong words marked the turning point in the euro area crisis
Source: ECB.

massive improvement in financial markets as the perceived likelihood of a break-up of the single currency fell sharply. Krugman (2019a) suggested that Draghi's saving of the euro from collapse in 2012–13 "arguably makes him the greatest central banker of modern times".

Using event study analysis, Krishnamurthy *et al.* (2017) find very large positive impacts on financial markets from the ECB's OMT-related announcements. In both Italy and Spain, 2- and 10-year government bond yields declined by around 200bps and 100bps respectively and there were also quite sizeable falls in corporate bond yields. Moreover, their stock markets increased by almost 15 per cent with gains closer to 20 per cent for financial stocks. Similar gains were evident for the broader European market and the authors estimate that the total gain in value for euro-area stocks and government and corporate bonds during OMT announcements was around €0.7 trillion, equivalent to around 7 per cent of the region's GDP. Altavilla *et al.* (2016) record similar declines in government bond yields and estimate that, towards the end of 2015, the OMT programme had boosted Italian and Spanish GDP by 1.5 per cent and 2 per cent respectively and inflation by around 1 per cent. There were also modest spillovers to Germany and France, where GDP was estimated to be 0.3 per cent and 0.5 per cent higher. Of course, the appropriate counterfactual is once again very important. If one assumes that EMU would have broken up without OMT, then the boost it provided to growth is obviously much higher. The "bang for the buck" of the OMT programme was clearly huge, given that the ECB never even had to use it and serves to reinforce the point that asset purchases are likely to be particularly powerful when the financial system is highly stressed and tail risks are high (IMF 2013a). It paved the way for the euro area to exit its double-dip recession in the first half of 2013 and, as noted above, was a key driver behind the robust UK economic recovery.

Despite the end of the crisis and a gradual economic recovery, growth remained modest, credit growth anemic and inflation well below target – leading to increased fears about deflation. Against this backdrop, the ECB finally embarked on a major QE programme involving government bonds in early 2015, around six years after the start of the US and UK programmes. Altavilla *et al.* (2015) note that the ECB placed particular emphasis on the portfolio rebalancing channel. Using an event study, they estimate that the initial round of QE lowered 10-year euro area government bond yields by 30–50bps, with the gain being around twice as high for countries with higher than average yields such as Italy and Spain. The signalling channel accounted for up to 10bps of the fall, with the rest coming from portfolio rebalancing. They also find that the programme fuelled quite a sizeable depreciation of the euro versus the USD (of between 5–12 per cent) and a rise in inflation expectations among investors. The stock market also registered modest gains. Econometric estimates by De Santis (2016) suggest that, by October 2015, the asset purchase programme had reduced 10-year euro-area sovereign bond yields by around 60bps, with the higher-yielding countries benefitting the most. Koijen *et al.* (2019) suggest that around 60 per cent of the ECB's bond purchases were from foreign investors, who did not reinvest the proceeds elsewhere in the euro area. This diminishes the portfolio rebalancing channel, but weakens the exchange rate.

The improvement in financial conditions due to asset purchases helped fuel an improvement in the economy, although the difficulty in quantifying the impact is further increased by the fact that they occurred around the same time as other monetary easing measures, and when fiscal austerity was largely coming to an end (which removed a major drag on growth). The ECB (2019) notes that the volume of lending to non-financial corporations became positive again in mid-2015 – with model-based estimates suggesting that around half of the 4.3 per cent annual volume growth by 3Q 2018 could be attributed to the effects of the asset purchases. Cova *et al.* (2015) estimate that the initial round of QE provided a peak boost to euro-area GDP and inflation of around 1.5 per cent and 1 per cent respectively. Andrade *et al.* (2016) estimate that the asset purchases were equivalent to a cut in official interest rates of around 1pp and boosted GDP by 1.1 per cent and raised inflation by around 0.4pp.[16]

In general, while the ECB's asset purchases clearly look to have supported growth, helped to improve the credit cycle and provided some boost to infla-tion, they have not been able to generate a sustainable recovery in the economy,

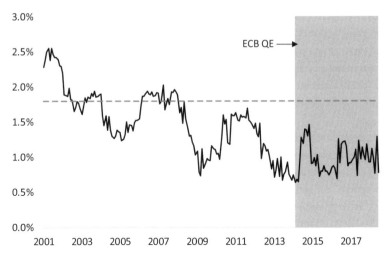

Figure 5.10. Euro area inflation has been consistently well below its target
Source: Eurostat, Federal Reserve Bank of St. Louis (FRED).

which (despite being one of the world's largest) remains heavily dependent on external developments. In addition, like other central banks, the ECB has struggled to raise inflation to its target. The underlying core measure of inflation has averaged just 1 per cent since the beginning of 2015 and has not risen above 1.5 per cent (see Figure 5.10) and inflation expectations remain very subdued. Many observers have suggested that the euro area is at risk of Japanification (El-Erian 2019), amid weak growth, poor demographics, rock bottom interest rates and extremely low inflation.

On first impressions, it may appear that the ECB and its President, Mario Draghi, are squarely to blame for the inability to generate a sufficiently strong recovery and raise inflation back to target, particularly given it did not embark on QE until around six years after the US and UK. Indeed, it is generally acknowledged that the ECB under Draghi's predecessor, Jean-Claude Trichet, was too slow to ease monetary policy in the aftermath of the GFC and made some major policy mistakes (including raising official interest rates in July 2008 and twice in 2011). However, since Draghi became President in November 2011, the ECB has eased policy significantly and despite major political opposition from Germany and other northern European countries, enacted the OMT and QE programmes – which most observers acknowledge saved the euro and staved off a deflationary spiral. Moreover, the situation of the ECB perhaps best of all exemplifies Mohamed El-Erian's famous proverb that central banks are the "only game in town". Even in the post-sovereign debt crisis period when financial markets have normalized, countries whose economies were most in need of fiscal stimulus such as Italy have been constrained by the euro area's fiscal rules while those countries with ample fiscal space such as Germany and the Netherlands have been loathe to use it. Meanwhile, progress has been very slow in enacting necessary improvements to the architecture of the single currency (Munchau 2019) such as a full banking union and some shared fiscal capacity, which could boost confidence and make the region more resilient to future economic shocks.

Perhaps one area where the current ECB is not immune from criticism is that political economy considerations, including calls from Germany and other northern European countries to end QE (*Financial Times* 2017a, 2017b, 2017c), may have influenced it to prematurely taper and then finish its asset purchases at the end of 2018. With growth in the euro area slowing sharply and inflation remaining subdued, the ECB restarted QE in September 2019 and cut interest rates further into negative territory. The large number of ECB members dissenting against the latest monetary easing and the renewed backlash in Germany, highlight once again the significant political economy constraints that could limit the ECB's future room for manoeuvre.[17]

In this chapter, I have argued that QE1 in the US and UK had large positive impacts on financial markets and both economies, helping them avoid worst-case scenarios such as another Great Depression or deflation and to subsequently embark on economic recoveries. While there remains some disagreement about the importance of the various channels in which QE worked, it is clear that it supported confidence and asset prices by reducing perceived probabilities of tail risk scenarios, calming financial markets and significantly reducing private and public sector borrowing costs. Critics that cite weak recoveries from the GFC as evidence that QE was ineffective overlook the enormous headwinds the economy faced.

Further rounds of QE in the US and UK helped to ease financial conditions and support growth, but appeared to exhibit some signs of diminishing returns, which is not surprising given that QE was no longer a new tool and some of its key channels would probably be less powerful outside of periods of market disruption. The QE programmes in Japan and the euro area also appear to have had positive impacts on growth. However, a key theme of all the central banks is that their QE programmes have been unable to generate robust and sustainable economic recoveries, enabling inflation to rise back to their targets. Indeed, inflation has remained below targets in most of the countries, particularly in Japan and the euro area. Some have argued that central banks should have been more aggressive in their use of QE and other unconventional monetary policies, suggesting that political economy constraints may have prevented more robust action. Given that the US was not particularly close to deflation and that significant uncertainty remained about the negative side effects when the Fed was pursuing QE, it is probably fair to say that the Bernanke Fed charted a relatively judicious course. Undoubtedly though, political economy issues have clearly prevented the ECB acting in a timely manner on a number of occasions. Only time will tell if this has contributed to a permanent Japanization of the economy. Of course, Japan's experience with QQE suggests that very aggressive monetary easing may not necessarily be a panacea.

In the next chapter, I discuss the international spillovers of QE and the political economy issues that have arisen.

6

INTERNATIONAL SPILLOVERS OF QUANTITATIVE EASING

I previously highlighted how, given that the USA is the world's largest economy and the USD is the global reserve currency, changes in its monetary policy – conventional or unconventional – have very large impacts across the global economy and financial markets. This is also the case for other major economies such as the euro area, Japan and China,[1] but to a much lesser extent. Reflecting this, any material changes in policy by these central banks garner significant international attention.

Strikingly, the announcement by the Fed of additional rounds of QE once the worst of the GFC had passed, such as QE2 in late 2010, gained significant attention overseas – much more than was typical for interest rate cuts. There was particularly strong criticism from politicians in emerging economies – with Brazilian politicians accusing the Fed of engaging in "currency wars" (Bernanke 2015c), suggesting it was deliberately trying to depreciate the USD to gain a competitive advantage in a beggar-thy-neighbour approach. This was an echo of the 1930s, a period marked by a significant deterioration in international trade relations amid the fallout from the Great Depression (James 2013). Chinese Prime Minister Wen Jiabao also blamed US QE for contributing to the sharp rise in global commodity prices (BBC 2011). Criticism was not confined to emerging markets, with German Finance Minister Wolfgang Schäuble echoing the currency manipulation accusations and suggesting that the Fed's policies were "clueless" (*Financial Times* 2010). At an IMF conference on unconventional monetary policy in 2015, Fed Governor Lael Brainard suggested "words that were used by foreign leaders in private meetings were even more colorful" and she noted that the reaction was equally as striking in the opposite direction when the Fed first announced its intention to taper its asset purchases in 2013 (foreign leaders were angry about the negative impact US tightening would have on their economies) (Brainard 2015a). Indeed, Rajan (2014) highlighted the risks from QE for emerging economies pertaining to both large capital inflows (during the easing phase) and outflows (during the tightening phase), whose timing is solely related to conditions in the source country (the US).

In this chapter, I examine the international spillovers from QE by the major central banks since the GFC, with a particular focus on the US. I examine the spillovers both to other developed economies and in particular to emerging markets and discuss some of the salient political economy issues. I begin by examining the evidence on the various spillovers before looking in more detail at capital flows to emerging markets and discussing the infamous "taper tantrum" episode and the impact on emerging economies of the Fed's policy normalization. I then summarize the impact of the Fed's QE on the global economy before finishing with the political issues.[2]

Brainard (2015b) suggests that international spillovers of unconventional monetary policy appear to occur through the same three channels as conventional monetary policy, where easing by a country should: (i) boost domestic demand, which will increase exports from the rest of the world; (ii) fuel currency depreciation, which should increase the competitiveness of the country's exports and lead to some switching away from imports from the rest of the world in favour of domestic producers; and (iii) fuel an easing in domestic financial conditions which, in tightly integrated global financial markets, should lead to easier financial conditions overseas. The author suggests that the reaction overseas (whether positive or negative) to spillovers from monetary policy changes by major economies since the GFC has typically depended on the relative strength of these three effects, as well as upon where foreign economies are in their economic cycles compared with the easing country and the flexibility of their monetary tools (for example, interest rates and exchange rates) to offset any divergent spillovers. I examine and evaluate the spillovers from US QE through Brainard's simple framework (Bernanke 2015c uses a similar framework).

(i) *Monetary easing boosts domestic demand*: Easier financial conditions due to monetary easing should boost domestic demand and result in higher exports from the rest of the world. US QE1, by helping to halt the downward spiral in the economy and generate a recovery, likely provided a very strong boost to global exports to the US, particularly when compared with plausible counterfactuals. Indeed, the IMF (2013a) highlights the extremely negative economic consequences for Latin America as a result of the US Great Depression between 1929–33 – a period in which it is now widely accepted that the Fed did not ease policy aggressively enough. The latter rounds of US QE (QE2 and QE3) – which occurred when the American economy was already expanding, albeit in a rather lacklustre way – are likely to have had a *relatively* less beneficial impact on exports to the US from the rest of the world.

(ii) *Monetary easing leads to currency depreciation*: Studies have typically found that as expected QE fuels domestic currency depreciation versus its peers. Using event study analysis, Neely (2011) suggests that the USD declined

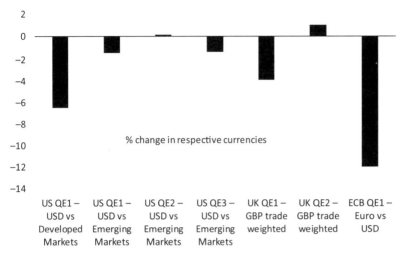

Figure 6.1. Currencies weakened amid QE-related announcements
Source: Neely (2011), Bowman *et al.* (2014), Haldane *et al.* (2016), Altavilla *et al.* (2015).
USD vs. Developed Markets from Neely (2011) is the USD versus an average of five major developed market currencies, USD vs. Emerging Markets from Bowman *et al.* (2014) is the USD versus an average of emerging market currencies, GBP trade weighted from Haldane *et al.* (2016) is the value of sterling vs. a basket of currencies weighted according to their share in UK trade, euro versus USD is from Altavilla *et al.* (2015).

on average by over 6 per cent against developed economy currencies during QE1-related announcements, while Bowman *et al.* (2014) find a depreciation of around 1.5 per cent against emerging market currencies (see Figure 6.1). The smaller fall against the latter probably reflects the fact that a number of emerging currencies are fixed or actively managed against the USD and the authorities likely resisted currency appreciation. The latter authors find that the USD did not depreciate against emerging market currencies on the announcements related to QE2, but fell by 1.5 per cent in QE3. In general, Glick and Leduc (2015) find that monetary policy surprises from the use of unconventional monetary policy have had larger impacts on the USD than those in the pre-GFC period, when the FFR was the main policy tool, although the IMF does not appear to have found evidence of this (IMF 2013c).

Studies for other countries also typically point to QE leading to currency depreciation. For the UK, using event studies Haldane *et al.* (2016) and Joyce *et al.* (2011a, 2011b) both report a depreciation of 4 per cent in sterling in trade weighted terms due to QE1, but the former find a modest appreciation on announcements related to QE2 (see Figure 6.1). For the euro area, Altavilla *et al.* (2015) find that the euro depreciated by around 12 per cent against the USD on announcements related to the ECB's QE1 (see Figure 6.1). In Japan, Hausman and Wieland (2014) find that the JPY depreciated by 3.5 per cent against the USD on the day of announcement of QQE, which followed a sharp previous depreciation amid the electoral victory of Shinzo Abe on a platform calling for aggressive monetary easing. Meanwhile, Goodhart and Ashworth (2012) highlight the relationship between relative changes in the size of central bank balance sheets due to unconventional monetary policies and the exchange rate. They find evidence of quite a strong relationship between the relative size of the Fed and ECB balance sheets and the exchange rate and similarly find some relationship between the BoE and ECB balance sheets and the exchange rate. However, they find less evidence of a relationship when looking at other countries.

As noted in Chapter 4, the BIS highlighted a sharp increase in the mention of the exchange rate by developed central banks, which they attribute to a greater emphasis on the exchange rate channel amid acknowledgement that the efficacy of the domestic channels of QE is waning. Currency depreciation to gain a competitive advantage is typically criticized for its beggar-thy-neighbour approach and the risk is that all central banks may increasingly engage in QE simply to avert a potential loss of competitiveness in what would be considered a classical currency war. Indeed, Hamada (2020) notes that before Abenomics, the strength of the JPY since the GFC had put Japanese industry at a disadvantage amid unconventional monetary easing by the other advanced economies. Shortly after assuming office, US President Donald Trump suggested that China and Japan devalue their currencies to gain a competitive advantage, and in June 2019 accused ECB President Mario Draghi of using monetary policy to weaken the euro. The risk is that countries may consider instituting trade tariffs against those that they view to be manipulating their currencies.

(iii) *Domestic monetary easing leads to easier financial conditions across the globe*: By lowering US interest rates across the yield curve during the process of QE, this will reduce the attractiveness of US government bonds for investors (both domestic and overseas) compared with their international counterparts, which should fuel increased purchases of overseas bonds. According to event study analysis by Bauer and Neely (2013), US QE1 reduced 10-year sovereign bonds on average in other developed markets by almost 50bps with much smaller impacts in US QE2 and QE3 (see Figure 6.2). Rogers *et al.* (2014) also find that US unconventional monetary policy changes have large international spillovers, lowering German and UK 10-year government bond yields by almost half the change in US yields. Their analysis suggests that spillovers are asymmetric, with US monetary policy having a much larger impact on non-US yields than the other

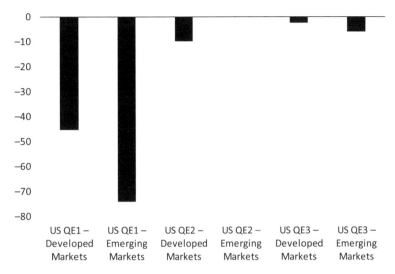

Figure 6.2. Changes in government bond yields during US QE announcements
Source: Bauer and Neely (2013), Bowman *et al.* (2014). US QE1, QE2 and QE3 versus Developed Markets is based on Bauer and Neely (2013), where Developed Markets is an equal weighted average of their estimated changes in 10-year government bond yields for Canada, Germany, Australia and Japan. US QE1, QE2 and QE3 vs. Emerging Markets is based on Bowman *et al.* (2014), where Emerging Markets is based on the JP Morgan GBI-EM global composite index.

way around. Bowman *et al.* (2014) estimate that US QE1 reduced sovereign bond yields in emerging markets by almost 80bps, but with modest impacts for QE2 and QE3 (see Figure 6.2). Similarly, Chen *et al.* (2012) find that US QE1 reduced 10-year government bond yields by 80bps on average in Asia, with a decline of around 10bps in QE2. For corporate bond yields they record declines of around 50bps and 15bps in QE1 and QE2 respectively. According to the IMF (2013b: 16):

The spillover effects of early bond purchase programs appear to be the largest. This could be due to the market stabilizing impact of such programs, not only in domestic economies, but also globally, given the systemic importance of the economies initiating the purchases. Spillovers were smaller once markets normalized. However, the lower spillover effects from later programs may also come from the fact that the announcements associated with these programs surprised markets less.

In terms of equities, in his event study of US QE1 announcements, Neely (2011) actually finds a decline of around 1.5 per cent on average for non-US developed equity markets, which compares with a gain of 3.4 per cent for the US market. The weakness in other developed countries may reflect the fact that their stock markets were being buffeted by other large negative events on QE announcement days, although currency movements may have played a role – a weaker USD would boost the international revenues of US companies through translation effects with the converse for the other developed economies whose currencies had strengthened against the USD. In contrast, event studies from Bowman *et al.* (2014) and Chen *et al.* (2012) found that emerging market and Asian equities increased by 10 per cent and 11 per cent respectively in US QE1. The former find a decline of 1 per cent in emerging market equities during QE2-related announcements and a gain of 4 per cent for QE3, while the latter record a gain of 1.5 per cent in Asian equities in QE2. In general, we noted in the previous chapter that event studies of QE announcements are likely to significantly underestimate the ultimate boost to equities from QE. This is particularly the case for US QE1, a major contributor to the economic recovery, which fueled a large rebound in both US and global equity markets.

In terms of commodities, using event study analysis, Glick and Leduc (2011) do not find evidence that US QE1 or QE2 fuelled rises in prices, which actually declined on average over their event study days, with the largest falls in QE1. Moreover, using regression analysis, the IMF (2012b) find little evidence that changes in global liquidity significantly affect commodity prices and oil prices in particular.[3] That being said, it seems highly likely that US QE did make a material contribution to higher global commodity prices given that it helped generate recoveries in the US and global economies and an improvement in risk appetite, which fuelled a switch by investors into riskier asset classes such as corporate bonds, equities and commodities. Nevertheless, one suspects QE critics overstate its contribution to surging commodity prices, given that there were a number of other important drivers. These include the huge Chinese stimulus package during the GFC, which included a large increase in commodity-intensive infrastructure investment; strong recoveries from the GFC in other emerging economies; and some supply shocks (Helbling 2012).[4]

Large, but not necessarily excessive, capital flows to emerging markets during the latter rounds of QE

In terms of international capital flows, Fratzscher *et al.* (2013) note that during the initial part of the financial crisis, the Fed's various policy measures helped to fuel a large global rebalancing of investor portfolios amid capital outflows from emerging markets and inflows into US bonds and equities, leading to an appreciation of the

USD. A key driver was also a general safe-haven demand for US assets and the USD, which tends to occur when global risks increase (Bernanke 2015c). Fratzscher *et al.* (2013) suggest that the Fed's various LOLR facilities may have contained a moral suasion component, with those receiving funds being more inclined to achieve their desired deleveraging by selling foreign rather than domestic assets and that by expanding the pool of collateral available to be used in its LOLR operations, the Fed may have increased the willingness of investors to hold US assets at a time of global liquidity shortages. As Figure 6.3 highlights, the USD strengthened sharply from the summer of 2008 to early March 2009, despite as previously noted falling on average over QE-related announcements (see Figure 6.1). It then declined over subsequent months and quarters during the actual QE1 asset purchases.

In contrast, Fratzscher *et al.* note that QE2 measures drove large capital outflows from the US, mainly into emerging market equities, and resulted in a depreciation of the USD (see Figure 6.3). The authors find that actual Fed operations, namely Treasury and MBS purchases, had comparatively larger effects on portfolio decisions and capital flows than their announcements, particularly for emerging markets and the other advanced economies. The IMF (2013a) note similar trends with Fed liquidity operations and QE announcements in the early part of the GFC fuelling capital inflows to the US and the later QE announcements boosting capital flows to emerging markets.

A key question was whether or not US QE2 and QE3 led to particularly excessive capital inflows into emerging markets which could create future risks to financial stability, particularly if there were large outflows when the Fed ultimately began to normalize policy. As Powell (2013: 1) notes:

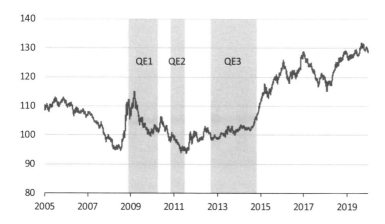

Figure 6.3. USD during QE periods
Source: Board of Governors of the Federal Reserve System, Federal Reserve Bank of St. Louis (FRED).

Emerging market economies have long grappled with the challenges posed by large and volatile cross-border capital flows. The past several decades are replete with episodes of strong capital inflows being followed by abrupt reversals, all too often resulting in financial crisis and economic distress.[5]

The IMF's characterization in early 2013 of the magnitude of overall capital flows to emerging markets seems to provide a generally fair and somewhat reassuring overall description: "Thus far, capital flows to emerging markets have been ample but not alarming. After a brief sudden stop over the crisis, flows have moved back close to the ample levels seen in the run up to the crisis" (IMF 2013a) (see Figure 6.4).

A breakdown of the data, however, suggests that portfolio inflows (particularly debt) typically accounted for a larger proportion of inflows to emerging economies in the post-crisis period when US QE was occurring than before the GFC (IMF 2013a) (see Figure 6.4). Portfolio inflows are typically much less sticky than other types of inflows such as foreign direct investment, and hence may pose greater risks of future outflows. The IMF (2013a) also notes that post-crisis flows involve significant amounts of debt-creating bond and bank lending inflows, which "tend to be more closely associated with credit growth and financial instability". Carstens (2015) highlights the fact that overseas holdings of local currency emerging market government bonds have increased from around 10 per cent of the total outstanding at the onset of the GFC to around 25 per cent from 2013.[6] Meanwhile, the destination of flows also appears to have shifted in

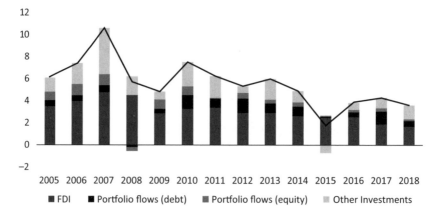

Figure 6.4. Emerging market capital inflows (% of GDP)
* Capital inflows are net purchases of domestic assets by non-residents.
Source: IMF.

the post-GFC period, with a greater proportion accounted for by Asia and Latin America and a much smaller share going to emerging Europe (IMF 2013a). All in all, during the period of US QE, capital inflows to emerging markets appear to have returned relatively close to pre-GFC levels but not beyond them, although there seems to have been some change in composition by region and towards riskier portfolio bond flows.

A more difficult question to answer, however, is what was the actual contribution made by QE to any of these trends in capital flows. Lavigne *et al.* (2014: 30) suggest that:

> QE appears to have increased capital flows to EMEs [emerging market economies], although there is no convincing proof that the overall effects are significantly different from conventional monetary easing. Moreover, diverging fundamentals between advanced economies and EMEs were likely at least as important.

In terms of the latter, they highlight the fact that growth and interest rate differentials favoured emerging economies. Powell (2018a) also highlights growth differentials as an important driver of capital flows to emerging economies and cites changes in commodity prices too.[7] Ahmed and Zlate (2013) do not find statistically significant effects of US QE on total net inflows of capital into emerging economies, although they find evidence that such policies have affected the composition of flows toward portfolio flows. Fratzscher *et al.* (2013) suggest that relative to the magnitude of swings in capital flows out of emerging markets following the collapse of Lehman Brothers in September 2008, and the subsequent capital flows surge to emerging markets in 2009 and 2010, the share of these movements explained by Fed monetary policy measures is comparatively modest. However, they argue that Fed policy has significantly exacerbated the pro-cyclicality of capital flows into and out of emerging markets.

The "taper tantrum" increased concerns about the normalization of Fed policy, but it ultimately proceeded relatively smoothly

The spillovers from US QE to emerging markets were particularly evident in May 2013 amid the large negative reaction in financial markets when Fed Chair Ben Bernanke discussed the possibility of a future tapering of asset purchases in its ongoing QE3 programme, despite the fact that he tried to stress the Fed's intention to maintain a highly accommodative monetary policy overall (Bernanke 2015c). This now infamous episode is commonly referred to as the "taper tantrum". Powell (2013: 10) notes that:

from May through August, US Treasury yields rose substantially as market participants reassessed the future course of US monetary policy. In response, EME bond and equity funds experienced very large outflows. EME yields rose as well, in some cases by more than those on Treasury securities, and many EME currencies depreciated.

He also highlighted the fact that "asset prices have fallen considerably more in economies with large current account deficits, high inflation, and fiscal problems than in countries with stronger fundamentals" and concluded "[t]hus, while a reassessment of US monetary policy may have triggered the recent retrenchment from EMEs, investors' concerns about underlying vulnerabilities appear to have amplified the reaction". Indeed, the IMF (2014b) note that, subsequent to the initial bouts of volatility, market differentiation increasingly occurred with investors exerting significant pressure on countries with larger external financing needs and macroeconomic imbalances such as Brazil, India, Indonesia, Turkey and South Africa. They suggest that these countries, commonly referred to as the "Fragile Five", saw, on average, bond yields rise 250bps, stock markets fall by 13.75 per cent, exchange rates depreciate by 13.5 per cent, and foreign exchange reserves fall by about 4 per cent between 22 May and end of August 2013.

The adverse impact from the mere discussion of a possible future tapering of asset purchases increased concerns that the actual process of tapering, followed eventually by interest rate increases and a reversal of the Fed's asset purchases, ran the risk of causing damaging spillovers to emerging economies (Powell 2013), with some fearing a repeat of the emerging market crises that had occurred in the latter decades of the twentieth century. In reality, the Fed's monetary policy normalization was gradual, when it did finally occur (Powell 2017). It did not announce a tapering of its asset purchases until December 2013 (which it gradually reduced over 2014 before ending in October), did not embark on interest rate increases until December 2015 and only began to unwind its asset purchases in October 2017 with the process finally ending in August 2019. While there have been periods of significantly higher financial market volatility and stress in emerging markets related to monetary policy normalization, including in 2015 amid a growing expectation that the Fed would begin raising interest rates (Bevilaqua & Nechio 2016) and in 2018 amid fears of faster than expected monetary tightening (Chitu & Quint 2018), there has not been a repeat of past emerging market crises. While Argentina and Turkey have experienced acute stress (Chitu & Quint 2018), in their cases there have been major country specific factors at play (Dubrowski 2018).

The largely successful normalization of monetary policy by the Fed likely reflects a number of factors which I discuss in Chapter 8. From the perspective of emerging markets, improved fiscal and monetary policy frameworks and more flexible exchange rate regimes likely reduced the vulnerabilities of many economies (Powell 2018a), as did the fact that in response to the taper tantrum, a number of countries made necessary policy adjustments and there was also a more realistic appraisal of risk by global investors (Powell 2017). From the Fed's perspective, the very careful communication of its policy intentions subsequent to the taper tantrum and the gradual nature of its policy normalization (Powell 2017) were key. In addition, the start of large QE programmes in Japan and the euro area from 2013 and 2015 respectively were important as they injected significant liquidity into global financial markets as the Fed was removing it. As the new Fed Chair Jerome Powell noted in May 2018: "it is notable that although the Fed has raised its target interest rate six times since December 2015 and has begun to shrink its balance sheet, overall US domestic financial conditions have gotten looser, in part due to improving global conditions and central bank policy abroad".

The verdict on international spillovers from US QE

The first round of US QE received relatively little criticism, neither domestic nor international. This probably reflected a widespread acknowledgement that extraordinary measures were needed to try to halt the GFC, avoid another Great Depression and help to generate a US and global economic recovery. According to Bernanke (2015c), the available evidence for the US suggests the boost to domestic demand from monetary policy easing largely offsets the negative impact on foreign exports from any USD depreciation that may occur (hence, channels (i) and (ii) of Brainard's framework typically offset each other). That said, in US QE1, the boost from the former likely *significantly* outweighed the latter as the stabilization and subsequent US economic recovery that QE helped to achieve, likely meant the boost to foreign exports was very large when compared with realistic counterfactuals. Meanwhile, event studies point to a USD depreciation on QE1 announcements, but not a particularly large one (see Figure 6.1). Moreover, as previously noted, the USD had strengthened significantly since the summer of 2008 amid safe-haven demand from global investors (Bernanke 2015c), peaking shortly before the final announcement of asset purchases in QE1 in March 2009. The subsequent depreciation over the remainder of 2009 during actual QE purchases merely reversed the majority of this appreciation (see Figure 6.3). Hence, even if this depreciation were entirely attributed to QE (and not a reversal of some of the previous safe haven flows), it is something of a stretch to make the case that it alone reduced the USD to excessively advantageous levels compared with previously. Finally, the significant reduction in tail risks and easier financial conditions in the US due to QE also contributed to a very significant improvement in global financial markets (channel (iii) of Brainard's framework). For example, Figure 6.2 highlights the sharp fall in overseas government bond yields during US QE1 announcements and global equity markets recovered strongly during actual QE1 asset purchases. All in all, US QE1 is likely to have been a very significant positive for the global economy and all its regions.[8]

The impact of additional rounds of US QE (QE2 and QE3) is not quite so clear cut for all countries. The adverse reactions of policymakers in some countries clearly suggests they did not think they would be beneficial. Of course, as noted in Chapter 3, the restarting by the Fed of QE in 2010 garnered significant domestic opposition too, particularly from the Republican party. It may have been that the announcements of additional rounds of QE seemed all the more extraordinary (and clearly reckless in the eyes of some) given that the financial crisis had passed and the US and global economies were growing again.

In terms of their economic impact, given that US growth, albeit lacklustre, was not particularly weak, the boost to domestic demand and, hence, over-seas exports is likely to have been significantly less beneficial than for QE1. Meanwhile, the dollar depreciated during QE2 (but not dramatically) and then rose over QE3 (Bernanke 2015c) (see Figure 6.3). Hence, it is hard to make the case that QE2 and QE3 drove a significant competitive advantage for the USD. On balance, it seems likely that the net effect on US domestic demand and the exchange rate would be roughly neutral for foreign exports – in line with Bernanke (2015c) who argued the two factors typically offset each other. Bernanke (2015c) also highlights the fact that the contribution to US growth from net exports was negative in 2010, broadly flat in 2011 and 2012, mod-estly positive in 2013 and modestly negative in 2014. Thus, he seems justified in arguing that it is hard to make the case that US QE2 and QE3 caused a significant USD depreciation that led to the US stealing demand from the rest of the world.

Hence, on the general assumption that for US QE2 and QE3 Brainard's first two channels were broadly neutral for global exports to the US, one must then examine the third channel, the overseas spillover from easier US financial conditions. With other developed economies such as the euro area, Japan and the UK struggling with extremely weak recoveries from the GFC when US QE2 and QE3 occurred, the boost provided to financial conditions and asset prices (while much less than in QE1, see, for example, Figure 6.2 for government bond yields) are likely to have been very timely and an overall positive for those coun-tries. Indeed, in their econometric model, Haldane *et al.* (2016) typically find that US QE has quite large positive impacts on GDP and inflation in the UK, Japan and the euro area through the boost to financial conditions. Hence, the overall impact of US QE2 and QE3 is likely to have been broadly beneficial for the other advanced economies as a whole.

Whether these easings in financial conditions and hence US QE2 and QE3 were beneficial for emerging markets was less clear. Indeed, Brainard (2015b) notes that, when the Fed launched QE2, a number of emerging countries were at a more advanced stage of the economic cycle than the US, being close to full employment and experiencing strong credit growth. Reflecting this, output gaps were largely closed or in positive territory in emerging economies (BIS 2016). Hence, they are unlikely to have welcomed any additional financial stimulus and the large increase in capital inflows (although, as was argued earlier, it is not clear that QE itself fueled a particularly excessive level of capital flows compared with pre-crisis). Nevertheless, Brainard highlights the fact that many countries with flexible exchange rates and robust monetary policy frameworks oriented to domestic objectives were able to offset the divergent spillovers on their economies.[9] In contrast, she suggests that some other countries without flexible exchange rates saw the increased capital flows as presenting problems for the management of their economies, while several countries with relatively flexible exchange rates, and which in particular were experiencing expansions because of elevated commodity prices, saw risks that strong capital inflows could fuel excessive currency appreciation and also result in an excessive loosening in credit conditions.

In general, economic weakness in developed countries and counter-cyclical fiscal and monetary easing by emerging economies to counter the fallout from the GFC had fuelled worsening current account balances and rapidly expanding credit growth that increased domestic financial vulnerabilities (IMF 2013d, 2014b). While emerging markets are a very heterogeneous group and questions can be raised about the appropriateness of various policy settings, it is probably fair to say that US QE2 and QE3 likely exacerbated these growing vulnerabilities in a number of emerging countries amid increased upward pressure on their currencies and looser financial conditions, which helped fuel higher asset prices and further increases in credit growth. Hence, with the trade channel likely to have been broadly neutral, this suggests that the latter rounds of QE may have been a net negative for some emerging economies.

However, given the very substantial positive boost provided by US QE1, it is still fair to say that the overall impact of US QE programmes on both advanced and emerging economies is likely to have been clearly positive. Indeed, as previously discussed, the Fed has now ended its balance sheet drawdown and this has not led to major crises in emerging markets as in the 1980s and 1990s. Summarizing their views, Lavigne *et al.* (2014: 23) note:

[t]he available evidence suggests that quantitative easing (QE) likely increased capital flows to EMEs and put somewhat unwelcome upward pressure on asset prices and exchange rates. However, the overall impact of QE on EMEs was likely positive because of the beneficial trade and confidence effects stemming from stronger economic activity in the countries adopting QE.

EM policy-makers called for greater coordination and consideration of external spillovers

Reflecting some of the negative spillovers on emerging markets from the latter rounds of QE, a number of emerging country policy-makers and academics have called for the Fed and other major developed central banks to take greater account of these spillovers in their decision-making. Rajan (2014: 4) writes:

Hence, my call is for more coordination in monetary policy because I think it would be an immense improvement over the current international non-system … In its strong form, I propose that large country central banks, both in advanced countries and emerging markets, internalize more of the spillovers from their policies in their mandate, and are forced by new conventions on the "rules of the game" to avoid unconventional policies with large adverse spillovers and questionable domestic benefits.

Rajan, who was the central bank governor of the Reserve Bank of India at the time, also argued that it is unfair for international organizations to overlook spillovers from unconventional monetary policies, while at the same time treating sustained currency intervention by some emerging economies with distinct opprobrium.

However, while highlighting the regular consultation the Fed has with foreign policy-makers[10] and expressing sympathy for the many difficulties they faced in recent years, Bernanke (2015c: 2) argues:

I think that some foreign policymakers were too willing, at least in public pronouncements, to accept the idea that countries other than the United States were the purely passive objects of the effects of Fed policy decisions, with little ability or responsibility to improve their own economic situations or to help make the international system work better.

He discusses this within the context of the famous Mundell–Fleming "trilemma" also referred to as the "impossible trinity", which states that policy-makers are only able to choose two out of the three following policy settings at any one time: free capital flows; an independent monetary policy; and an exchange rate target/fixed exchange rate.[11] He argues that concerns about currency wars appear to reflect frustration with this trilemma amid the ongoing desire of emerging market policy-makers to both manage the value of their exchange rates against the USD in order to maintain export competitiveness and to continue to attract capital inflows to fuel economic development. The upshot being that they are constrained in their ability to independently set their own monetary policy in order to offset the impacts on their domestic economies from major US monetary policy changes.[12]

Bernanke (2015c) notes that, over time, the main focus on the international spillovers of monetary policy has switched from currency wars to financial spillovers, which were particularly evident during the taper tantrum. He cites the work of Helene Rey (2013, 2014) who suggests there is a "global financial cycle" – of which US monetary policy is an important driver – which involves the strong common movement of risk appetite, capital flows, asset prices, leverage and credit growth across countries. Rey (2013, 2014) argues that even countries with flexible exchange rates and independent monetary policies are unable to offset the impact of the large financial spillovers from this global financial cycle on their domestic economies. While acknowledging the existence of this global financial cycle, Bernanke cautions that only limited evidence exists on whether this common movement in asset prices and other measures of risk-taking is excessive or through which channels the spillovers occur. He suggests that the existence of the financial spillovers argument does not invalidate the view that countries with flexible exchange rates and independent monetary policies are still better placed to offset the impacts on domestic output from changes in monetary policy overseas. Hence, he suggests that monetary and exchange rate policies should focus on macroeconomic objectives, with the problem of financial spillovers being addressed by other tools such as macroprudential policies,[13] financial regulation, targeted capital controls, potential USD borrowing constraints, etc. Bernanke also highlights the fact that the Fragile Five countries were particularly badly affected during the taper tantrum amid their greater structural issues and macroeconomic imbalances. Reflecting this, he suggests that countries can better insulate themselves from financial spillovers by improving their regulatory frameworks and macroeconomic and structural policies. Indeed, Fratzscher *et al.* (2013) find substantial differences in the extent to which different countries' capital flows and asset prices react to Fed QE measures and suggest that those with high-quality institutions and more active monetary policies were better insulated from spillovers. They conclude that "there may indeed be a case both for domestic policy reforms as well as for more coordination at the global level in order to deal with policy spillovers and externalities".

In terms of the prospects for international policy coordination, Blanchard *et al.* (2013) quip that it "is like the Loch Ness monster – much discussed but rarely seen". Recognizing the practical limitations of proposals favouring the global coordination of monetary policy, Brainard (2015b) notes that "in 2013 the Group of Seven (G7) instead adopted a more circumscribed but achievable set of commitments. Each member committed that its monetary settings – unconventional as well as conventional – would be oriented to meeting its 'respective domestic objectives using domestic instruments,' and 'not target[ing] exchange rates'". This is based on the view that "keeping one's house in order" benefits all (Borio 2011) and Brainard argued that the agreement is likely to be an important constraint against beggar-thy-neighbour policies. However, in a far cry from even this limited form of policy cooperation, the international monetary and trade systems have subsequently come under significant pressure amid severe criticism from US President Donald Trump since his election in 2016. He has accused a number of advanced and emerging economies of engaging in beggar-thy-neighbour behaviour via mercantilist trade policies and manipulating the value of their currencies through QE and other easy money policies. The US has increased trade tariffs on several items, significantly increased tariffs on Chinese imports and threatened other countries with tariffs. Hence, given the current political backdrop, any material increase in international policy coordination seems highly unlikely in the near-term.

An in-depth discussion on the future of the international monetary and financial system is well beyond the scope of this book. An important paper presented at the Fed's annual Jackson Hole Economic Policy Symposium by BoE Governor Mark Carney sets out the key issues. Carney (2019b) argues that in the new world order of increased globalization, financial linkages and USD dominance (despite the declining share of the US in the global economy and sharply rising share of emerging economies), "a reliance on keeping one's house in order is no longer sufficient. The neighborhood too must change". He argues that the deficiencies in the current system impact emerging markets most directly through the loss of monetary policy control, but that everybody is impacted because of the downward pressure on the global equilibrium interest rate amid the vast accumulation of USD-denominated foreign exchange reserves by emerging markets (this was discussed in Chapter 2 in relation to the pre-GFC "global savings glut"). This lowers domestic equilibrium interest rates (see Chapter 1), meaning that monetary policy must be set at even easier settings (for example, through the use of QE and other unconventional policies) in order to sufficiently stimulate the economy.

Over the medium-term, Carney advocates a number of reforms to the existing system. He suggests that emerging economies can increase sustainable capital flows by addressing "pull" factors (reinforcing monetary policy credibility, increasing the resilience of banks, deepening domestic capital markets to reduce the reliance on foreign currency debt and expanding the use of macroprudential tools to guard against excessive credit growth) and that advanced economies should moderate "push" factors, including risks in their own financial systems that can spillover to emerging markets. He argues for more effective and impactful IMF surveillance of cross-border spillovers and calls for an increase in the IMF administered global financial safety net to reduce the need for emerging economies to accumulate foreign exchange reserves as insurance against less sustainable capital flows. Over the longer-term, he suggests that more fundamental changes are needed such as a move to a multipolar system with multiple global reserve currencies.[14] He argues that by increasing the supply of safe assets this would reduce downward pressure on the global equilibrium interest rate, while a more diversified system would reduce spillovers from the core (the US) and, hence, lower the synchronization of trade and financial cycles.

A key conclusion of this chapter is that US QE overall was a major positive for the rest of the global economy, with the significant benefits of QE1 to the US economy and global financial markets more than offsetting any negative impacts that a number of emerging economies may have experienced with the latter rounds of US QE. Moreover, the Fed has successfully unwound its asset purchases and raised interest rates without causing a major crisis in emerging markets such as was seen in the latter decades of the twentieth century. Some criticisms of the Fed's QE by emerging economies have been somewhat unfair, while others echo long-held criticisms of the US dominated international monetary system. While significant improvements do need to be made to the international monetary system, a significant step-up in international policy cooperation does not seem likely anytime soon. Indeed, there has been a significant deterioration in international trade relations since Donald Trump became US President. He has accused a number of countries of engaging in mercantilist trade policies and of using monetary policy to weaken their currencies to gain a competitive advantage. Meanwhile, a move to a multipolar system of reserve currencies seems some way off given the overwhelming dominance of the USD and the large network effects that act to sustain this. At the same time, the most likely candidates to become reserve currencies alongside the USD, the euro and the Chinese Renminbi, for various reasons seem some way off from being able to assume the role (Gopinath 2020). In the next chapter, I discuss the domestic criticisms and negative externalities of QE.

7

CRITICISMS AND NEGATIVE EXTERNALITIES OF QUANTITATIVE EASING

QE has received significant criticism on numerous fronts owing to fears it would fuel surging inflation, currency debasement and financial instability and amid accusations that it has been responsible for a huge rise in inequality *within* countries. One senior German politician even suggested it was partly responsible for the rise in right-wing extremist political groups. In this chapter, I highlight and examine the many criticisms aimed at QE and other easy money policies by politicians, the media, the general public and some economists. The growing criticism of central banks has raised important questions about the appropriate level of coordination with governments in future downturns and reopened the debate about the desirability of their independence, which I highlight and discuss.

Some fears of an inflation surge

Perhaps the most feared negative externality of QE when it was first announced in the US and UK was that it would generate runaway inflation, with some commentators describing it as "money printing" and making comparisons with the German Weimar Republic in the early twentieth century and more recently Zimbabwe, where, in cooperation with their governments, the central banks financed huge increases in government spending, eventually resulting in hyperinflation. In the event, QE did not fuel surging inflation and, as previously highlighted in Chapter 5, the main central banks have in fact actually struggled to raise inflation back up to their 2 per cent targets.

There appear to be a number of reasons why the early rounds of QE in the US and UK did not lead to the surge in inflation that some feared:

(i) Although there are a number of similarities and the dividing lines can become increasingly blurred (Turner 2013), US and UK QE typically differed in some important respects to the monetary financing of government fiscal deficits, which occurred in Weimar Germany and Zimbabwe. Crucially, with QE the decision to purchase assets by central banks was made *independently* of governments and was taken with the intention of increasing aggregate demand and so preventing inflation falling materially below their targets. As Miles (2012) notes in relation to the BoE, "The decision of the MPC to embark on asset purchases on an enormous scale was not done because it had abandoned the inflation target, it was done because of the inflation target". Moreover, central banks stressed that QE was temporary and would be reversed once economic circumstances improved. In contrast, with monetary financing of government deficits, central bank asset purchases have typically been done amid pressure from the government to fund massive spending increases and without a great deal of concern for the inflationary consequences (at least, perhaps, until the large negative economic and social consequences of soaring inflation become evident). Meanwhile, increases in the monetary base are typically permanent.

(ii) Significant spare capacity, such as extremely elevated unemployment rates and low capacity utilization at factories, was exerting large downward pressures on inflation.

(iii) Despite massive increases in the size of the monetary base amid QE, as previously discussed, this failed to fuel much of a rise in broader measures of money supply and lending to the private sector.

(iv) There remained sustained downward *structural* pressure on inflation from globalization and technological trends.

(v) Inflation expectations remained well anchored around central bank targets. This was very important. It is reasonable to assume that reason (ii) weighed down on inflation expectations, together with the collapse in consumer, business and investor confidence (this actually raised the risk of inflation expectations falling significantly below target). The greatest potential risk of an upward jump in inflation expectations and, hence, inflation came from reason (i) – if investors, businesses and households began to believe (whether or not it was justifiable) that central banks were beginning to engage in more reckless policies and had given up on their inflation targets. Former Fed Governor Lyle Gramley spoke to these types of fears in June 2009:

I don't think they [the Fed] can afford to go out and aggressively buy longer-term Treasuries or even step-up aggressively their purchases of mortgage debt ... There is this fear going around in financial markets that the Fed is going to monetize the debt, and we're going to have big inflation. I don't believe that for a minute, but the perception is a reality that the Fed is going to have to deal with.

(Bull 2009 in D'Amico & King 2011)

This is why the central banks went to great lengths to stress their ongoing commitment to their inflation targets, the differences between QE and the outright monetary financing of government deficits and their confidence that once recovery came they had the necessary tools to control any risks stemming from the huge growth in the liability side of their balance sheets. They were also quite measured in their discussions around supporting inflation expectations.[1]

Inflation has remained below targets

The inability of central banks to raise inflation back up to their targets since the GFC, despite economic recoveries, was an overriding theme in Chapter 5 and has served to challenge economists' understanding of the inflation generation process.

In particular, the enormous QE programme enacted by Japan since 2013 has come pretty close to most definitions of outright monetary financing of government deficits. It was enacted at the behest of the new Abe administration as a key plank of its Abenomics programme; annual purchases of government bonds have exceeded government deficits and the BoJ now owns over 40 per cent of all outstanding government debt. Moreover, few realistically expect the BoJ's government bond purchases will ever be reversed. Despite this, both inflation and inflation expectations have remained quiescent and well below the BoJ's 2 per cent inflation target. This has clearly challenged the earlier views of many leading academic economists that central banks could always create sufficient inflation. Bernanke (2002) notes:

> Like gold, U.S. dollars have value only to the extent that they are strictly limited in supply. But the U.S. government has a technology, called a printing press (or, today, its electronic equivalent), that allows it to produce as many U.S. dollars as it wishes at essentially no cost. By increasing the number of U.S. dollars in circulation, or even by credibly threatening to do so, the U.S. government can also reduce the value of a dollar in terms of goods and services, which is equivalent to raising the prices in dollars of those goods and services. We conclude that, under a paper-money system, a determined government can always generate higher spending and hence positive inflation.

Admittedly, if Japan were to completely "throw caution to the wind" one suspects they could generate significant inflation through a complete collapse in the currency, although this would probably come at the expense of a major financial crisis.

Meanwhile, as economic recoveries from the GFC have progressed in the advanced economies, inflation and wage growth have remained pretty subdued despite sharp falls in unemployment rates, which reached their lowest in around fifty years in the US and UK and well below most previous estimates of their natural rates or NAIRUs. In Chapter 1, I described how belief in the Phillips Curve, which posited a long-run inverse relationship between the unemployment rate and wages/inflation, broke down during the 1970s amid both soaring unemployment and inflation. Nevertheless, the data have typically tended to show evidence of a shorter-term trade-off between the unemployment rate and wages/inflation, which economists refer to as the short-run Phillips curve (FRBSF 2008). In the long run, the Phillips curve is thought to be vertical at the natural rate of unemployment/NAIRU, with inflation accelerating if policymakers attempt to push unemployment below its natural rate. Economists use a version of the short-run Phillips curve called the "expectations augmented Phillips Curve", that includes inflation expectations as a determinant of inflation, to help forecast inflation (FRBSF 2008). The addition of inflation expectations reflected an attempt to explain the breakdown of the relationship in the 1970s (Cunliffe 2017). The fact that labour-market slack appears to be having a much-diminished impact on domestic wages and inflation in the recovery from the GFC points to a significant flattening and shift of the short-run Phillips curve (much larger falls in the unemployment rate are needed to raise wages/inflation than previously and a given level of the unemployment rate is consistent with lower inflation, see Figure 7.1). For an excellent exposition of recent changes in the Phillips curve, particularly from a UK perspective, see Cunliffe (2017).

There are a number of possible explanations for this, all of which could have made some contribution:

(i) In the aftermath of the massive negative shock of the GFC, workers are less willing to push for higher wages and/or firms have become more cautious about increasing their fixed costs by granting higher pay rises.

(ii) Globalization has continued to hold prices and wages down. Borio and Filardo (2007) suggest that global measures of economic slack have gained in importance as a driver of domestic inflation and Forbes (2019) finds that global factors (including commodity prices, world slack, exchange rates, and global value chains) are significant drivers of inflation in a cross-section of countries and their role has increased since the GFC. Moreover, the continued threat of offshoring production by firms probably continues to restrain pay demands of workers.

(iii) Technological advances may be increasingly having a greater downward impact on price pressures, likely lowering inflation through numerous channels. These include the automation of production processes and customer service tasks, the disruption of traditional industries (for example Uber, Airbnb, WhatsApp, Netflix, LinkedIn, etc.) and the broader competitive pressures brought about by large e-commerce companies such as Amazon.[2] Once again, the threat of automation and remote working may also be restraining worker pay demands in certain industries.

(iv) The successful anchoring of inflation expectations over recent decades around inflation targets, which may mask and suppress price changes in response to unemployment (see Ng *et al.* 2018). A point highlighted by Powell (2018b).

(v) The natural rate of unemployment/NAIRU may have fallen and, indeed, most central banks have been lowering such estimates. In the US, the Fed's estimate has fallen from around 5.5 per cent in the years following the GFC to around 4 per cent at present. In the UK, the BoE's estimate has fallen from around 5 per cent before the GFC to 4.25 per cent at present.

Financial stability risks?

Another major criticism of QE and other easy money policies was that they would create major financial instability by driving a hunt for yield among

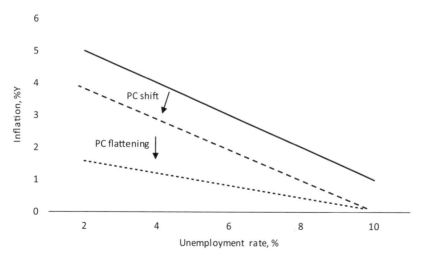

Figure 7.1. The Phillips Curve seems to have flattened and shifted
Source: Ashworth (2020).

investors, fuelling asset price bubbles and encouraging a further accumulation of debt when the private sector should be repairing its finances after the pre-GFC splurge. Krugman (2015) argued that many of those uncomfortable about unconventional monetary policies switched their concerns to financial stability once it became clear that the threatened inflation was not going to materialize.

Most asset prices in developed economies, whether of equities, government bonds, corporate bonds or housing, have risen sharply since the onset of QE, and in a number of cases, are now at, or close to, record highs. The IMF's October 2019 *Financial Stability Report* highlights stretched valuations in some markets, an increasing hunt for yield in a number of sectors and suggests that financial vulnerabilities are building in some areas. However, it is not clear that there are major bubbles posing serious financial stability risks. Indeed, central bankers acknowledge that some improvement in risk taking was a key aim of these policies[3] (Bernanke 2018) and one must acknowledge that the significant economic improvement that QE in part helped to generate has provided a fundamental underpinning behind a significant portion of these asset price gains (Bernanke 2018). In terms of private sector non-financial debt, as a share of GDP it is some way below its pre-GFC peaks in the US (Bernanke 2018) and UK and at broadly similar levels in the euro area and Japan.[4] Hence, it is hard to make the case that QE has reignited another major private sector credit cycle in the economies enacting it. Admittedly, as Cunliffe (2019) notes, the aggregates do mask some sectoral trends. In particular, the ratio of debt-to-GDP for US non-financial corporations has risen sharply and the proportion of this owed by highly leveraged companies has returned to pre-GFC levels of around 40 per cent (Cunliffe 2019). Summarizing the US Fed's latest thinking, Chair Powell suggested in August 2019: "We have not seen unsustainable borrowing, financial booms, or other excesses of the sort that occurred at times during the Great Moderation, and I continue to judge overall financial stability risks to be moderate. But we remain vigilant" (Powell 2019a).

While private sector debt ratios have not really risen in the major developed economies since the GFC, global debt levels have amid a rapid expansion in borrowing by emerging markets. Private non-financial sector debt in emerging markets has risen from around 75 per cent of GDP in 4Q 2008 to almost 140 per cent at present, with a particular surge in China to over 200 per cent of GDP. The key driver of the increase has been non-financial corporate debt. Using regression analysis, Lo Duca *et al.* (2014) find that US QE had a large impact on global corporate bond issuance, particularly in emerging markets. The size and speed of the rise in debt levels increase the financial stability risks stemming from emerging markets and the potential spillback to developed economies could be greater than in the past given that the share of the emerging world in the global economy has increased by around 10 percentage points since the GFC.

Of course, it would clearly be unfair to blame all or even much of the increase in debt on QE by the US and other developed economies given that emerging markets had eased monetary policy significantly to stimulate their economies after the GFC and given that credit-intensive growth has been part of the development model in countries such as China (Bernanke 2018).

A particular area of risk could be the large rise in total overseas USD borrowing by non-US borrowers. BIS data show this has increased sharply from $5.8 trillion in Q4 2008 to $9.4 trillion in Q4 2014, when US QE finally ended, and to almost $12 trillion at present, with a large increase in non-financial sector debt securities outstanding from $1.2 trillion in Q4 2008 to $2.4 trillion in Q4 2014 and $3.2 trillion at present. In emerging markets, total USD borrowing has increased from $1.6 trillion (7.5 per cent of GDP) in 4Q 2008 to $3 trillion (10 per cent of GDP) at the end of US QE and to $3.8 trillion at present (11 per cent of GDP). Of this, the value of non-financial sector debt securities outstanding has risen from around $0.5 trillion to $1.1 trillion in 4Q 2014 and $1.8 trillion at present. The increases in USD borrowing were particularly large in emerging Asia (China) and to a lesser extent Latin America. If the USD were to strengthen significantly against other currencies, some of these overseas USD borrowers could be at risk of future default given that their revenues will be in their local currencies. Bernanke (2015c) suggests that emerging market governments should "monitor and possibly constrain" the USD borrowing of their banks and companies, suggesting the stress testing of their liabilities for currency risk.

Some critics also point to a number of undesirable medium-term and longer-run unintended consequences of prolonged ultra-easy monetary policy on the financial system (Borio 2012; White 2012). Borio (2012) argues that it makes it easier to delay the recognition of losses on bank loans (evergreening), can lessen incentives to reduce excess capacity in the financial sector, can atrophy markets and mask market signals, and, over time, it can undermine the earnings capacity of financial intermediaries: low short-term interest rates and a flat yield curve due to central bank government bond purchases compress the net interest margins of banks (whose standard business model is based on maturity transformation where they borrow short-term and lend longer-term); low long-term interest rates damage the business models of insurance companies and pension funds. Cunliffe (2019) suggests insurance companies and pension funds are having to invest in riskier assets to maintain sufficient returns and they may have to accelerate changes to their business models, which will result in less risk-sharing with a larger proportion of pensioners retaining their own longevity and investment risks. White (2012) argues that easy monetary conditions could fuel malinvestments and prevent the re-allocation of capital to more productive firms and sectors and, in association with regulatory and technical developments, encourage the development of a riskier and more procyclical "shadow banking sector", the complexity and non-transparency of which he notes, is highlighted by the Financial Stability Board (FSB) (2012). The shadow banking sector, referred to by the FSB since 2019 as "non-bank financial intermediation", has increased its share of total global financial assets to over 48 per cent at present, slightly higher than its pre-GFC peak of around 47 per cent (FSB 2020).

In conclusion, a reasonable argument can be made that we are now more than a decade since the beginning of QE and the Fed has successfully wound down its asset holdings. Therefore, it does not appear as though QE has created major or abnormal financial stability risks, particularly over and above those that would come from a prolonged period of conventional monetary policy easing. Moreover, after the mistakes made in allowing the housing bubble to build prior to the GFC, central bank officials argue that they are significantly more alert to the build-up of financial stability risks this time around, helped by the significant reforms and improvements to the financial system in the aftermath of the GFC and the introduction of macroprudential tools in a number of countries.

However, critics still have some justification in arguing that it is still too early to make a definitive judgement. Indeed, the difficulty in correctly identifying the housing bubble and massive vulnerabilities that had built in the financial system prior to the GFC suggests that a fair degree of caution is warranted. As former Fed Governor Kevin Warsh suggested in 2018: "A decade should have been plenty sufficient to provide strong, compelling evidence of the wisdom or folly of the QE seriatim experiment. But, it is not. For the central bank community evaluating QE, we are still in the thick of history". Indeed, that the QE programmes in the euro area and Japan are ongoing complicates any contemporary evaluation as it is possible that they may have limited the negative impact on global financial markets from the winding down of the Fed's QE programme. Significant negative fallout could increasingly materialize if the euro area and Japan were to unwind their programmes, although this admittedly seems way off in the future, if it happens at all. In truth, while it is always difficult to identify the exact trigger beforehand, the next major global downturn is probably the most likely event that could reveal any major financial vulnerabilities created by QE that we do not already know about. As renowned investor Warren Buffet famously said "Only when the tide goes out do you discover who's been swimming naked". A key area of potential risk could be the less regulated parts of the financial system.

Misallocation of resources and weakened productivity

Productivity growth (for example, output per hour worked) has been very weak in the developed economies in the aftermath of the GFC, although it had already begun to slow somewhat before the GFC. There is probably some merit in the argument that QE and other easy money policies have created some distortions and misallocation of resources and, hence, may have weakened *underlying* productivity growth. The argument is probably more pertinent for the later rounds of QE done outside of the GFC,[5] where financial markets were not hugely distorted and the boost to growth was much more modest and for those economies that have been implementing QE and other unconventional monetary policies over an extended period, namely the euro area and Japan. Admittedly, it will probably take a number of years for a clearer picture to emerge and the post-GFC data is still subject to (potentially) significant data revisions.

Chapter 1 highlighted how significant inflation variability, as occurred in the 1970s, can be a key source of inefficiency and, potentially, QE could also have caused its own misallocation of resources. In large modern capitalist economies such as the US, price signals from goods and services (inflation), labour (via wages), and financial assets such as the 10-year US Treasury yield, are key in the efficient allocation of real resources and capital across the economy. Warsh (2018) comments "[m]y overriding concern about continued QE, then and now, involves the misallocations of capital in the economy". He notes that "price signals are everything" and argues that the yield on the 10-year US Treasury bond set in open financial markets is the most important price signal in the world as it is the risk-free rate on which all other financial assets are priced. He argues that we are creating major tail risks if, as a result of asset purchases, we do not know the true risk-free rate and notes that it was a risk he was willing to take when the Fed did QE in the crisis, but suggests that the argument is less clear-cut outside of crises.

Shirai (2018b) suggests the decline in functioning of the Japanese government bond market amid the BoJ's QQE programme is a growing concern given its role as a benchmark for pricing loans and corporate bonds and she notes that concerns are also increasing regarding the functioning of the Japanese equity market. Due to the BoJ's ongoing purchases of equity ETFs, she suggests there is less downside risk in the stock market, some small-cap stocks are overvalued and there is a potential adverse impact on corporate governance as a result of the BoJ's growing presence as a silent investor without exercising its voting rights. Strikingly, the BoJ now owns around 5 per cent of total stock market capitalization and is a top-ten shareholder in 40 per cent of all listed companies (*Financial Times* 2019b). Perhaps with Japan and the euro area in mind where interest rates are in negative territory, Summers and Stansbury (2019) suggest "[t]here is something unhealthy about an economy in which corporations can profitably borrow and invest even if the project in question pays a zero return". Of course, a perennial problem is that it is very difficult to know in "real-time" the level of malinvestment that may potentially be occurring as a result of distorted price signals and excessively cheap credit (Warsh 2018).

Meanwhile, lower interest rates across the yield curve may have weighed on productivity through three other key channels:

(i) by keeping "zombie" (non-viable) firms alive. This prevents necessary restructuring and ties up bank capital and lending in these companies, preventing economic resources from being redirected to more productive firms and sectors. In a study of advanced economies, Banerjee and Hofmann (2018) find that while lower rates boost aggregate demand and raise employment and investment in the short run, the higher prevalence of zombies they leave behind misallocate resources and weigh on productivity growth.

(ii) by fuelling a large increase in the liabilities of defined benefit pension plans (which are typically discounted using a longer-term government or corporate bond yield), which meant that some firms had to divert funds from more productive uses such as investment and research & development, to plugging these larger pension fund gaps. Goodhart and Ashworth (2012) highlight the sharp increase in liabilities of UK defined benefit pension plans and suggested that the diversion of funds to filling this gap raised the risk of lower business investment and productivity. Bunn *et al.* (2018a) find that firms that are required to make deficit recovery contributions by The Pensions Regulator have lower investment expenditure compared with other firms, and more so if they are financially constrained; and

(iii) by flattening the yield curve this will have adversely impacted the profitability of banks which could have reduced their incentives to lend to firms. Cunliffe (2019) notes that the net interest margins of Japanese banks have been falling for over a decade and that we have seen a similar, albeit smaller, effect in other advanced economies.

Rising wealth inequality and large distributional issues

Bunn *et al.* (2018b) note that "Distributional issues have increased in prominence since the financial crisis, with income and wealth inequality becoming headline news". The "Occupy Wall Street" movement, which began in 2011 and spread to many countries, began to focus attention on rising inequality in the developed world, with BoE Chief Economist Andy Haldane acknowledging that "Occupy touched a moral nerve among the many" (Haldane 2014). The trend of rising inequality over the past several decades in some developed economies was famously documented by Thomas Piketty in his 2014 book *Capital in the Twenty-First Century*, which showed that the top decile in the US now accounted for almost 50 per cent and over 70 per cent of total income and wealth respectively (see Figure 7.2 and Piketty 2014).

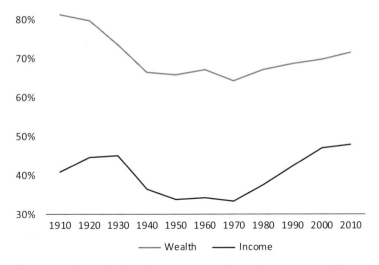

Figure 7.2. Inequality has been rising sharply over the past several decades (income and wealth shares of US top 10 per cent)
Note: data on inequality can vary depending on the source, but the general theme has been one of rising inequality over recent decades.
Source: Piketty (2014).

A key criticism of QE and other easy money policies is that they have helped fuel a further increase in inequality amid surging house prices and stock markets. UK Prime Minister Theresa May suggested in a 2016 speech that:

> while monetary policy – with super-low interest rates and quantitative easing – provided the necessary emergency medicine after the financial crash, we have to acknowledge there have been some bad side effects. People with assets have got richer. People without them have suffered. People with mortgages have found their debts cheaper. People with savings have found themselves poorer. (May 2016)

Even some hedge fund bosses have criticized QE for increasing wealth inequality (Marshall 2015).

Debelle (2017) notes that monetary policy has always had distributional consequences but suggests the greater focus on it during the period of unconventional policy may reflect the fact that concerns about income inequality are greater during periods when wage growth is stagnant for most of the population. He also suggests another possible explanation is that, if a key transmission channel of unconventional monetary policy is through asset prices (including house prices), then the wealth channel may be having a greater role than historically. One suspects the greater focus also reflects the fact that monetary policy helped the better off at a time when there has been significant fiscal austerity in the developed economies which has primarily impacted poorer segments of the population. Goodhart and Lastra (2018) argue that QE and other unconventional monetary policies are now seen in the context of the winners and losers from globalization. They suggest that this may reflect the fact that the trends in interest rates over the past three decades have been so large and persistent,[6] whereas previously it was believed that interest rates and inflation would fluctuate around a norm, so that temporary benefits to one side or the other would eventually cancel out. According to Borio and Zabai (2016: 32):

> Things have changed post-crisis. On the one hand, the financial crisis has put the spotlight on the growing inequality that had been growing for decades (e.g. Piketty (2014)). On the other hand, the extreme monetary policy settings have focused attention on central banks' role, not least given their greater and explicit reliance on boosting asset prices and given the impact of persistent exceptionally low interest rates on savers.[7]

In general, central banks have typically tried to play down the negative distributional impacts of their unconventional policies (Broadbent 2018). Based on standard Gini coefficients[8] both Bunn *et al.* (2018b) and Lenza and Slacalek (2018) argue that QE did not have much impact on either income or wealth inequality in the UK and euro area respectively, suggesting it actually reduced it slightly on both measures.[9] The finding of a reduction in *income* inequality comes mainly through the boost provided to growth and the resultant improvement in labour markets, with both studies highlighting the benefits to the job prospects of the young and less educated who are typically more negatively impacted during economic downturns than the older and more educated. This is a reasonable argument which I would not dispute. The claim that QE has not increased w*ealth* inequality is somewhat surprising though. An important factor influencing the results appears to be the fact that home ownership is quite broadly spread across the respective populations, so that many households benefitted from rising house prices. However, as Cribb (2013) notes regarding the use of Gini coefficients, "summarizing inequality in just one number can mask different patterns in changing inequality". Indeed, it seems eminently clear that those who do not own their homes (renters, the young) and who presumably do not have much financial wealth either, have experienced large relative declines in their wealth compared with homeowners and those with extensive financial assets as a result of QE and other easy money policies. In the UK, around

20 per cent of households are private renters and around 17 per cent are in social housing (ONS 2019), while in the US over one-third of the population are renters, including almost two-thirds of under 35s (Pew Research Center 2017). According to Borio and Zabai (2016) "The direct impact of policy on asset prices, especially equities, is quite visible. And if one focuses on the richest (e.g. the top 1 per cent) and poorest segments of the population, it is hard to argue that policy does not raise wealth inequality".

A seemingly more plausible argument for central banks would be to more openly acknowledge that there are some negative impacts on wealth inequality from QE and other unconventional monetary policies (as is the case with conventional monetary policy), but to suggest that in the circumstances when they were used this was probably a price worth paying given that it potentially helped avoid another depression during the GFC and had very positive impacts on growth and the labour market (of course, some would suggest that this is a very credible argument for US and UK policy-makers to make about QE1, but perhaps less so for subsequent rounds). Former BoE Deputy Governor Paul Tucker provides a generally fair account of events:

> I think, for example, that central banks have been far too defensive about whether there have been distributional effects from quantitative easing. Rather than giving lots of papers saying, "The biggest effects on inequality are coming from elsewhere," which I believe to be true as a matter of economics, I think it would be more prudent and central bankers would be listened to more, if they said, "Well, it's not why we did it, but yes, it's had the effect. It's helped people keep jobs, particularly people in more insecure jobs. It has pushed up asset prices, and probably helped the rich. It probably has squeezed people who live off their income from savings ..." (Tucker 2018)

Other distributional consequences have also gained significant attention. According to Mckinsey (2013), QE and other easy money policies lowered the net interest income of the household sector in the US, UK and the euro area by around $630 billion between 2007 and 2012. They note sharp differences across demographic groups, however, with younger households that are typically net debtors benefitting but older households with interest earning savings suffering. This negative consequence of ECB monetary policy has received particularly vehement criticism in Germany. Finance Minister Wolfgang Schäuble suggested in 2016 that the ECB's easy money policies were partly behind the rise of the right-wing *Alternative für Deutschland* (AfD) party and, after the ECB's decision in September 2019 to restart QE and cut interest rates further into negative territory, German newspapers depicted ECB President Mario Draghi as Count

Dracula sucking the money out of Germans' savings accounts (*Financial Times* 2019c).

There are several reasons why the negative reaction may have been so strong in Germany. First, Germans did not see themselves as being part of the pre-GFC speculative bubble that occurred in Anglo-Saxon countries and others in Europe and the economy emerged from the GFC in relatively robust shape and has generally performed strongly. Hence, unlike many other countries, the German public has probably been less willing to view low interest rates on their bank accounts as a painful, but unavoidable, side-effect of extraordinary monetary policies necessary to support a recovery from the crisis. Second, for historical reasons, the German population has a strong aversion to easy money policies and, as discussed in Chapter 3, hostility to the ECB has consistently grown as it has enacted ever more extraordinary monetary policies over the past decade. Third, OECD data show that around 40 per cent of the financial assets of German households are invested in currency and deposits – which is well above the OECD median and compares with just 13 per cent in the USA. Moreover, the positive offset from wealth increases may have been lower than in other countries despite strong gains in the German stock market and house prices since the GFC. Only around 10 per cent of German household financial assets are directly held in equities, half the OECD median and less than a third of the US number (OECD 2019) and German home ownership rates of around 50 per cent are also very low compared with other OECD countries (Andrews & Sanchez 2011).

Another key criticism in the UK regarding the distributional impacts of QE was the impact it had on the income derived from pensions (Altmann 2012). This has clearly been an issue in all developed countries given the collapse in interest rates on government bonds, although pension laws exacerbated the plight of many UK pensioners. Until a change of UK law, in 2014, workers in defined-contribution pension schemes were required to purchase an annuity with their accumulated pension savings on retirement. An annuity provides a regular income during retirement, the size of which depends on factors such as the value of pension savings and prevailing market interest rates. The collapse in the latter meant that many retirees had to permanently lock themselves into a much lower than expected income stream. According to the National Association of Pension Funds (NAPF), a 65-year-old male with a pension fund of £100,000 could have bought an annuity of around £7,810 per annum in early 2008, but this sum had fallen to just £6,112 by March 2012 – a real-terms decline of around one-third (Goodhart & Ashworth 2012). Of course, the BoE would argue that its policies, by helping to drive a recovery in the economy and asset prices after the GFC, helped boost the value of pension pots as well as other assets such as houses.

Central bankers have often pointed out that governments have fiscal tools at their disposal to offset any negative distributional consequences from monetary policy. A key problem highlighted in Chapter 3 was that for most of the post-GFC period central banks have been "the only game in town" (El-Erian 2017) as governments have been either unable or unwilling to ease fiscal policy (in fact, as highlighted in Chapter 3, many actually tightened policy significantly). With the efficacy of QE programmes likely declining over time and some of the negative side-effects increasing, one suspects that more supportive fiscal policy from governments could have provided a more optimal policy trade-off than some of the latter rounds of QE. It could have boosted growth and labour markets, but without some of the associated consequences for wealth inequality due to rising asset prices. Tucker (2019: 529–30) acknowledges:

> For central bankers, the dominating concern, given their mandate, was to restore growth in aggregate incomes and jobs in order to bring inflation back toward target. With hindsight, however, they should have been more active in highlighting the costs of their policy. Had they done so, it would have been clearer to the public and civil society that the political authorities had the means to mitigate some of the distributional consequences, and that a different mix of monetary and fiscal policy was worth considering.

Admittedly, the argument in favour of easier fiscal policy is easier to make in hindsight. It also glosses over the fact that, in the US, the Obama administration's hands were largely tied after the loss of Congress to the Republicans in late 2010, hence, fiscal stimulus was not really a plausible alternative to US QE2 and QE3. Meanwhile, the UK coalition government faced a budget deficit of 10 per cent of GDP and fears that the euro area sovereign debt crisis could spread to its shores when it came to power in May 2010. Hence, it had little room to support the economy with easier fiscal policy as an alternative to QE2. With all this in mind, it perhaps supports the view of some leading US economists (such as Paul Krugman and Alice Rivlin) who argued that the initial fiscal stimulus programmes enacted at the time of the GFC should have been even larger and spread over more years. It was when the fiscal stimulus programmes started to wind down in 2010 and 2011 that the economic recoveries lost some momentum, leading to the restarting of the US and UK QE programmes. Of course, a counter-argument could be that with deficits and government debts soaring at the height of the GFC, financial markets may not, at the time, have stomached even larger fiscal stimulus programmes. However, this seems unlikely, particularly if the US and UK had paired extra fiscal stimulus with plans for future fiscal consolidation once the economic recoveries had gained traction.

Meanwhile, a key riposte of ECB President Mario Draghi to criticisms from Germany and other northern European countries about the negative externalities from the ECB's policies has been that they would not have been quite so necessary if countries such as Germany and the Netherlands with significant fiscal space had used some of it. Indeed, Germany has run a budget surplus since 2012 which had risen to around 1 per cent of GDP by 2015 and 2 per cent by 2018. Given that it is by far the euro area's largest economy, a more expansionary fiscal policy would have boosted other euro area economies and by raising German wages and inflation would have increased the relative competitiveness of other countries in the bloc.

Populism

The accusation by German finance minister Wolfgang Schäuble that the ECB's policies were in part responsible (he suggested around 50 per cent) for the rise of the right-wing populist AfD party in Germany (*Financial Times* 2016) was perhaps one of the most pointed criticisms aimed at a major central bank in recent times. Without wanting to dwell too much on the specific accusation, many observers have highlighted other seemingly more important factors behind the growth in the AfD's support, such as Chancellor Merkel's decision to allow large numbers of refugees from the Syrian conflict to resettle in Germany and large regional inequalities (*Guardian* 2019a). Indeed, cross-sectional regression analysis of the results of the 2017 federal election by Roth and Wolff (2017) finds that seven variables explain over 70 per cent of the variation in the vote for the AfD. Particularly important explanatory variables were: the East–West divide, with the former East Germany voting much more heavily for the AfD (even after controlling for socio-economic factors); districts with higher percentages of older voters, foreigners and the less educated favoured the AfD; districts with higher disposable income were less predisposed to the AfD. Of lesser importance, districts with higher church membership were less inclined to vote AfD, with the opposite for more rural areas.

Moreover, it is also worth bearing in mind that had the ECB not saved the euro area from probable collapse with its OMT programme in 2012, one suspects that the ensuing economic catastrophe would have provided a far more fertile breeding ground for populist parties in Germany and across the European continent, potentially of far greater extremes. Also, by helping to generate an economic recovery and reducing unemployment through its QE programmes, the ECB has probably helped to keep something of a lid on populist pressures compared with the counterfactual, particularly in the peripheral countries where European fiscal rules prevented much, if any, support from fiscal policy.

Ironically, some have warned that the constant criticism of the ECB in Germany risks fuelling a broader populist turn against the European project among the German public. They highlight the constant criticism of the EU in the UK media in the decades before it voted in the referendum to leave (*Financial Times* 2019d, 2019e). The ECB's new Executive Board member from Germany, Isabel Schnabel (Sabine Lautenschlager's replacement), has also warned against this risk (*Financial Times* 2019f) and has refuted the major criticisms aimed at the ECB's policies (Schnabel 2020).

Threats to central bank independence

Amid the successful economic performance of the developed economies during the Great Moderation, central bankers came to be held in extremely high esteem by investors, the media and members of the general public with an interest in such matters. Particularly feted was Alan Greenspan, Fed Chair between 1987 and early 2006, famously nicknamed the "Maestro", which was the title of a biography about him (Woodward 2001). However, the reputations of central bankers have suffered since the GFC. As Goodhart and Lastra (2018) note:

> central banks, alongside most others, failed to foresee or head off the Global Crisis and their focus on a narrowly construed price stability-oriented monetary policy made them ignore or insufficiently calibrate the perils of financial instability … Although their immediate response in 2008/09 was exemplary, and did succeed in preventing another Great Depression, their record afterwards, from 2010 to 2016, was consistently one of failing to forecast the sluggishness of growth of either output or inflation, casting some doubt on their competence, economic understanding and capacities.

Reflecting the growing discontent, former ECB Chief Economist Otmar Issing suggests that "The independence of central banks has again become a prominent subject in academia, politics and the media. However, this time, in contrast to the past, critical voices dominate" (Issing 2018). In addition to the criticisms regarding the distributional consequences of QE and other easy money policies, I highlighted in previous chapters the increasing politicization of central banks. This included fierce criticism of the Fed by opposition Republicans during latter rounds of QE, immense pressure placed on the BoJ to support Prime Minister Abe's "Abenomics" programme and the ever-growing hostility towards the ECB from large parts of the German establishment. Balls *et al.* (2018) note that the US Congress only narrowly rejected an "Audit the Fed" plan to curtail the Fed's independence and highlight the significant criticisms of its decisions and independence from President Trump (in recent decades US Presidents had previously eschewed commenting on Fed policy). In the UK, the authors highlight the fierce criticism aimed at the BoE over its analysis in the run up to the Brexit referendum and note that the opposition Labour party launched a review of the BoE.

Goodhart and Lastra (2018) suggest that an additional aspect to concerns about central bank independence comes from the decision to grant them extra responsibility for financial stability in the aftermath of the GFC. They suggest this has further complicated their lives in a number of respects and that "the blurring of independence in the fields of financial stability may raise questions for central banks' independence in the future". Indeed, according to Balls *et al.* (2018) "these new powers may require the central bank to coordinate closely with the government and other regulatory institutions, and to venture into politically treacherous areas with first-order distributional consequences such as housing policy". Tucker (2018) worries that too much is now being expected of central banks:

> We hope they'll solve all of the macroeconomic and financial problems that we have. I worry that some central banks have powers that make it possible for them to enter territory which really belongs to the politicians. The slogan is, 'Central banks are the only game in town', and I don't think that's sustainable.

The UK perhaps best exemplifies Tucker's fears, with the opposition Labour Party suggesting including a target for productivity growth[10] in the BoE's mandate and powers for helping to tackle climate change (*Guardian* 2018, 2019b).

Summers (2017) argues that the case for central bank independence today is much weaker than it was twenty years ago and suggests that "institutional evolution in major countries is both likely and desirable over the next couple of decades". I highlighted in Chapter 1 how central bank independence came about in response to the Great Inflation of the 1970s. Summers notes, however, that the problem in the current era in most countries is too little inflation. He argues that, as a result of the current institutional set up (which shields central banks from political pressure), the best current thinking on economies in a liquidity trap emphasizes that central banks will not be believed when they promise to be irresponsible and allow inflation to continue to rise once the economy recovers. In summary, he suggests "central bank independence is defended as reducing inflation expectations by reducing the inflation temptation. When inflation expectations are too low, this argument boomerangs".

Summers also suspects that the costs of central bank independence have increased because of the growing importance of treasury–central bank cooperation and amid the increased responsibilities of central banks. He suggests that

"Fiscal monetary cooperation is a much more significant issue when an economy is in a liquidity trap, near the liquidity trap, or facing the possibility of getting into the liquidity trap at some point in the future" and notes the importance of cooperation in areas of debt management, exchange rate policy and crisis prevention and response. Summers concludes that:

> over time we will see some 'drawing close together' of Treasuries and central banks and perhaps more devices like inflation targets where politically accountable officials establish frameworks in which central banks can act … And central bankers will find themselves in closer consultation with governments and engaged in more joint endeavours.

McCulley and Pozsar (2013) suggest that the relationship between the fiscal and monetary authority is dynamic over time. In the case of the Fed and the US Treasury, they suggest the relationship is heavily circumstance-dependent: "close during periods of world war, deleveraging and deflation, and distant during periods of peacetime, leveraging and inflation".

Greater cooperation needed at the lower bound

Greater cooperation between central banks and their governments is certainly needed when economies are around the ZLB. This could allow for a more optimal mix of economic policies. A key argument made by some is that central banks have been far too inclined to constantly reach for even easier monetary policies which has taken the pressure off governments to stimulate the economy with fiscal policy and enact economic reforms that would boost the economy's long-run potential. While acknowledging the "flawed" mix of policies which are "creating avoidable risks in the world economy and financial system", Tucker (2019: 536–7) notes:

> however, it is a mistake to stipulate or imply that central banks should sit on their hands in order to induce governments to act. To do so would be to set aside their legal mandates from elected assemblies, flouting our democratic values and the rule of law. It is one thing for central banks to be the only game in town, but quite another for them to abrogate the sovereign power, taking it to themselves. Constrained as they were, therefore, to do as much as they could within their powers, they ended up looking like something they are not: the macroeconomic policymakers. And they were left exposed to being held responsible for something they simply cannot deliver: prosperity.

He argues that a Fiscal Constitution is needed, which should include, among other things:

> the role of the fiscal authority [government] in macroeconomic sta-
> bilization when monetary policy is close to the effective lower bound
> and the economy faces deep recession; how the distributional effects
> of central banks' actions will be tracked; and, in the financial services
> sphere, whether a capital-of-last resort policy will be in place for when
> all else has failed or whether a policy of "no bailouts" will be credibly
> absolute.

Tucker suggests that a possible negative externality of central bank independence has been an underinvestment in fiscal institutions (both research and practice) and suggests that there is no reason why central banks should not speak about the downsides to their policies and about their limited role in healing the economy. Cognizant of the various threats to central bank independence that greater central bank-government cooperation could engender, Balls *et al.* (2018) argue that formal monetary-fiscal coordination mechanisms should be limited to the ZLB, triggered by the central bank and should protect democratic control over fiscal policy.

More experimental and riskier policies

As discussed earlier and in Chapter 5, prior fears about soaring inflation have not come to pass with QE and other unconventional monetary policies. At the same time, there has been disappointment in QE's most recent impacts and sharp criticisms about its distributional consequences. It also now appears close to being largely exhausted, particularly in Japan and the euro area where government bond yields are in or close to negative territory across much of the yield curve. Against this backdrop, one suspects there is a reasonable chance that central banks could ultimately opt for, or be pressured into, much more aggressive and experimental measures if there is another major global slowdown in the coming years. As Borio and Zabai (2016: 34) conclude:

> As the central bank's policy room for maneuver narrows, so does its
> ability to deal with the next recession, which will inevitably come. The
> overall pressure to rely on increasingly experimental, at best highly
> unpredictable, at worst dangerous, measures may at some point become
> too strong.

Already in 2015, UK opposition Labour leader Jeremy Corbyn called for a "People's QE", where the central bank would create money to finance government investment in infrastructure (Elliott 2015) and Balls *et al.* (2018) note that "Even mainstream academic voices have begun breaking long-held taboos by calling for monetary financing of governments ('helicopter money')".

Perhaps the leading recent proponent has been former UK Financial Services Authority Chairman and academic Adair Turner, who suggested in his book *Between Debt and The Devil* (2015) that developed economy central banks should embark on outright monetary financing of government debt in order to fuel more sustainable economic recoveries (unlike QE, the creation of new monetary base by the central bank would be permanent). Turner suggested three possible options: (i) central bank financed tax cuts or government spending increases – he noted that this was the same as Ben Bernanke's 2002 recommendation that the BoJ should perform a modern day version of Milton Friedman's helicopter drop of cash (Friedman 1969), paying for tax cuts or new government spending with central bank created money with no new government debt incurred; (ii) central bank write-offs of their government debt holdings; and (iii) the financing of a recapitalization of banking systems by a permanent increase in central bank money.

Turner acknowledged that monetary financing is a taboo policy for good reasons, comparing it with a dangerous medicine, which, when taken in small amounts, can help cure severe illness but, when taken in excess, can be fatal. As a result, he argues that there is a strong case for making the use a "one off" response to exceptional circumstances, returning to the usual prohibition on monetary financing once robust growth has returned and inflation is back on target. To prevent misuse he suggests the decision to use monetary finance and in what size should be made by independent central banks in light of their judgements on the prospects for inflation relative to their targets (in a similar way to how they currently make decisions on interest rates and unconventional policies), but the decisions on how to spend the money, such as tax cuts or government spending increases, would be made by politicians. He accepts that significant coordination between fiscal and monetary authorities would be required but suggests that such discussions are nothing new and are inevitable and appropriate when economies face debt overhangs and deflationary pressures. Turner argues that there is no reason why monetary financing should fuel excessive inflation and suggests that, by putting money into the hands of households and firms, it avoids the need to stimulate growth through the indirect transmission channels of credit growth and higher asset prices as in QE (hence, it could be designed to avoid the inequality problems associated with QE).

Perhaps the greater longer-term risk is that QE and more aggressive monetary policies could ultimately be employed in normal times, when the economy is not in or even close to recession. Selgin (2020: 13–22) suggests there is a growing movement to have the Fed and other central banks engage in what he refers to as "fiscal" QE, whose purpose is to prop-up particular markets or finance government programmes rather than to combat recessions when conventional monetary policy has been exhausted. He highlights calls by 2016 US Green Party Presidential candidate Jill Stein for the Fed to use QE to solve the student debt problem through a loan "jubilee" and by proponents of the US Green New Deal – a huge public spending programme unveiled in 2019 by some left-leaning Democrats – that it be funded by QE. Selgin suggests that some supporters of the Green New Deal have been heavily influenced by Modern Monetary Theory (MMT). The latter has been growing in popularity with those on the left of politics in the US who favour large government fiscal expansions to finance environmental and social programmes. One of its key tenets is that a government with its own currency can never go bankrupt as the central bank can always print enough money to finance budget deficits and outstanding debt (Davies 2019). However, MMT has been heavily criticized by most mainstream economists (Krugman 2019b; Rogoff 2019; Summers 2019). Selgin suggests that fiscal QE is unlikely to be a welfare enhancing way for the government to raise money, but suggests that its appeal to some politicians lies in the fact that it *appears* to be a cheap source of finance and because it offers opportunities to fund spending programmes that may not survive the normal budget appropriations process.

Selgin argues that the Fed's post-GFC operating framework exposes it to greater pressure from a future Congress to engage in fiscal QE. I highlighted in Chapter 1 that, before the GFC, central bank trading desks would adjust the amount of reserve balances in the banking system so that the interest rate at which banks could borrow from each other overnight was equal to the target interest rate set by the central bank policy committee. However, this became very difficult as the massive lending programmes and asset purchases amid QE led to surging reserve balances. As Selgin notes, the Fed thus moved to a "Floor" system where it would administratively set the interest rate on reserve balances which would serve as its target rate and instrument of monetary control. Selgin argues that the previous system provided the Fed with a powerful argument against being forced by Congress to fund government spending through fiscal QE, as any reserve balances created would push overnight borrowing rates for banks below the Fed's target interest rate and thus hamper the Fed's ability to control inflation. However, he notes that under the "Floor" system increased reserve balances do not influence interest rates and, hence, it is harder for the Fed to mount the defence that Congress is hampering its ability to control inflation.

In truth, at the time of writing, it seems hard to imagine fiscal QE occurring on a material scale in the future in the major developed economies. That said, it must be acknowledged that hardly any economists fifteen years ago would have believed that the major central banks would engage in massive QE, let alone some moving official interest rates into negative territory. Indeed, it is not wholly unrealistic to envisage a scenario where some well-intentioned independent central banks and their governments engaged in limited monetary financing of the kind recommended by Turner (2015) which ultimately resulted in the regular monetary financing of government deficits. For example, imagine a scenario in which both growth and inflation remained somewhat subdued over several years despite several limited monetary financings of government deficits. The respective responsibilities of central banks and governments would be becoming increasingly blurred at a time when populist politicians and policies would probably be in the ascendancy. Such politicians would likely, over time, increasingly staff the central banks with like-minded officials.

In summary, fears that QE would fuel runaway inflation have failed to materialize, with insufficient inflation being a key problem. This, however, may have opened the door to the use of more experimental and aggressive policies in the future, with the risk this could ultimately result in much higher inflation. Similarly, fears about a significant increase in financial instability have not come to pass, although it is still too early to make a final judgement. It could be the next significant downturn that uncovers any major financial vulnerabilities that we do not currently know about. Unconventional monetary policies may have contributed to the post-GFC slowdown in productivity across the advanced economies, but it may be some time before a clearer picture emerges. Meanwhile, QE and easy money policies have had quite large distributional impacts and have likely contributed to some rise in wealth inequality. While QE has been beneficial overall, central banks should more readily acknowledge some of the negative side-effects and limitations of their policies. The question of central bank independence is likely to remain a hot topic for some time, but greater cooperation between central banks and governments is surely necessary in the next downturn and should lead to a more optimal policy mix. In the final chapter, I discuss the exit from QE and provide some thoughts on policies for the next downturn.

8
EXITING QUANTITATIVE EASING AND POLICIES FOR THE NEXT SLOWDOWN

Central bank commentary during the initial QE programmes regarding their eventual cessation amid economic recovery, typically focused on assurances to investors and the general public that they had the necessary tools to control any risks stemming from the huge growth in the liability side of their balance sheets. In particular, there were some fears that an economic recovery would encourage commercial banks to use their huge reserve balances to unduly expand lending, which would further increase activity and could fuel a jump in inflation and in inflation expectations. Fed officials noted that there would be some automatic shrinkage in reserve balances amid an economic recovery as its emergency lending programmes would no longer be needed. They also stressed that by moving to the "floor" system of paying interest on reserve balances (see Chapter 7), policy rates could be raised at the appropriate time, tempering the incentives of banks to make new loans. They also highlighted other new tools at their disposal to drain reserves from the banking system if necessary (Bernanke 2009a, 2009d, 2009c, 2009e; Kohn 2009).

An important consideration for policy-makers when contemplating the ending and ultimate reversal of their QE programmes was the debate (highlighted in Chapter 5) about whether "Stock" or "Flow" effects of asset purchases had the most powerful effect on financial markets. As a reminder, Stock effects are a persistent change in prices and yields of government bonds in response to permanent changes in the supply of bonds available to be purchased by private investors (with expectations of future changes in supply being discounted into prices and yields as soon as the QE programmes are announced), whereas Flow effects reflect changes in prices and yields in response to the actual ongoing purchases of government bonds by central banks (D'Amico & King 2011). The general consensus of financial market practitioners and policy-makers was that Stock effects were key, and academic research has generally supported this view. This was important as it suggested that significant stimulus would likely remain in place for a considerable period after the end of asset purchases and

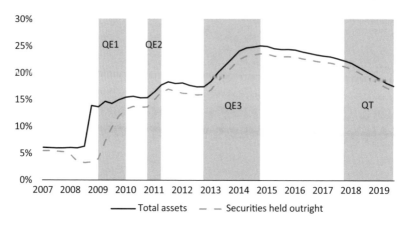

Figure 8.1. The Fed's balance sheet: assets (% of GDP)
Source: Board of Governors of the Federal Reserve System, Bureau of Economic Analysis, Federal Reserve Bank of St. Louis (FRED).

even when they were being reversed. In contrast, if Flow effects had dominated, there could have been a material tightening in financial conditions once QE ended and even more so when it ultimately went into reverse.

The process of unwinding or reversing QE is often referred to as balance sheet normalization or QT. A central bank can achieve this in two main ways. The most passive approach is to stop reinvesting the principal payments they receive when assets they hold, such as government bonds, mature. The time this takes will depend on the maturity profile of its assets. A more proactive and aggressive approach involves selling back their assets such as government bonds to investors. Once the various asset purchase programmes have finished, central banks have typically continued to reinvest the principal payments received on their assets in order to prevent a reduction in policy stimulus in the passive way.[1] Admittedly, even in this approach there is some tightening if the economy and/ or stock of government debt continues to increase. This is because the central bank's bond holdings as a share of GDP or total government debt outstanding is in decline (see, for example, the period between QE3 and QT in Figure 8.1). Moreover, the amount of excess reserves will also decline in this scenario as demand for other liabilities such as currency by the general public continues to grow over time (Rosengren 2019). This occurred in the US between the end of its QE3 programme in late 2014 and before the onset of the reduction in its balance sheet in late 2017 (see Figure 8.2).[2]

Given elevated levels of government debt in the aftermath of the GFC, some commentators questioned why central banks do not simply cancel their holdings of government debt. This was also an argument put forward by Turner (2015)

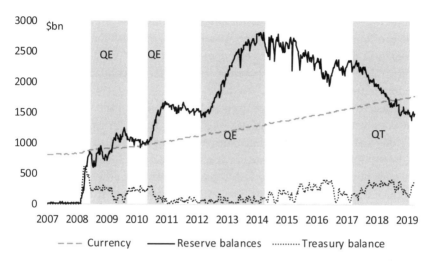

Figure 8.2. The Fed's balance sheet: liabilities
Source: Board of Governors of the Federal Reserve System.

as an option for the monetary financing of government deficits for economies struggling to emerge from a slump (see Chapter 7). This is not quite as straightforward and appealing as it first sounds, however, particularly for economies that are already in recovery. It would leave the central banks without assets on their balance sheet, although the liabilities of the reserve balances they created to buy the government bonds would remain. If the central bank were to raise interest rates in the future, it may not have sufficient income to pay the interest due on these reserves. It would have to use its seignorage to cover these interest costs with any additional deficit needing to come from the government, which could potentially threaten central bank independence. Either way, the consolidated public sector (government plus the central bank) would be no better off in income terms, while the *net* size of its liabilities would remain the same but would now be in the form of reserve balances rather than government bonds (Sheard 2014).[3]

Those central banks that began considering the eventual unwinding of their extraordinary monetary easing typically suggested that they first intended to raise interest rates to at least some minimum level before they would begin to reduce the size of their balance sheets. In the US, this ultimately was 1–1.25 per cent in the case of the Fed, while in the UK the BoE has suggested that it will not start reducing the size of its balance sheet until the Bank rate has reached 1.5 per cent (Hauser 2019). The thinking behind this reflected the desire to restore the primacy of interest rates as their main monetary policy tool, a key reason being their greater certainty about the impact that interest rate increases have on the economy compared with the reversal of QE, of which they had no prior experience (Yellen 2017), and also owing to the fact that interest rates are more flexible and better suited to responding to short-term economic fluctuations (Broadbent 2018).

Some feared that QT could have an equal, but opposite impact on the economy to QE, which, if correct, would have implied a significant tightening in financial conditions and quite a sizeable hit to growth. Indeed, the 2013 taper tantrum (see Chapter 6) in response to the mere discussion of a potential future *reduction* in the pace of asset purchases by Fed Chair Ben Bernanke served as a warning about the risks inherent in winding down the extraordinary post-GFC monetary easing. In truth, the Fed had few good historical precedents to guide its actions, with the unwinding of the BoJ's balance sheet in 2006 after its initial QE programme perhaps the most pertinent. This occurred in a relatively orderly fashion with little negative impact on the economy or financial markets. There were two main reasons cited for this. First, the BoJ had concentrated its purchases on short-dated assets mainly from banks and it simply allowed these to passively run-off as they matured. Second, the BoJ was very clear and transparent in its communications regarding its policy actions (Greenwood 2017; IMF 2010; BIS 2019). A key difference for the Fed, however, was that it had intentionally focused on purchasing longer-dated government bonds from non-banks amid criticisms about the efficacy of the BoJ's initial QE programme. Moreover, its balance sheet unwinding was likely to occur against a less ebullient global backdrop. Nevertheless, it seemed likely that the Fed's QT would have a materially smaller impact in the opposite direction than QE. In particular, as previously discussed, a major boost from QE came by helping to calm highly dysfunctional financial markets and supporting confidence through reducing major tail risks, but the unwinding of QE was only likely to occur in normal times when financial markets and the domestic and global economies are performing relatively well (Broadbent 2018).

Meanwhile, there was significant uncertainty regarding what the new long-term equilibrium size of the various central bank balance sheets should be, which was an important consideration as it would indicate the point at which central banks should end QT. As Powell (2019b: 3) noted:

> The committee has long said that the size of the balance sheet will be considered normalized when the balance sheet is once again at its smallest level consistent with conducting monetary policy efficiently and effectively. Just how large that will be is uncertain, because we do not yet have a clear sense of the normal level of demand for our liabilities.[4]

It was generally agreed that the balance sheet would be bigger than before the GFC in absolute terms, as economies are now much bigger and, hence, the level of currency demanded by households should have risen given the greater level of transactions. But it was also thought likely that the equilibrium size of balance sheets should have risen as a share of GDP too. This is because demand from commercial banks for safe, liquid assets such as reserves held at the central bank was likely to be structurally higher than before the GFC, both by choice and as a result of new regulations in the aftermath of the crisis. Brainard (2019) notes that currency demand has also grown notably relative to GDP since the GFC in the US, a surprising trend also evident in a number of other countries (Ashworth & Goodhart forthcoming). From a supply perspective, Powell (2019b) notes that the Fed's chosen operating regime for controlling interest rates also plays a role in determining the quantity of reserves because in the "Floor" system adopted during the crisis the central bank does not actively manage the supply of reserves in the banking system. Hence, he suggests the latter must be "ample" so that they can meet typical reserve demands of banks and those stemming from other volatile factors.

The US Federal Reserve as first-mover

After ending its QE3 programme in 2014, the Fed finally raised interest rates for the first time in December 2015, raised them again in December 2016 and then further to 1–1.25 per cent by June 2017. It began the process of unwinding its asset purchases in October 2017, reducing the size of its balance sheet passively by not reinvesting the principal repayments it received on its assets such as government bonds and mortgage-related securities when they matured. Over time, it allowed the total monthly amount of principal payments it would not reinvest to gradually increase from $10 billion in October 2017 to $50 billion from October 2018. In May 2019, it began to slow the pace of principal payments it would not reinvest and it finally ended its programme of balance sheet draw-down in August 2019 which was a couple of months earlier than expected.[5] By the time QT ended, the Fed's balance sheet had shrunk by over $700 billion or almost 20 per cent since its peak and reserve balances had fallen by over $1,300 billion or almost 50 per cent (see Figures 8.1 and 8.2).

The process of winding down the Fed's balance sheet was relatively successful with the fears of some commentators not materializing. Based on event study analysis, Broadbent (2018) found little upward impact on US government bond yields from QT-related announcements between January and September 2017 and Bullard (2019) notes "seemingly small observed impacts from unanticipated announcements of QT policy actions during 2017". Indeed, US financial

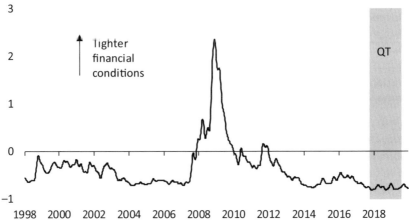

Figure 8.3. QE reversal didn't have a major impact on US financial conditions
Source: Federal Reserve Bank of Chicago, Federal Reserve Bank of St. Louis (FRED).

conditions did not seem to tighten much during the announcement phase or the subsequent period when balance sheet drawdown and additional interest rate hikes occurred (see Figure 8.3). While there have been periods of general financial market volatility such as the large stock market sell-off in late 2018, other factors were more likely the main cause (Dudley 2019; Rosengren 2019). Moreover, problems in specific emerging markets such as Argentina and Turkey were primarily country-specific (see Chapter 6). Over the actual QE unwind period as a whole, the S&P 500 was up around 15 per cent, while 10-year government bond yields were actually materially lower. The economy also performed quite strongly with quarterly real GDP growth averaging around 2.5 per cent at an annual rate. Of course, as per usual there were a number of other important events occurring during the Fed's balance sheet drawdown such as corporate tax reform, a fiscal stimulus package and deregulation. These provided offsetting support to the economy and financial markets and indeed it seems likely that much less monetary tightening would have occurred in their absence. That said, the balance of evidence suggests that QT did not have much of a negative impact on either financial conditions or the broader economy.

As discussed earlier, generally speaking, the unwinding of QE was likely to have a smaller impact given that many of its original benefits came during the GFC when financial markets were hugely dysfunctional and major tail risks abounded. There were also a number of other reasons why QT, when it finally occurred, did not have a major negative impact on financial markets and the US economy. Yellen (2017) highlights the fact that it had been well communicated over the previous several years and Broadbent (2018) notes the very gradual pace of balance sheet unwind and the importance of the FOMC's emphasis that if it were to tighten monetary conditions, the official interest rate would be commensurately lower than it would otherwise have been.

Large ongoing QE programmes from the ECB and BoJ also helped to offset the reductions in global liquidity from the Fed's actions and limited the rise in US and other developed economy government bond yields. In terms of global liquidity, Lane (2019) highlights how the growth of euro-denominated loans by banks outside of the euro area has outpaced USD-denominated loans to non-US borrowers since 2015. BIS data also show that the value of euro-denominated bonds issued outside of the euro area has grown solidly since late 2013. Moreover, Lane notes that the introduction of ECB QE in 2015 "was followed by a striking swing from a sustained period of net portfolio flows into the euro area to sizeable net portfolio flows out of the euro area" with the net outflows almost entirely accounted for by portfolio flows into long-dated foreign bonds. He suggests that euro area investors favoured developed economy sovereign bonds, most notably US Treasuries, but also UK and Japanese government bonds. Coeure (2018) comments that euro area residents accounted for nearly 30 per cent of total US Treasury purchases during the first half of 2018 up from 25 per cent in 2017. Meanwhile, BIS data suggests that the growth of JPY-denominated loans and bonds issued outside of Japan has accelerated during the Fed's balance sheet drawdown, although the stock is admittedly tiny compared to those in USD and even the euro. Unlike the euro area, the beginning of QQE in Japan did not fuel a large swing in net portfolio outflows out of Japan; there were actually large net inflows into Japanese equities (Coeure 2017). However, there have generally been large net portfolio outflows since 2015 into overseas equities and to a lesser extent long-term foreign bonds. Overall, euro area and Japanese investors combined increased their holdings of US Treasury securities by around $270 billion during the Fed's balance sheet drawdown, which was equivalent to around sixty per cent of the reduction in the Fed's holdings of Treasuries during this process.

Not everything has gone entirely according to plan for the Fed, however. In the aftermath of the end of QT, there was a very sharp jump in interest rates in US repurchase (repo) markets in September 2019, where financial institutions borrow funds from each other for short time periods in exchange for collateral such as Treasury securities. The repo rate at which they borrow increased to around 10 per cent, which was well in excess of the target FFR it typically tracks (which was around 2 per cent), while the effective FFR also moved above the target rate. The jump raised concerns that the Fed had lost control of monetary policy and elicited some broader fears as a spike in repo rates had preceded the GFC (*Financial Times* 2019g, 2019i; *The Economist* 2019a, 2019b). While a number of shorter-term demand and supply factors have been identified as contributing to the jump in interest rates, it also appears that the structural supply of reserve balances after the balance sheet drawdown ended was not sufficient i.e. the Fed had reduced the size of its balance sheet too much (*The Economist* 2019a, 2019b; *Financial Times* 2019g, 2019i, 2019j, 2019k).

The Fed responded by injecting new reserve balances into the system through repurchase operations in September, and in October announced that it would also purchase short-term US Treasury bills to increase reserve balances over the next several months (Selgin 2019; Williams 2019). Fed Chair Powell (2019c) stressed that "these actions are purely technical measures to support the effective implementation of monetary policy as we continue to learn about the appropriate level of reserves. They do not represent a change in the stance of monetary policy". He also suggested that Treasury bill purchases should not be confused with the large-scale asset purchases that were carried out during and after the GFC:

> In those programs, we purchased longer-term securities to put down-ward pressure on longer-term interest rates and ease broader financial conditions. In contrast, increasing the supply of reserves by pur-chasing Treasury bills only alters the mix of short-term assets held by the public and should not materially affect demand and supply for longer-term securities or financial conditions more broadly.
>
> (see FOMC 2019: 3–4)

While this episode is unlikely to have much if any impact on the economy, it clearly suggests that risks and uncertainties remain as a result of the Fed's decade of extraordinary balance sheet policies. Indeed, it serves to reinforce the view of Warsh (2018) that "For the central bank community evaluating QE, we are still in the thick of history".

Policies for the next global slowdown

The US expansion that began in 2009 is the longest on record, the Japanese recovery since late 2012 is one of the longest since the end of the second world war and expansions in the euro area and the UK have been underway since 2013 and 2011 respectively. Hence, at some point in the not too distant future it seems highly likely there will be another recession in the developed world. With official central bank interest rates currently around the ZLB in the US and UK and in negative territory in the euro area and Japan, there will be very little scope for central banks to use conventional monetary policy to support growth.

As a result, central banks will have to resort to unconventional monetary policies such as QE and forward guidance once again. But, as previously discussed, even here the space to ease policy is quite modest and significantly less than it was in the years following the GFC. In the US, 2-year, 10-year and 30-year government bond yields are currently only modestly positive, while in the euro area and Japan yields are in or close to negative territory. Presumably, these interest rates would have moved yet lower in the event of an economic slowdown even before any central bank action. Japan and the euro area are in what Bernanke (2017a) described as a "sort of 'super liquidity trap'" and the size of their central bank balance sheets are already at record levels as a share of GDP. Political economy issues are also becoming very problematic for the ECB, and BoE Governor Mark Carney acknowledged that they were a particular issue for asset purchases amid concerns about their distributional effects (Carney 2020). Moreover, as previously noted, the negative externalities from asset purchases and other unconventional monetary policies have been increasing and this could become a particular issue for those countries where a sizeable portion of the yield curve is already in or around negative territory.

Amid the monumental changes in monetary policy over the past decade, the Fed and ECB are currently undertaking major reviews of their monetary policy-making processes. The three key areas of focus for the Fed are its monetary policy strategy, tools and communication practices. Being the first review of its kind by the Fed, it is a little difficult to gauge the likely conclusions. Chair Powell suggested:

> We believe that our existing framework for conducting monetary policy has generally served the public well and the review may or may not produce major changes. Consistent with other central banks with these reviews, the process is more likely to produce evolution rather than revolution. We seek no changes in law and we are not considering fundamental changes in the structure of the Fed, or in the 2 per cent inflation objective. (Powell 2019b: 9)

The Fed's review of its monetary policy *strategy* has been a source of particular interest for investors. Given the rather limited firepower left for central banks to deal with future downturns, fears have increased that persistent undershoots of inflation versus their targets will become more likely. These persistent shortfalls carry the risk that longer-term inflation expectations become unanchored or permanently anchored below targets (Clarida 2019) and raise the spectre of a "Japanification" of the Western economies, with the euro area already appearing to be a prime candidate. Policies under consideration by the

Fed to counter this threat are what are commonly referred to as "make-up" strategies, where, instead of at present just aiming to hit the 2 per cent inflation target over the medium-term, the Fed would aim for inflation to average 2 per cent over the economic cycle or over the period when interest rates are at the ZLB. The latter was suggested by former Fed Chair Bernanke and garnered significant attention (Bernanke 2017b, 2017c, 2019). It would mean that if inflation is below the 2 per cent target for a period when interest rates are at the ZLB, the central bank would have to keep monetary policy looser for longer than normal so that inflation eventually moves above target and offsets prior undershoots. In current inflation targeting regimes, central banks do not have to make-up for prior inflation under- or overshoots. A potential benefit of the new policy would be that it would reduce expected interest rates and boost anticipated inflation, which by reducing real interest rates should fuel stronger economic growth. Bernanke notes that it would obviate the need for and be superior to forward guidance and would not require a major shift away from the current framework.

A cautionary point stressed by Fed officials, however, is that while these make-up strategies typically produce superior economic outcomes in terms of its mandate when simulated in macroeconomic models, it is less clear that they would work in practice if firms and households found them hard to understand and/or were not confident the stimulus would come through (Clarida 2019; Powell 2019c). Powell (2019b) notes that policy-makers considered these policies in the wake of the GFC, but had doubts about whether the general public would believe the central bank's promise of "good times to come" with part of the problem being the time inconsistency problem (as discussed in Chapter 1), where the general public may doubt the Fed's willingness to tolerate future above target inflation. In truth, given the difficulty central banks have faced in raising inflation back to their targets in the aftermath of the GFC, one suspects that both investors and the general public could be quite sceptical about their ability to hit their inflation targets in the next economic downturn, never mind engineer above target inflation. This would particularly be the case if the downturn were severe and if they once again were "the only game in town" in the words of Mohamed El-Erian (El-Erian 2017).

The general consensus is that fiscal policy will have to play a much larger role in trying to help economies recover from the next downturn. There has already been some loosening in the fiscal policy stance in recent years, most notably in the US where we have seen large fiscal easing since 2018 amid President Trump's corporate tax reform and fiscal stimulus package. The UK fiscal stance is also becoming decidedly more expansionary. In the euro area, ECB President Mario Draghi and his successor Christine Lagarde have called on countries with fiscal room such as Germany and the Netherlands to ease fiscal policy and reduce the burden placed on monetary policy to support the region's economy. The ECB also changed the fiscal policy portion of its post-meeting introductory statement for the first time in a number of years to include such a message (Draghi 2019b). Draghi has acknowledged the diminishing returns and negative side-effects of unconventional monetary policies and has suggested the latter would have been much less if fiscal policy had been more supportive. He noted that countries adopting similar levels of monetary stimulus but more active fiscal policies since the GFC have been able to achieve higher inflation rates and that easier fiscal policy would increase the efficacy of current unconventional policies and reduce the need for some of them to remain in place (Draghi 2019b, 2019c). There are some tentative signs that the debate in Germany may be beginning to shift slightly in favour of a more supportive fiscal policy (*Financial Times* 2019h). In general, there seems to be a growing recognition in western economies that more investment is needed in areas such as infrastructure and to fight climate change, although given such spending is typically slow to enact, tax cuts will also likely form part of any future fiscal stimulus programmes.

But even the room for fiscal stimulus may be less than in previous downturns in most countries given the already poor state of public finances. The US is currently running a fiscal deficit of over 5 per cent of GDP at a time of respectable growth and its government debt is over 100 per cent of GDP, while in Japan government debt is almost 250 per cent of GDP. In the euro area, current government debt is around 85 per cent of GDP (see Figure 8.4), although there are large cross-country differences with debt levels of around 60 per cent, 100 per cent and 130 per cent of GDP in Germany, France and Italy respectively. Unfortunately, the generally poor state of public finances comes at a time where ageing populations will increasingly exert structural pressures on the public finances. Against this backdrop, there is clearly a risk that in the face of a further deterioration in the public finances, financial markets could react negatively at some point to fiscal stimulus (Bartsch *et al.* 2019) and political economy issues could become very difficult again as in the aftermath of the GFC. Indeed, Fed Chair Powell recently cautioned that the high and rising debt in the US could, over time, restrain the willingness or ability of fiscal policy-makers to support the economy during a downturn (Powell 2019c). Of course, in the event that any significant fiscal easing was putting upward pressure on government bond yields, an increased benefit of central bank QE would be to reduce or place a ceiling on them. Countries may even consider adopting Japanese-style yield curve control, maintaining government bond yields of various maturities at a certain level. Former Fed Chair Ben Bernanke had suggested this as a potential monetary policy option (Bernanke 2016b).

If the next downturn were very severe and unconventional monetary policies together with available fiscal stimulus were proving inadequate to restore

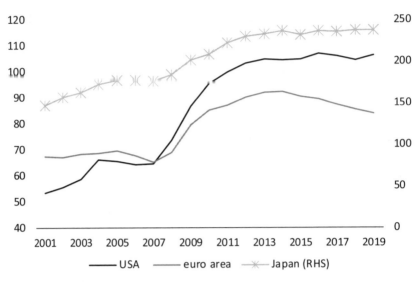

Figure 8.4. General gross government debt levels (% of GDP)
Source: IMF.

a meaningful recovery, central banks may eventually come under pressure to experiment with more adventurous and aggressive monetary policy measures. One suspects that pressure could build for central banks to engage in the out-right monetary financing of government deficits and debt in order to fund tax cuts or increased government spending along the lines suggested by Turner (2015). Envisaging the potential for such a future scenario, several former leading policy-makers such as Ben Bernanke and his former deputy Stanley Fischer have recently recommended templates for how this could be achieved without putting central bank independence and long-term fiscal discipline at risk (Bernanke 2016c; Bartsch *et al.* 2019). At this stage, monetary financing of government deficits would appear to be the most likely direction of travel if more aggressive "unconventional unconventional" monetary policies are eventually required in what Bernanke (2016c) calls a "presumably last-resort" option for policy-makers. One other major extension of the current set of unconventional monetary policies suggested by some is to move official central bank interest rates more *materially* into negative territory. However, the ability to switch funds into cash would seem to remain an impediment to this occurring anytime in the foreseeable future, in addition to the increasingly negative signal it could send to the general public.

CONCLUSION

Despite massive expansions in central banks' traditional roles as lenders of last resort during the GFC and a reduction in official interest rates to their zero or effective lower bounds, the western economies stood on the precipice of another Great Depression. Against such a backdrop, the Fed and BoE embarked on massive QE programmes, which together with large fiscal stimulus packages, helped quell the crisis and enable their economies to avoid worst-case scenarios and stage economic recoveries. These initial rounds of QE had significant positive impacts on financial markets and economic activity by further lowering various longer-term interest rates, reducing elevated tail risks, improving liquidity in dysfunctional financial markets and boosting the confidence of investors and the general public.

Future major rounds of QE occurred in the US, UK, Japan and the euro area at different times over subsequent years, although given that various financial crises had passed, it was primarily enacted to boost sluggish growth, reduce the risks of deflation and help to raise inflation to central bank targets. A key feature of the policy environment when these programmes were enacted was that, with the exception of Japan, central banks had become the "only game in town" in supporting their economies through QE and other unconventional tools. Indeed, amid soaring government debt levels and varying degrees of pressure from politics and/or financial markets, crisis era fiscal stimulus programmes made way for significant fiscal tightening which created material economic headwinds. These subsequent QE programmes did have positive impacts on financial markets and growth, although there seemed to be signs of diminishing returns compared with the programmes enacted during the crisis and the negative side effects are likely to have increased over time, particularly for those countries where much of the yield curve has moved into negative territory. An overarching theme has been that these rounds of QE were unable to generate *robust* recoveries and raise inflation up to central bank targets, suggesting that it is not quite as powerful a tool as many may have thought before the GFC. Some economists argue that it should have been done in greater amounts, although political economy constraints already appear to have been high in the US and the euro area and few could credibly accuse the BoJ of being overly timid.

At various times, QE has received significant criticism amid fears of its likely consequences. The primary concern, when first initiated, that it would fuel run-away inflation has clearly not materialized, with insufficient inflation a key feature of the post-crisis economic landscape. Another prominent fear was that its ongoing use would create major financial stability risks, in a similar way as easy money had prior to the crisis. At this stage, despite areas of seeming overvaluation in some asset markets and material indebtedness in certain sectors, it is not clear that QE and other unconventional policies have created major bubbles and significant financial stability risks. Admittedly, the jury is still out and it may not be until the next major global slowdown that any such vulnerabilities emerge. A major ex-post criticism of the latter QE programmes in particular has been that they have fuelled large rises in inequality. Central banks have typically tried to play this down, although it is hard to argue against the fact that the rich with assets such as housing and equities have benefited relative to the poor who have few, if any, assets. Central banks would have been better served acknowledging some of these negative side-effects, as it may have placed more onus on governments to be more supportive with fiscal policy, or at the very least provide some additional support to the disadvantaged. There are some signs that central banks are now more readily highlighting the increasing side effects of their policies and calling on fiscal policy to be more supportive.

Criticism of QE did not come solely from domestic sources. There was also significant international criticism about its spillovers. In its early programmes, the Fed was accused of seeking a competitive advantage through covert currency depreciation and its QE2 and QE3 programmes were criticized for, among other things, fuelling massive capital flows into emerging markets. With a number of emerging economies already growing very strongly, these latter programmes may have been on net negative for these countries. However, given the huge benefits provided to the US economy and global financial markets from the Fed's QE1 programme, US QE was still on balance likely to have been a net positive overall for the developing countries. Meanwhile, amid worsening international trade relations over recent years, the BoJ and ECB have faced criticism from US President Trump who suggested they were purposely engaging in currency depreciation with their ongoing QE policies.

Economic recoveries in the developed economies have be in train for a significant period now and, hence, the next downturn may not be too far away. Unfortunately, the major central banks no longer have much ammunition to throw at it. Governments will have to step up to the plate with significant fiscal stimulus. But even here there could be some limitations given that government debt is close to record levels as a share of peacetime GDP in most countries and deficits are already high in some nations. In particular, political economy issues against fiscal easing could increase again as was the case after the crisis. If the existing toolkit of unconventional monetary policies together with the available fiscal stimulus are unable to dig economies out of a future major downturn, central banks may come under significant pressure to enact increasingly aggressive and experimental policies such as the outright monetary financing of government deficits to fund tax cuts or increased government spending.

Before the crisis, central bankers had been held in extremely high regard after more than two decades of generally robust economic performance and surging asset prices. Despite their undoubted success in staving off another Great Depression, their reputations have suffered amid their perceived role in contributing to the GFC, their inability to generate strong post-crisis recoveries and amid the various criticisms of their unconventional policies. As a result, debates have increased about whether they should remain independent in the future and with the current inflation problem being that it has consistently been too low, some leading economists have suggested that the original arguments in favour of central bank independence have now been turned on their heads.

The inability of the vast majority of economists and financial market commentators to foresee the GFC reinforced the view that greater humility must be shown regarding our ability to forecast major economic events. Nevertheless, after the unprecedented changes in central banking and monetary policy since the GFC, I feel reasonably confident in predicting that the next decade could be just as eventful.

NOTES

1 Monetary policy-making since the end of Bretton Woods

1. This did not mean that policy-makers no longer engaged in exchange rate management. As Eichengreen (1996) notes, countries continued to manage their currencies to prevent both excessive weakness and strength and the G5 acted in concert to weaken the USD with the Plaza Accord in 1985.
2. For example, a country experiencing balance of payments difficulties and at risk of breaking their exchange rate peg would often have to raise interest rates in an attempt to moderate aggregate demand and reduce imports and also to attract foreign capital.
3. For an excellent exposition of Bretton Woods and the International Monetary System both before and after the world wars, see Eichengreen (1996). For a concise summary of Bretton Woods and its demise, see Bordo (2017).
4. This is where Ricardian equivalence holds and the general public does not increase spending in response to tax cuts because they expect a future offsetting rise in taxes.
5. He found that between 1861–1957 the rate of change of nominal wages in the UK could be explained by both the level and rate of change of unemployment.
6. It is more important to look at *real* rather than *nominal* interest rates when gauging the easiness or tightness of monetary policy, as the former is key for borrowing and lending decisions (see page 12).
7. Also see Issing (2005) who discusses why the Great Inflation did not happen in Germany.
8. For an excellent overview of how thinking on monetary policy has shifted since Paul Volcker became Fed Chair in 1979, see Bernanke (2005a). See also Balls *et al.* (2018), Debelle (2017), Den Haan *et al.* (2017), Draghi (2018) and Issing (2018) who discuss the evolution of monetary policy in favour of independent central banks in the context of criticism they have received in the aftermath of the Great Financial Crisis and amid some discussion about whether they should or will remain independent in the future. Also see Jevcak (2014) for an excellent summary of how monetary policy frameworks have evolved since the collapse of Bretton Woods, Gavin (2018) for a useful summary of the monetary policy regimes in the US since 1965, Goodfriend (1997) for a summary of twentieth-century US monetary policy and Issing (2010) for his reflections on developments in monetary policy in the twentieth century.
9. Monetary policy rules or commitments can include maintaining a fixed exchange rate, targeting specific rates of money growth or inflation (as we would see in subsequent decades) or Taylor Rules (see page 13).
10. Alesina and Summers acknowledge the endogeneity problem, however, where a greater degree of central bank independence may simply be acting as a proxy for a greater aversion to inflation in particular societies i.e. it is this that could be driving low inflation, not necessarily central bank independence per se.

11. Issing (2005) notes that the German Bundesbank was the first to pioneer the practice in December 1974. The policy of targeting the growth rate in monetary aggregates reflected the increased importance assigned to monetary developments in controlling inflation and was typically referred to as "intermediate" targeting, given that the rate of growth of money was an intermediate target on the way to achieving the ultimate goal of controlling inflation (Jevcak 2014).

12. Procedures have been put in place in an attempt to shield the Fed from political interference with its seven Governors appointed to staggered single fourteen-year non-renewable terms which should reduce the incentive for members to try and set policy in order to gain favour with the President (Thoma 2017). However, Thoma notes that few Governors serve their full-terms and as a result most Presidents have the opportunity to appoint the majority of the governors by the end of their second term.

13. The BoJ had previously suggested that the inflation rate it views as being consistent with price stability in the medium to long-term is "in a positive range of 2 percent or lower in terms of the year-on-year rate of change in the CPI" with "a goal of 1 percent for the time being" (Shirikawa 2012).

14. The ZLB is where a central bank has reduced interest rates to zero and it was assumed prior to the GFC that they could not be lowered any further (since the GFC some central banks have enacted modestly negative interest rates). With an inflation target of 2 per cent, the real interest rate would be –2 per cent if the inflation target is hit when official nominal interest rates are at the ZLB. In contrast, in such circumstances the real interest rate would be 0 per cent with an inflation target of 0 per cent under conditions of strict price stability.

15. This latter point is important and I return to it in Chapter 7 in the context of a discussion of the criticisms and negative externalities of QE.

16. See Balls *et al.* (2018) pages 80–128 for an excellent summary of the objectives, decision making processes and communications of the G-20 central banks.

17. For example, the Fed's FRB/US model.

18. For a summary of monetary policy implementation in the US see: www.newyorkfed.org/markets/domestic-market-operations/monetary-policy-implementation

19. The natural rate of unemployment, u* or NAIRU (non-accelerating inflation rate of unemployment) is the rate of unemployment at which inflation is stable. If unemployment is above this rate, it will put downward pressure on wages and prices, while the opposite is true if unemployment is below this rate (Schuele & Wessel 2019).

20. For a useful summary on the Natural Rate of Interest, see Williams (2003).

21. The potential level of GDP is how much the economy could produce if its resources were fully and efficiently utilized (Coibion *et al.* 2018).

22. Greenspan (1997) highlights the uncertainty around estimates of the equilibrium real interest rate and potential output of the economy. Orphanides (2000, 2002, 2003) also highlights the fact that the NAIRU, potential output and hence, the output gap are subject to significant ex-post revisions.

2 Key monetary policy trends and events in the decades before the Great Financial Crisis

1. Stock and Watson (2003) also highlight the decline in output volatility in G7 countries, whilst noting material timing differences in the falls.

2. Also see Stock and Watson (2003) for a useful discussion on the various drivers and Hakkio (2013) for an excellent summary paper on the Great Moderation.

3. For example, the US Savings and Loans crisis, 1987 stock market crash, 1990–91 Gulf War, 1997 Asian Financial Crisis, bursting of the US IT bubble in 2001, September 11, 2001 terrorist attacks on the US, to name a few.

4. It has been commonly acclaimed that at the peak of the boom, the value of the land under the Emperor's Palace in Tokyo was worth more than that of the US state of California.

5. For a more detailed discussion of the drivers behind the asset bubbles and their bursting, see Ueda (2000).

6. The problem was exacerbated for financial institutions by the Japanese practice of "cross-shareholdings", whereby banks would own equity in the companies which they lent to (Baxter 2009). Ueda (2012) notes that deposit-taking banks held 11.7 per cent of total stock market value at the bubble's peak.

7. For an excellent summary of the history of the Japanese economy over the period 1984–2004, see Wakatabe (2012). Also see IMF (2009) which provides a helpful chronology of the key policy measures enacted by the authorities since the bursting of the asset bubbles and Koo (2009).

8. For a summary of the global IT boom and its bursting, see Greenspan (2001) and Meyer (2001). For a summary of the boom in US IT investment and faster productivity growth, see Ferguson (2000).

9. The negative feedback loop in Japan of falling asset prices, financial instability and weak economic growth has often been referred to as "Japanization" (Ueda 2012).

10. In general, individuals with low credit scores will apply for non-prime mortgages. Bernanke (2013) describes non-prime mortgages as consisting of sub-prime and Alt-A mortgages. Low or no documentation typically means that borrowers have had to provide little or no proof of their incomes and/or credit history. Bernanke (2013) notes that the situation was perverse, as individuals with low credit scores should normally have to provide greater evidence of their incomes.

11. For more details see: www.boj.or.jp/en/mopo/mpmsche_minu/minu_2001/g010319.htm/.

12. It was assumed at the time that official nominal central bank interest rates could not be reduced below zero, although in the aftermath of the GFC a number of central banks have moved interest rates modestly into negative territory. The ability of the private sector to switch commercial bank deposits into physical cash has been one reason why central banks have been averse to moving rates more materially into negative territory. Note, a central bank can theoretically enact QE at any level of official nominal short-term interest rates, not just the ZLB.

13. See www.boj.or.jp/en/announcements/release_2001/k010319c.htm for additional details on the BoJ's new procedures.

14. See Ugai (2006) for a detailed description of the policy duration effect.

15. Ueda (2012) highlights the fact that depository institutions (commercial banks) accounted for 59 per cent of Japanese financial assets in 2001, which was similar to the euro area but compared with just 25 per cent in the United States, which has a much more market-based financial system. Reflecting this in part, we will see in Chapters 3, 4 and 5 how US QE after the GFC focused more on financial markets rather than the banking system.

16. Ueda (2010) notes that the banks could have sold these equities in the market themselves, however, given the lack of market liquidity, they may have been reluctant to sell stocks and lower prices themselves.

17. As I discuss in Chapter 4, central bank purchases are likely to have a more powerful effect if they favour longer-dated bonds.

3 The Great Financial Crisis and the onset of quantitative easing

1. The growth of securitization in financial markets meant that financial institutions could sell on the mortgages they made, which also resulted in a significant reduction in the quality of lending standards.

2. For an excellent short summary of the US sub-prime mortgage crisis, see Duca (2013). See also, DiMartino and Duca (2007).

3. Amid its role as the global reserve currency, around half of all global trade is invoiced in USDs despite the fact that the US itself only accounts for around 10 per cent of global trade (Carney 2019a). As a result, overseas financial institutions need USDs to facilitate this non-US trade.

4. Although the NBER Business Cycle Dating Committee did not make the official determination until December 2008.

5. The decision by the US authorities to allow Lehman Brothers to go into bankruptcy raised major political economy issues. However, an in-depth discussion is beyond the scope of this book. Bernanke (2013) acknowledges that Lehman Brothers was probably too big to fail, but suggests that because it had become insolvent the Fed had no legal way to save it. Ball (2018) disputes this, however. He argues that the Fed could have saved Lehman, but that it chose not to amid political pressures and because they underestimated the damage its bankruptcy would cause.

6. See www.treasury.gov/initiatives/financial-stability/TARP-Programs/Pages/default.aspx#

7. The closed capital account means that Chinese citizens are prevented from investing abroad and foreign investors are largely restricted from accessing China's financial markets (Liu *et al*. 2019).

8. For an excellent summary of the build-up to the GFC and the Fed's performance during it, see Bernanke (2013). For a more detailed discussion, see Bernanke (2015a). Also see Irwin (2013), which provides a very interesting international perspective from a leading financial journalist and Geithner (2014), which contains former US Treasury Secretary Tim Geithner's reflections on the GFC. For a timeline of the GFC from a US perspective, see www.stlouisfed.org/financial-crisis/full-timeline.

9. The GSEs were created by the government to help support the housing market. Their main role has been to purchase *prime* mortgages made by financial institutions and either hold them in their own portfolios or guarantee and package them together into MBS to sell to investors. The firms are owned by private shareholders, but were placed under government control in September 2008 amid major financial difficulties owing to the housing crisis. For more details, see www.fhfa.gov/SupervisionRegulation/FannieMaeandFreddieMac/Pages/About-Fannie-Mae---Freddie-Mac.aspx

10. Covered bonds are issued by banks and other financial institutions and are backed by collateral such as mortgage loans (Packer *et al*. 2007).

11. The purchases of government bonds occurred in secondary markets rather than directly from governments in the SMP to further emphasize the distinction with the monetary financing of government deficits.

12. For example, in the absence of the requirement that countries benefitting from OMT were in a financial rescue programme, falling sovereign yields amid the bond purchases may have reduced the motivation of countries to make the difficult decisions necessary to improve their public finances. Also, the fact that the bond purchases were short-dated meant that governments would only have a relatively limited period in which to regain the confidence of financial markets.

13. In 2015, the ECJ ultimately ruled in favour of the legality of the ECB's OMT programme, suggesting that "This programme for the purchase of government bonds on secondary markets does not exceed the powers of the ECB in relation to monetary policy and does not contravene the prohibition of monetary financing of Member States" (Court of Justice of the European Union 2015).

14. For a superb and detailed discussion of the ECB's non-standard policy measures following the GFC, see Cour-Thimann and Winkler (2012). Also see Brunnermeier *et al*. (2016) and Irwin (2013) which include excellent expositions of the political economy issues.

15. For a detailed discussion on the Fed's balance sheet and developments since the financial crisis, see Bernanke (2009a, 2009b, 2009c, 2013) and Board of Governors of the

Federal Reserve System (2019). For a useful and interesting summary of the historical developments in central bank balance sheets, see Haldane *et al.* (2016). The authors note that large expansions in central bank balance sheets historically had typically been to finance wars.

16. For an excellent discussion of the Fed's various QE programmes, see Bernanke (2013, 2015a), Irwin (2013) and Kuttner (2018). For a short overview, see Ashworth (2013).

17. Until a change of law announced in 2014, UK workers in defined-contribution pension schemes were required to purchase an annuity with their accumulated pension savings on retirement. This meant many retirees had to lock in the extremely low prevailing interest rates.

18. See Kuroda (2016a, 2016b, 2016c, 2016d) for further details.

19. It charged a negative interest rate on only a very small portion of current account balances held by commercial banks at the BoJ in order to reduce short-term market interest rates further, but without damaging the profitability of banks whose current account balances were expanding rapidly amid the massive asset purchases. A reduction in profitability could have reduced their ability and/or willingness to lend and offset any boost from lower interest rates.

20. For example, the 10-year US Treasury yield is an important driver of government bond markets globally. If it were rising sharply, perhaps owing to expectations that the Fed was going to move the FFR higher over coming years, this would drive equivalent yields higher in other countries to varying degrees. In such a scenario, the BoJ may have to purchase more bonds than typically would be the case to keep the 10-year JGB at its target rate. Dell' Ariccia *et al.* (2018) note that a possible advantage of adopting a target is that if it is credible, investors may coalesce around it without requiring purchases by the central bank.

21. In addition to government bonds, the ECB's Asset Purchase Programme (APP) included the third covered bond purchase programme (CBPP3), launched in October 2014; the asset-backed securities purchase programme (ABSPP), launched in November 2014; and the corporate sector purchase programme (CSPP), launched in June 2016. The purchase of government bonds represented over 80 per cent of the APP, the CBPP3 constituted 10 per cent, the ABSPP 1 per cent and the CSPP 7 per cent (ECB 2019).

22. For a useful summary of ECB QE and some of the political economy issues, see Brunnermeier *et al.* (2016). Also see Dell' Ariccia *et al.* (2018), Constancio (2018), Praet (2018) and Mersch (2016) for excellent summaries of the use of unconventional monetary policy by the ECB since the GFC.

4 How quantitative easing works

1. See "Quantitative easing explained" (YouTube 2010) and Malekan (2018).

2. Gagnon *et al.* (2011) suggest this may occur because those investors most willing to bear this type of risk are those left holding it, or even if investors do not differ greatly in their attitudes to bearing the risk of holding longer-term bonds, they may require reduced compensation for bearing the risk when they have less of it in their portfolios.

3. When there are few buyers and sellers in a market (for example, during a financial crisis), it may be difficult for an investor to sell an asset at the time and price they desire due to the lack of market liquidity. Hence, an investor considering entering such a market would want to be compensated by a higher liquidity risk premium. This would mean that the price of assets would be lower and their yields higher. An improvement in market liquidity would lead to a rise in asset prices as investors demand a lower liquidity risk premium.

4. See "Back to basics: what is monetarism?" (IMF 2014a). www.imf.org/external/pubs/ft/fandd/2014/03/basics.htm

5. For very useful summaries and discussions on how QE works, see Bean (2009), Gagnon *et al.* (2011), Gagnon (2016), Joyce *et al.* (2011a) and Krishnamurthy and Vissing-Jorgensen (2011, 2013). Also see Ashworth (2013) for a short summary.

6. The C/D ratio represents the value of currency (banknotes) in circulation as a proportion of total deposits held at commercial banks. The R/D ratio represents the value of reserve balances held by commercial banks at the central bank as a proportion of their total deposits. In banking crises, the C/D ratio typically rises as the general public switch out of bank deposits into cash. Similarly, the R/D ratio rises as banks choose to keep a greater proportion of their funds as reserve balances at the central bank rather than make new loans to the private sector. A rise in either the C/D or R/D ratio reduces the money multiplier.

7. It is widely assumed by investors that the US government would never default on its own bonds, given that in theory it has limitless capacity to produce currency. This is why US government bonds are considered risk-free assets (admittedly, government bonds still have duration risk which I discussed earlier). Agency debt and agency MBS are also generally considered risk-free assets, particularly since the GSEs were taken into de facto government ownership during the GFC.

8. He explains this by suggesting that given the realization that central banks can use QE in the future, investors would have discounted into the current price of bonds its future use in states of the world where the liquidity and term premiums rise.

9. Various academic proposals have been put forward to abolish the effective lower bound on interest rates caused by the ability to switch into cash. Rogoff (2016) argues that countries should do away with high denomination notes such as $20, $50, $100 bills in the US, which would make hoarding cash prohibitively expensive. Buiter and Rahbari (2015) proposed abolishing cash entirely or either enacting a tax on it or devaluing it against central bank reserves.

5 Measuring the effectiveness and impact of quantitative easing

1. Some authors use windows of up to a couple of hours in their event studies, while others use these smaller windows to confirm that their selected events were what actually impacted asset prices.

2. For a superb discussion of the various methods used to estimate the impact of QE, see Bhattarai and Neely (2016). For a concise summary, see Gagnon (2016).

3. They disagree, however, about the specific channels within portfolio rebalancing through which this occurred. Gagnon *et al.* (2011) stress the reduction in term premiums via the reduction of duration risk in investors' portfolios. In contrast, Krishnamurthy and Vissing-Jorgensen (2011) highlight the importance of the "safety channel", which falls under the "preferred habitat" explanation. This is where certain investors have a preference for what are commonly referred to as "safe assets" which are highly liquid and there is little chance of default (for example, longer-term US government bonds). Greenlaw *et al.* (2018) note that given certain safe assets such as government bonds can be used as collateral in repurchase transactions, this endows them with additional value to certain investors. By reducing the supply of these safe assets in the hands of private investors, central banks increased their price and reduced their interest rates. Note, given their view that the rather narrow safety channel accounted for a significant portion of the reduction in medium- and long-term sovereign yields, Krishnamurthy and Vissing-Jorgensen argue that the spillovers to mortgage and lower-grade corporate bonds were limited. They suggest that purchases of non-Treasury assets such as agency MBS have the most beneficial effect on mortgage and lower-grade corporate bond yields.

4. Examining the channels through which QE works is not merely a matter of academic interest. Kuttner (2018) notes that a change in the term premium may have a smaller effect on economic activity than a lowering of future short-term interest rates via the policy signalling channel, a result found by Kiley (2014) and the IMF (2013a). The latter suggest this may be owing to the fact that the portfolio rebalancing channel may be expected to be more temporary and reversible, in part because of the volatile market conditions on which this channel relies.

5. Longer-term real interest rates are typically inferred from the yields on inflation protected bonds such as Treasury Inflation Protected Securities (TIPS) in the US.

6. He examined the USD against the Australian dollar, GBP, the Canadian dollar, the euro and the JPY.

7. In their econometric modelling, Hesse *et al.* (2017) find significant and persistent positive effects of US and UK QE on equity prices.

8. Liu (2016) notes that around two-thirds of FTSE All-Share sales are generated abroad.

9. For very useful summaries of the various studies of the impact of QE on GDP and inflation, see Borio and Zabai (2016), Gagnon (2016), IMF (2013a) and Bhattarai and Neely (2016) for the US.

10. Paul Krugman, discussing the effects of asset purchases at an IMF conference in November 2015, suggested "I would say that on the whole time series methods here are really pretty unpersuasive ... I find the cross-sectional [studies] across advanced countries a little bit more persuasive and the countries that did a lot of QE have done a bit better than a scatter plot of fiscal policy versus GDP would suggest. US has done better. UK has done better than you would expect from a simple fiscal tightening versus GDP scatter plot. But it's not overwhelming it's not dramatic". At the same conference, Adam Posen agreed with using a cross-sectional approach for evaluating QE. He highlighted the substantial differences in credit flows and unemployment between the countries that used QE and the euro area countries that needed QE but were constrained from getting it, even once adjustment is made for differences in fiscal policy.

11. The potentially relevant events were the August 2011 Purchasing Managers' Indices for Manufacturing and Services. Note, the authors did not include the final £50 billion of asset purchases in July 2012 as their paper had already been written by that point.

12. Note that QE1 and QE2 in the UK were *broadly* equal in size.

13. For an excellent summary of QE and other unconventional monetary policies enacted in the US, see Kuttner (2018). See also Bernanke (2013, 2015a).

14. Previously, it took around fifteen years for the monetary base to triple to its value in March 2013, a period which included the first QE programme between 2001 and 2006.

15. A point well made at a November 2015 IMF conference by Japan expert Adam Posen: "I think more interestingly and the way I would interpret the data is they have shifted the regime in a meaningful way but that hasn't resulted in the upward movement in inflation we expected. So, I think if you look fairly at the data and the results of what's gone on, we have moved from an area where inflation, just to be very crude about it, inflation was roughly fluctuating around −0.5 per cent to −1 per cent pretty steadily for many, many years and nominal wages were declining, to a realm where inflation is fluctuating between +0.5 per cent and +1 per cent and nominal wages are rising ... but I think, as the Bank of Japan has tried to show, there are some meaningful changes in behaviour that go with that in terms of price setting, in terms of wage behaviour but we are not there yet" (Posen 2015).

16. For an excellent summary of the ECB's asset purchase programme, see European Central Bank (2019).

17. For an excellent summary of QE and other unconventional monetary policies enacted in the euro area, Japan and the UK, see Dell' Ariccia *et al.* (2018).

6 International spillovers of quantitative easing

1. China's largely closed capital account provides some external insulation from the impacts of changes in its monetary policy and some internal insulation from changes in other countries' monetary policies.
2. For an excellent short summary paper of the spillover effects of QE on emerging markets, see Lavigne *et al.* (2014). See also Bernanke (2015c), Brainard (2015b, 2017), IMF (2013a, 2013b, 2013c) and Powell (2013, 2017, 2018a).
3. When controlling for other factors, they find that liquidity supply shocks explain less than 10 per cent of the variation in oil prices for the period since the crisis. This would suggest that large increases in monetary base from QE may not have been a very important driver of higher commodity prices.
4. Emerging economies are more sensitive to rising commodity prices than their developed peers given the greater share of household spending devoted to food and energy. But there are winners and losers. Commodity producers (like Brazil) benefit from higher prices, while importers (such as India) prefer lower prices.
5. Citing the work of Ghosh *et al.* (2016), Carney (2019b) notes that one-fifth of all surges in capital flows to emerging economies have ended in financial crises.
6. Local currency emerging market bonds are where foreign investors have purchased bonds in the currency of the issuing country (for example, Brazil) and, hence, bear foreign exchange risk. This compares with the more traditional foreign/hard currency emerging market bonds which are denominated in USD.
7. The rise in commodity prices fuelled strong increases in capital flows to emerging market commodity producers. Of course, interest rate differentials and global commodity prices are in part impacted by US QE.
8. This was the conclusion of Fed Governor Brainard, who highlighted the fact that easing through unconventional means was broadly welcomed in 2008 and 2009 (Brainard 2015b).
9. For example, countries already at full-employment could raise interest rates and/or allow their currencies to appreciate to offset the stimulus and prevent their economies from overheating.
10. Bernanke (2015c) acknowledges "Admittedly, consultation is not the same as active coordination of policies. But Fed decisions were certainly informed by what my colleagues and I heard from colleagues around the world".
11. For a useful summary of this, see *The Economist* (2016). Note, most countries opt for free capital flows and an independent monetary policy. China and Hong Kong are notable exceptions. The former opted for an independent monetary policy and fixed exchange rate until recently, which meant that it had a closed capital account. It now manages the currency and has a largely closed capital account. Hong Kong has a fixed exchange rate with the USD and free capital flows, but this means it does not have an independent monetary policy (it has to adopt the interest rate policy of the Fed as, otherwise, its fixed exchange rate peg might break).
12. Bernanke (2015d) notes that the euro area is the same size as the US, but the US seemed to get much more criticism, most likely reflecting the international use of the USD.
13. These include maximum loan-to-value or loan-to-income ratios on new residential mortgages, countercyclical capital buffers, leverage ratios, etc. For a summary of macroprudential policy, see Gadanecz and Jayarem (2015).
14. Carney (2019b) suggests the creation of a "Synthetic Hegemonic Currency", which would be a digital currency backed by several global reserve currencies.

7 Criticisms and negative externalities of quantitative easing

1. Also see Ashworth (2013) for a summary of why inflation did not accelerate during QE.
2. For more on the impact of technology on inflation, see www.dallasfed.org/research/events/2018/18ted.aspx
3. As is the case with conventional monetary policy easing.
4. For statistics on credit to the private non-financial sector in different countries, see www.bis.org/statistics/totcredit.htm?m=6%7C380%7C669. For statistics on overseas USD borrowing by non-US borrowers, see www.bis.org/statistics/gli.htm?m=6%7C333%7C690.
5. Clearly, by averting a collapse in the financial system and another Great Depression, QE1 provided a large boost to productivity versus the likely counterfactuals.
6. For example, as I highlighted in Chapter 2, interest rates have moved sharply lower since the mid-1980s.
7. See Figure 1 on page 13 of Bunn et al. (2018b) for a superb summary table showing the various transmission channels of monetary policy to income and wealth distributions.
8. The Gini coefficient or Gini index measures the extent to which the distribution of income or wealth among individuals or households within an economy deviates from a perfectly equal distribution. A reading of zero reflects perfect equality while 100 represents perfect inequality (OECD 2002).
9. The main calculations from Bunn et al. (2018b) combined the impacts of both interest rate cuts and QE, although splitting them out separately they also suggest that QE had little impact on the Gini coefficients.
10. The ability to influence productivity growth is typically thought to be in the domain of governments, given that its main drivers are the size and quality of the capital stock, technology, the skills and education of the workforce and how well all these factors are combined.

8 Exiting quantitative easing and policies for the next slowdown

1. This did not always occur. For example, in 2010 the Fed initially did not reinvest the principal payments on its agency securities and agency MBS (see Bernanke 2010).
2. See Sheard 2017 for an excellent Q&A on the unwinding of QE and Sheard 2014 for Q&A on QE in general.
3. Turner (2015) acknowledges the complications that may arise with the monetary financing of deficits when the central bank eventually begins to raise interest rates. One solution he suggests is to raise the required reserve ratio under which the banks receive no interest on their reserve balances.
4. As discussed in Chapter 3, the main liabilities of central banks are currency in circulation with the general public and the reserve balances held by commercial banks at the central bank. The value of central bank assets equals the value of its liabilities.
5. For a history of the Fed's balance sheet normalization, see www.federalreserve.gov/monetarypolicy/policy-normalization-discussions-communications-history.htm

REFERENCES

Adrian, T. *et al.* 2014. "Treasury Term Premia: 1961–present", Liberty Street Economics.

Ahmed, S. & A. Zlate 2013. "Capital flows to emerging market economies: a brave new world?" Board of Governors of the Federal Reserve System.

Alesina, A. & L. Summers 1993. "Central Bank independence and macroeconomic performance: some comparative evidence". *Journal of Money, Credit and Banking* 25(2), 151–62.

Alon, T. & E. Swanson 2011. "Operation Twist and the effect of large-scale asset purchases". FRBSF Economic Letter.

Altavilla, C., G. Carboni & R. Motto 2015. "Asset purchase programmes and financial markets: lessons from the euro area". European Central Bank Working Papers, No. 1864.

Altavilla, C., D. Giannone & M. Lenza 2016. "The financial and macroeconomic effects of the OMT announcements". *International Journal of Central Banking* 12(3): 29–57.

Altmann, R. 2012. "Quantitative Easing is silently stealing older people's assets". *Daily Mail.* www.dailymail.co.uk/debate/article-2103728/Quantitative-Easing-silently-stealing-older-peoples-assets.html

Andrade, P. *et al.* 2016. "The ECB's asset purchase programme: an early assessment". ECB Working Paper No. 1956.

Andrews, D. & A. Sánchez 2011. "The evolution of homeownership rates in selected OECD countries: demographic and public policy influences". *OECD Journal: Economic Studies* 2011/1.

Antolin-Diaz, J. 2013. "Understanding the ECB's monetary policy". Fulcrum research papers, Fulcrum Asset Management.

Ashworth, J. 2013. "Quantitative easing by the major western central banks during the global financial crisis". *The New Palgrave Dictionary of Economics*, Palgrave Macmillan.

Ashworth, J. 2020. *Quantitative Easing.* Newcastle upon Tyne: Agenda Publishing.

Ashworth, J. & C. Goodhart (forthcoming). "The surprising recovery of currency usage". *International Journal of Central Banking.*

Ball, L. 2018. *The Fed and Lehman Brothers: Setting the Record Straight on a Financial Disaster.* Cambridge: Cambridge University Press.

Balls, E., J. Howat & A. Stansbury 2018. "Central bank independence revisited: after the financial crisis, what should a model central bank look like?" MRG.CBG Working Paper, Harvard University.

Baltensperger, M. & B. Call 2018. "Euro-area sovereign bond holdings: an update on the impact of quantitative easing". Bruegel blog. www.bruegel.org/2018/11/euro-area-sovereign-bond-holdings-an-update-on-the-impact-of-quantitative-easing.

Banerjee, R., D. Latto & N. McLaren 2012. " Using changes in auction maturity sectors to help identify the impact of QE on gilt yields". *Bank of England Quarterly Bulletin* Q2.

Banerjee, R. & B. Hofmann 2018. "The rise of zombie firms: causes and consequences". *BIS Quarterly Review*, September.

Bank for International Settlements 2016. *Eighty-Sixth Annual Report*, 1 April 2015–31 March 2016. Basel, 26 June 2016. www.bis.org/publ/arpdf/ar2016e.htm.

REFERENCES

Bank for International Settlements 2019. "Large central bank balance sheets and market functioning". Report prepared by a study group chaired by Lorie Logan (Federal Reserve Bank of New York) and Ulrich Bindseil (European Central Bank), Markets Committee Papers No 11. www.bis.org/publ/mktc11.htm.

Bank of England 2011. Minutes of the Monetary Policy Committee Meeting, 7–8 September.

Bank of Japan 2019. Financial System Report, April 2019.

Barro, R. & D. Gordon 1983. "Rules, discretion and reputation in a model of monetary policy". *Journal of Monetary Economics* 12(1), 101–21.

Bartsch, E. *et al.* 2019. "Dealing with the next downturn: From unconventional monetary policy to unprecedented policy coordination", Blackrock Investment Institute.

Bauer, M. & C. Neely 2013. "International channels of the Fed's unconventional monetary policy". Federal Reserve Bank of San Francisco Working Paper Series, Working Paper 2012-12.

Bauer, M. & G. Rudebusch 2013. "The signaling channel for Federal Reserve bond purchases". Federal Reserve Bank of San Francisco Working Paper Series.

Baxter, R. 2009. "Japan's cross-shareholding legacy: the financial impact on banks". Federal Reserve Bank of San Francisco.

BBC 2011. "China rules out faster yuan rise despite soaring prices".

Bean, C. 2009. "Quantitative Easing – an interim report". Speech to the London Society of Chartered Accountants, London.

Bernanke, B. & F. Mishkin 1997. "Inflation targeting: a new framework for monetary policy?" *Journal of Economic Perspectives* 11(2), 97–116.

Bernanke, B. 1999. "Japanese monetary policy: a case of self-induced paralysis?" Presentation at the ASSA meetings, Boston, MA.

Bernanke, B. 2002. "Deflation – making sure 'it' doesn't happen here". Speech before the National Economists Club, Washington, DC.

Bernanke, B. 2003. "An unwelcome fall in inflation". Remarks before the Economics Roundtable, University of California, San Diego, CA.

Bernanke, B. 2004. "The Great Moderation". Speech at the meetings of the Eastern Economic Association, Washington, DC.

Bernanke, B. 2005a. "What have we learned since October 1979?" *Federal Reserve Bank of St Louis Review* 87(2), Part 2.

Bernanke, B. 2005b. "The global saving glut and the U.S. current account deficit". Remarks at the Sandridge Lecture, Virginia Association of Economists, Richmond.

Bernanke, B. 2007. "The subprime mortgage market". Speech at the Federal Reserve Bank of Chicago's 43rd Annual Conference on Bank Structure and Competition, Chicago, Illinois.

Bernanke, B. 2009a. "The crisis and the policy response". Speech at the Stamp Lecture, London.

Bernanke, B. 2009b. "The Federal Reserve's balance sheet". Speech at the Federal Reserve Bank of Richmond 2009 Credit Markets Symposium, Charlotte, North Carolina.

Bernanke, B. 2009c. "The Federal Reserve's balance sheet: an update". Speech at the Federal Reserve Board Conference on Key Developments in Monetary Policy, Washington, DC.

Bernanke, B. 2009d. "Federal Reserve policies to ease credit and their implications for the Fed's balance sheet". Speech at the National Press Club Luncheon, Washington, DC.

Bernanke, B. 2009e. "Frequently asked questions". Economic Club of Washington, DC, Washington DC.

Bernanke, B. 2010. "The economic outlook and monetary policy". Speech at the Federal Reserve Bank of Kansas City Economic Symposium, Jackson Hole, WY.

Bernanke, B. 2012. Transcript of Chairman Bernanke's Press Conference April 25, Board of Governors of the Federal Reserve System.

Bernanke, B. 2013. *The Federal Reserve and the Financial Crisis.* Princeton, NJ: Princeton University Press.

Bernanke, B. 2014. "A conversation: the Fed yesterday, today and tomorrow". Brookings Institution, 16 January.

Bernanke, B. 2015a. *The Courage To Act: A Memoir of a Crisis and Its Aftermath*. New York: Norton.

Bernanke, B. 2015b. "Why are interest rates so low? Part 4: term premiums". Brookings Institution, 13 April.

Bernanke, B. 2015c. "Federal Reserve policy in an international context". Speech at the Sixteenth Jacques Polak Annual Research Conference, Unconventional Monetary and Exchange Rate Policies hosted by the IMF, Washington, DC.

Bernanke, B. 2015d. "Federal Reserve policy in an international context". Mundell–Fleming Lecture, Sixteenth Jacques Polak Annual Research Conference hosted by the IMF, Washington, DC.

Bernanke, B. 2016a. "What tools does the Fed have left? Part 1: negative interest rates". Brookings Institution, 18 March.

Bernanke, B. 2016b. "What tools does the Fed have left? Part 2: targeting longer-term interest rates". Brookings Institution, 24 March.

Bernanke, B. 2016c. "What tools does the Fed have left? Part 3: helicopter money". Brookings Institution, 11 April.

Bernanke, B. 2017a. "Some reflections on Japanese monetary policy". Brookings Institution, 24 May.

Bernanke, B. 2017b. "Monetary policy in a new era". Speech at conference on Rethinking Macroeconomic Policy, Peterson Institute, Washington, DC.

Bernanke, B. 2017c. "Temporary price-level targeting: an alternative framework for monetary policy". Brookings Institution, 12 October.

Bernanke, B. 2018. "Conversation at Lessons Learned From 10 Years of Quantitative Easing". American Enterprise Institute.

Bernanke, B. 2019. "Evaluating lower-for-longer policies: temporary price-level targeting". Brookings Institution, 21 February.

Bernanke, B. 2020. "The new tools of monetary policy", American Economic Association Presidential Address.

Bevilaqua, J. & F. Nechio 2016. "Fed policy liftoff and emerging markets". FRBSF Economic Letter.

Bhattarai, S. & C. Neely 2016. "A survey of the empirical literature on U.S. unconventional monetary policy". Research Division Federal Reserve Bank of St. Louis Working Paper series.

Blanchard, O. & J. Simon 2001. "The long and large decline in U.S. output volatility". *Brookings Papers on Economic Activity* 32(1), 135–74.

Blanchard, O., J. Ostry & A. Ghosh 2013. "Overcoming the obstacles to international macro policy coordination is hard". *Vox EU*. https://voxeu.org/article/obstacles-international-macro-policy-coordination.

Blinder, A. 2013. *After the Music Stopped*. London: Penguin.

Bloomberg 2018. "ECB wins EU top court fight over legality of QE program".

Board of Governors of the Federal Reserve System 2010. FOMC Minutes, 2–3 November.

Board of Governors of the Federal Reserve System 2019. Monetary Policy Report, 22 February, Washington, DC.

Bordo, M. 2017. "The operation and demise of the Bretton Woods system: 1958 to 1971". *Vox EU*. https://voxeu.org/article/operation-and-demise-bretton-woods-system.

Borio, C. 2011. "Central banking post-crisis: what compass for uncharted waters?" BIS Working Papers No. 353.

Borio, C. 2012. "The financial cycle and macroeconomics: what have we learnt?" BIS Working Papers No. 395.

Borio, C. & A. Filardo 2007. "Globalisation and inflation: new cross-country evidence on the global determinants of domestic inflation". BIS Working Papers No. 227.

Borio, C. & A. Zabai 2016. "Unconventional monetary policies: a re-appraisal". BIS Working Papers No. 570.

Bowman, D. *et al.* 2011. "Quantitative easing and bank lending: evidence from Japan". International Finance Discussion Papers 1018, Board of Governors of the Federal Reserve System (US).

Bowman, D., J. Londono & H. Sapriza 2014. "US unconventional monetary policy and transmission to emerging market economies". International Finance Discussion Papers, Board of Governors of the Federal Reserve System.

Brainard, L. 2015a. Remarks on "Unconventional monetary policy and cross-border spillovers". The Sixteenth Jacques Polak Annual Research Conference sponsored by the IMF, Washington, DC.

Brainard, L. 2015b. "Unconventional monetary policy and cross-border spillovers". The Sixteenth Jacques Polak Annual Research Conference sponsored by the IMF, Washington, DC.

Brainard, L. 2017. "Cross-border spillovers of balance sheet normalization". National Bureau of Economic Research's Monetary Economics Summer Institute, Cambridge, USA.

Brainard, L. 2019. "Navigating cautiously". Remarks at the Julis-Rabinowitz Center for Public Policy and Finance and the Bendheim Center for Finance, Woodrow Wilson School of Public and International Affairs, Princeton University, New Jersey.

Brave, S. & R. Butters 2011. "Monitoring financial stability: a financial conditions index approach". *Economic Perspectives*, Federal Reserve Bank of Chicago Q1, 22–43.

Broadbent, B. 2018. "The history and future of QE". Speech to the Society of Professional Economists, London.

Brunner, K. & A. Meltzer 1973. "Mr. Hicks and the monetarists". *Economica* 40(157): 43–9.

Brunnermeier, M., H. James & J.-P. Landau 2016. *The Euro and the Battle of Ideas*. Princeton, NJ: Princeton University Press.

Brunnermeier, M. & Y. Koby 2019. "The reversal interest rate". Submitted.

Buiter, W. & E. Rahbari 2015. "High time to get low: getting rid of the lower bound on nominal interest rates". Citi Research.

Buiter, W. & A. Sibert 2007. "The central bank as the market maker of last resort: from lender of last resort to market maker of last resort". *Vox EU*. https://voxeu.org/article/subprime-crisis-what-central-bankers-should-do-and-why.

Bull, A. 2009. "FED Focus – Fed seen extending, not increasing Treasury buys". Thomson Reuters, 16 June.

Bullard, J. 2019. "When quantitative tightening is not quantitative tightening". Federal Reserve Bank of St. Louis.

Bunn, P., P. Mizen & P. Smietanka 2018a. "Growing pension deficits and the expenditure decisions of UK companies". Bank of England Staff Working Paper No. 714, February.

Bunn, P., A. Pugh & C. Yeates 2018b. "The distributional impact of monetary policy easing in the UK between 2008 and 2014". Bank of England Staff Working Paper No. 720, March.

Business Insider 2010. "Full text of the letter where House and Senate Republicans attack the Fed over QE".

Carney, M. 2019a. "Pull, push, pipes: sustainable capital flows for a new world order". Speech at the Institute of International Finance Spring Membership Meeting, Tokyo.

Carney, M. 2019b. "The growing challenges for monetary policy in the current international monetary and financial system". Speech given at the Jackson Hole Symposium.

Carney, M. 2020. "A framework for all seasons?" Bank of England Workshop on the Future of Inflation Targeting.

Carstens, A. 2015. "Challenges for emerging economies in the face of unconventional monetary policies in advanced economies". Stavros Niarchos Foundation Lecture, Washington, DC.

Chen, Q. *et al.* 2012. "International spillovers of central bank balance sheet policies", BIS Papers chapters, vol. 66, 220–64.

Chitu, L. & D. Quint 2018. "Emerging market vulnerabilities – a comparison with previous crises". ECB Economic Bulletin 8.

Christensen, J. & G. Rudebusch 2012. "The response of interest rates to U.S. and U.K. quantitative easing". Federal Reserve Bank of San Francisco Working Paper Series.

Christensen, J. & G. Rudebusch 2013. "Modelling yields at the zero lower bound: are shadow rates the solution?" Federal Reserve Bank of San Francisco Working Paper Series.

Churm, R. *et al.* 2015. "Unconventional monetary policies and the macroeconomy: the impact of the United Kingdom's QE2 and Funding for Lending Scheme". Bank of England Staff Working Paper No. 542.

Clarida, R., J. Galí & M. Gertler 2000. "Monetary policy rules and macroeconomic stability: evidence and some theory". *Quarterly Journal of Economics* 115, 147–80.

Clarida, R. 2019. "The Federal Reserve's review of its monetary policy strategy, tools, and communication practices". Remarks at the 2019 US Monetary Policy Forum, New York.

Clouse, J. *et al.* 2000. "Monetary policy when the nominal short-term interest rate is zero". *BE Press Journal of Macroeconomics: Topics in Macroeconomics* 3(1): 1–65.

Coeure, B. 2017. "The international dimension of the ECB's asset purchase programme". Speech at the Foreign Exchange Contact Group meeting, Frankfurt.

Coeure, B. 2018. "The international dimension of the ECB's asset purchase programme: an update". Speech at a conference on Exiting Unconventional Monetary policies, Paris.

Coibion, O., Y. Gorodnichenko & M. Ulate 2018. "Real-time estimates of potential GDP: should the Fed really be hitting the brakes?" Center on Budget and Policy Priorities.

Constancio, V. 2018. "Past and future of the ECB monetary policy". Speech at the Conference on Central Banks in Historical Perspective: What Changed After the Financial Crisis? Malta.

Cour-Thimann, P. & B. Winkler 2012. "The ECB's non-standard monetary policy measures: the role of institutional factors and financial structure". *Oxford Review of Economic Policy* 28(4), 765–803.

Court of Justice of the European Union 2015. The OMT programme announced by the ECB in September 2012 is compatible with EU law.

Cova, P., P. Pagano & M. Pisani 2015. "Domestic and international macro-economic effects of the Eurosystem expanded asset purchase programme". Banca d'Italia Working Paper 1036.

Cribb, J. 2013. "Income inequality in the UK". Institute for Fiscal Studies.

Cunliffe, J. 2017. "The Phillips curve: lower, flatter or in hiding?" Speech to the Oxford Economics Society.

Cunliffe, J. 2019. "Financial stability and low for long". Bank of England.

Daines, M., M. Joyce & M. Tong 2012. "QE and the gilt market: a disaggregated analysis". Bank of England Working Paper No. 466.

D'Amico, S. *et al.* 2012. "The Federal Reserve's large-scale asset purchase programs: rationale and effects". Federal Reserve Board, Washington, DC.

D'Amico, S. & T. King 2011. "Flow and stock effects of large-scale Treasury purchases". Federal Reserve Board, Washington, DC.

Davies, G. 2016. "What investors should know about R star". *Financial Times* blog.

Davies, G. 2019. "What you need to know about modern monetary theory". *Financial Times* blog.

Debelle, G. & S. Fischer 1994. "How independent should a central bank be?" Conference Series [Proceedings] 38, 195–225.

Debelle, G. 2017. "Central bank independence in retrospect". Address at "Bank of England Independence: 20 Years On" conference, London.

De Haan, J. & W. Kooi 1997. "What really matters: conservativeness or independence?" *Banca Nazionale del Lavoro Quarterly Review* 50(200), 23–38.

Dell' Ariccia, G., P. Rabanal & D. Sandri 2018. "Unconventional monetary policies in the euro area, Japan, and the United Kingdom". Hutchins Center Working Paper No. 48. Brookings Institution.

Den Haan, W. *et al.* 2017. "Is the era of central bank independence drawing to a close?" *LSE Business Review* https://blogs.lse.ac.uk/businessreview/2017/01/10/is-the-era-of- central-bank-independence-drawing-to-a-close/

De Santis, R. 2016. "Impact of the asset purchase programme on euro area government bond yields using market news". European Central Bank Working Paper Series No. 1939.

DiMartino, D. & J. Duca 2007. "The rise and fall of subprime mortgages". Economic Letter, Insights from the Federal Reserve Bank of Dallas.

Draghi, M. 2012. "Verbatim of the remarks made by Mario Draghi". Speech at the Global Investment Conference, London.

Draghi, M. 2018. "Central bank independence", First Lamfalussy Lecture, Banque Nationale de Belgique, Brussels.

Draghi, M. 2019a. European Central Bank press conference, Frankfurt, July.

Draghi, M. 2019b. European Central Bank press conference, 12 September, Frankfurt.

Draghi, M. 2019c. Remarks at farewell event in his honour.

Dubrowski, M. 2018. "Is this time different? Reflections on recent emerging-market turbulence". Bruegel blog post.

Duca, J. 2013. "Subprime mortgage crisis". Federal Reserve History.

Dudley, B. 2010. "The outlook, policy choices and our mandate". Remarks at the Society of American Business Editors and Writers Fall Conference, City University of New York, Graduate School of Journalism, New York.

Dudley, B. 2019. "Stop worrying about the Fed's balance sheet". Bloomberg Opinion.

Dynan, K., D. Elmendorf & D. Sichel 2005. "Can financial innovation help to explain the reduced volatility of economic activity?" FEDs Working Paper No. 2005–54.

The Economist 2008. "A \$586 billion stimulus plan for China's economy: China seeks stimulation".

The Economist 2016. "The Mundell–Fleming trilemma: two out of three ain't bad".

The Economist 2019a. "Money markets and the Fed: hitting the ceiling".

The Economist 2019b. "Money markets: making the world go round".

Eichengreen, B. 1996. *Globalizing Capital: A History of the International Monetary System*. Princeton, NJ: Princeton University Press.

El-Erian, M. 2017. *The Only Game In Town*. New Haven, CT: Yale University Press.

El-Erian, M. 2019. "Investors in Europe should hunker down for trouble ahead". *Financial Times*.

Elliott, L. 2015. "Is Jeremy Corbyn's policy of 'quantitative easing for people' feasible?" *The Guardian*. 14 August.

European Central Bank 2010. "The 'Great Inflation': lessons for monetary policy". ECB Monthly Bulletin, May.

European Central Bank 2015. Introductory statement to the press conference (with Q&A), 22 January 2015.

European Central Bank 2016. Introductory statement to the press conference (with Q&A), 10 March 2016.

European Central Bank 2019. "Taking stock of the Eurosystem's asset purchase programme after the end of net asset purchases". Prepared by Felix Hammermann, Kieran Leonard, Stefano Nardelli and Julian von Landesberger.

Faria-e-Castro, M. 2018. "Fed payments to Treasury and rising interest rates". Federal Reserve Bank of St. Louis "On the Economy" blog.

Federal Reserve Bank of San Francisco (FRBSF) 2008. "Dr. Econ, what is the relevance of the Phillips curve to modern economies?" *Fed Education*, March. www.frbsf.org/education/ publications/doctor-econ/2008/march/phillips-curve-inflation.

Ferguson, R. 2000. "Technology, macroeconomics, and monetary policy". Remarks by Roger W. Ferguson, Jr. at the Rochester Institute of Technology, New York.

Financial Stability Board 2012. "Securities lending and repo: market overview and financial stability issues". Basel, April.

Financial Stability Board 2020. "Global Monitoring Report on Non-Bank Financial Intermediation 2019". January. www.fsb.org/2020/01/global-monitoring-report-on-non-bank-financial-intermediation-2019/

Financial Times 2010. "Fed critics run risk their attacks will backfire". 6 December.

Financial Times 2015a. "European Central Bank unleashes quantitative easing". 22 January.

Financial Times 2015b. "How Europe's power couple split over QE". 23 January.

Financial Times 2016. "Germany blames Mario Draghi for rise of rightwing AfD party". 10 April.

Financial Times 2017a. "Bundesbank chief Weidmann calls for end to ECB stimulus". 5 April.

Financial Times 2017b. "Jens Weidmann fuels debate on ending ECB monetary stimulus". 26 Janaury.

Financial Times 2017c. "Draghi refuses to call end to ECB crisis measures". 26 October.

Financial Times 2019a. "The Bank of Japan risks falling out of sync on global easing". 5 August.

Financial Times 2019b. "BoJ's dominance over ETFs raises concern on distorting influence". 31 March.

Financial Times 2019c. "Backlash against ECB stimulus is misplaced". 17 September.

Financial Times 2019d. "Germany pulls back from recent overt criticism of ECB". 1 December.

Financial Times 2019e. "Brexit is a warning to Germany's ECB-bashers". 5 November.

Financial Times 2019f. "Germany's ECB nominee expresses doubts over fresh bond buying". 3 December.

Financial Times 2019g. "Why is the Federal Reserve pouring money into the financial system?" 17 September.

Financial Times 2019h. "Eurozone wakes up to ECB's fiscal message as economy weakens". 16 September.

Financial Times 2019i. "How the Federal Reserve could fix the repo market". 2 October.

Financial Times 2019j. "Repo glitches expose flaws in Fed's approach". 4 October.

Financial Times 2019k. "'Repo ructions highlight failure of post-crisis policymaking". 5 November.

Fisher, P. 2010. "The corporate sector and the Bank of England's asset purchases". Speech to the Association of Corporate Treasurers.

FOMC 2019. Transcript of Chair Powell's press conference, 30 October.

Forbes, K. 2019. "Inflation dynamics: dead, dormant, or determined abroad?" BPEA Conference Draft, Fall.

Fratzscher, M., M. Lo Duca & R. Straub 2013. "On the international spillovers of US quantitative easing". ECB Working Paper Series No. 1557.

Friedman, M. 1969. *The Optimum Quantity of Money and other Essays*. Chicago, IL: Aldine.

Friedman, M. & A. Schwartz 1982. *Monetary Trends in the United States and the United Kingdom: Their relation to Income, Prices and Interest Rates, 1867–1975*. Chicago, IL: University of Chicago Press.

Gadanecz, B. & K. Jayarem 2015. "Macroprudential policy frameworks, instruments and indicators: a review". Bank for International Settlements.

Gagnon, J. *et al.* 2011. "The financial market effects of the federal reserve's large-scale asset purchases". *International Journal of Central Banking*, March.

Gagnon, J. 2016. "Quantitative easing: an underappreciated success". Peterson Institute for International Economics, Policy Brief.

Gagnon, J. & B. Sack 2018. "18–19 QE: a user's guide". Peterson Institute for International Economics, Policy Brief.

Gavin, W. 2018. "Monetary policy regimes and the real interest rate". *Federal Reserve Bank of St. Louis Review.*

Geithner, T. 2014. *Stress Test: Reflections on Financial Crises*. London: Random House Business.

Ghosh, A., J. Ostry & M. Qureshi 2016. "When do capital inflow surges end in tears?" *American Economic Review* 106(5): 581–5.

Giannone, D., M. Lenza & L. Reichlin 2008. "Explaining the Great Moderation: it is not the shocks". ECB Working Paper Series No. 865.

Giannone, G. *et al.* 2012. "Non-standard monetary policy measures and monetary developments". In J. S. Chadha & S. Holly (eds), *Interest Rates, Prices and Liquidity: Lessons from the Financial Crisis*, 195–221. Cambridge: Cambridge University Press..

Glick, R. & S. Leduc 2011. "Central bank announcements of asset purchases and the impact on global financial and commodity markets". Federal Reserve Bank of San Francisco Working Paper Series, Working Paper 2011–30.

Glick, R. & S. Leduc 2015. "Unconventional monetary policy and the dollar: conventional signs, unconventional magnitudes". Federal Reserve Bank of San Francisco Working Paper Series, Working Paper 2015–18.

Goodfriend, M. 1997. "Monetary policy comes of age: a 20th-century odyssey". *Federal Reserve Bank of Richmond Economic Quarterly* 83(1).

Goodhart, C. 2010a. "The changing role of central banks". BIS Working Papers No. 326.

Goodhart, C. 2010b. "Money, credit and bank behaviour: need for a new approach". *National Institute Economic Review* 214: F73.

Goodhart, C. & J. Ashworth 2012. "QE: a successful start may be running into diminishing returns". *Oxford Review of Economic Policy* 28(4), 640–70.

Goodhart, C., E. Bartsch & J. Ashworth 2016. "Central banks and credit creation: the transmission channel via the banks matters". *Sveriges Riksbank Economic Review* 3, 55–68.

Goodhart, C. & R. Lastra 2018. "Potential threats to central bank independence". In S. Eijffinger & D. Masciandaro (eds), *Hawks and Doves: Deeds and Words – Economics and Politics of Monetary Policymaking*. VoxEU.

Gopinath, G. 2020. "Digital currencies will not displace the dominant dollar", *Financial Times* 6 January.

Greenlaw, D. *et al.* 2018. "A skeptical view of the impact of the Fed's balance sheet". NBER Working Paper No. 24687.

Greenspan, A. 1996. "The challenge of central banking in a democratic society". Remarks by Chairman Alan Greenspan at the Annual Dinner and Francis Boyer Lecture of the American Enterprise Institute for Public Policy Research, Washington, DC.

Greenspan, A. 1997. "Remarks at the 15th Anniversary Conference of the Center for Economic Policy Research at Stanford University", California.

Greenspan, A. 2001. Semi-annual monetary policy report to the US Congress.

Greenspan, A. 2002a. "Economic volatility". Remarks by Chairman Alan Greenspan at a symposium sponsored by the Federal Reserve Bank of Kansas City, Jackson Hole, WY.

Greenspan, A. 2002b. "Issues for monetary policy". Remarks before the Economic Club of New York.

Greenspan, A. 2005. Testimony of Chairman Alan Greenspan: Federal Reserve Board's semi-annual Monetary Policy Report to the Congress Before the Committee on Banking, Housing, and Urban Affairs, U.S. Senate.

Greenwood, J. 2017. "The Japanese experience with QE and QQE". *Cato Journal* 37(1).

Grilli, V., D. Masciandaro & G. Tabellini 1991. "Political and monetary institutions and public financial policies in the industrial countries". *Economic Policy* 6(13), 341–92.

Gross, W. 2010. "The Ring of Fire". PIMCO Investment Outlook.

Guardian 2009. "Obama signs $787bn economic stimulus bill". 17 February.

Guardian 2012. "Federal Reserve announces new monetary stimulus plan – US politics". 13 September.

Guardian 2018. "Labour to propose Bank of England remit to boost productivity". 19 June.

Guardian 2019a. "The AfD is gaining strength in Germany. A reformed EU can stop it". 3 September.

Guardian 2019b. "Labour to give Bank of England role in tackling climate crisis". 24 June.

Hakkio, C. 2013. "The Great Moderation 1982–2007". Federal Reserve History, 22 November.

Haldane, A. 2014. "Unfair shares". Speech at the Bristol Festival of Ideas, Bristol.

Haldane, A. *et al.* 2016. "QE: the story so far". Bank of England Working Paper No. 624.

Hamada, K. 2020. "Does inattention explain today's low inflation?" *Japan Times*. 3 January.

Hancock, D. & W. Passmore 2011. "Did the Federal Reserve's MBS purchase program lower mortgage rates?" Federal Reserve Board, Finance and Economics Discussion Series, Washington, DC.

Hauser, A. 2019. "Waiting for the exit: QT and the Bank of England's long-term balance sheet". Speech at the European Bank for Reconstruction and Development, London.

Hausman, J. & J. Wieland 2014. "Abenomics: preliminary analysis and outlook". *Brookings Papers on Economic Activity* 48(1): 1–76.

Hayashi, F. & E. Prescott 2002. "The 1990s in Japan: a lost decade". *Review of Economic Dynamics* 5(1), 206–35.

Helbling, T. 2012. "Commodities in BOOM". IMF Finance & Development.

Hesse, H., B. Hofmann & J. Weber 2017. "The macroeconomic effects of asset purchases revisited". BIS Working Papers No. 680.

Hilpert, H. 2003. "Japan: is the crisis over?" *CESifo Forum* 4(4): 49–61.

Holston, K., T. Laubach & J. Williams 2016. "Measuring the natural rate of interest: international trends and determinants". Federal Reserve Bank of San Francisco Working Paper Series.

IMF 2009. "'Lost Decade' in translation: what Japan's crisis could portend about recovery from the Great Recession". IMF Working Paper No. 282.

IMF 2010. "Managing the exit: lessons from Japan's reversal of unconventional monetary policy". IMF Working Paper No. 114.

IMF 2012a. "Bank of Japan's quantitative and credit easing: are they now more effective?" IMF Working Paper No. 2.

IMF 2012b. "2012 spillover report". Policy Papers, July.

IMF 2013a. "Unconventional monetary policies: recent experiences and prospects". Policy Papers, April.

IMF 2013b. "Unconventional monetary policies: recent experiences and prospects – background paper". Policy Papers, April.

IMF 2013c. "Global impact and challenges of unconventional monetary policies". Policy Papers, April.

IMF 2013d. "Global financial stability report: lower for longer". Global Financial Stability Report, October.

IMF 2014a. "Back to basics: what is monetarism?" *Finance & Development* 51(1).

IMF 2014b. "Emerging market volatility: lessons from the taper tantrum". IMF Staff Discussion Note.

IMF 2019. "Global financial stability report: lower for longer". Global Financial Stability Report, October.

Irwin, N. 2013. *The Alchemists: Inside the Secret World of Central Bankers.* London: Headline.

Issing, O. 2005. "Why did the Great Inflation not happen in Germany?" *Federal Reserve Bank of St Louis Review* 87(2), part 2.

Issing, O. 2010. "The development of monetary policy in the twentieth century – some reflections". Working Paper Research, National Bank of Belgium.

Issing, O. 2018. "The uncertain future of central bank independence". In S. Eijffinger & D. Masciandaro (eds), *Hawks and Doves: Deeds and Words – Economics and Politics of Monetary Policymaking.* VoxEU.

Ito, T. 1997. "Japan's economy needs structural change". *Finance & Development*, June 1997.

James, H. 2013. "International cooperation and central banks". *VoxEU.* https://voxeu.org/article/international-cooperation-and-central-banks.

Jevcak, A. 2014. "Monetary policy frameworks: gradual implementation of steadily evolving theory". ECFIN Economic Brief, European Commission.

Jordan, T. 2017. "Central bank independence since the financial crisis: the Swiss perspective". CFS Presidential Lectures, Frankfurt.

Joyce, M., M. Tong & R. Woods 2011a. "The United Kingdom's quantitative easing policy: design, operation and impact". *Bank of England Quarterly Bulletin* Q3.

Joyce, M. *et al.* 2011b. "The financial market impact of quantitative easing in the United Kingdom". *International Journal of Central Banking*, September.

Kan, K., Y. Kishaba & T. Tsuruga 2016. "Policy effects since the introduction of quantitative and qualitative monetary easing (QQE)". Bank of Japan.

Kapetanios, G. *et al.* 2012 "Assessing the economy-wide effects of quantitative easing". Bank of England Working Paper No. 443.

Keynes, J. 1964 [1936]. *The General Theory of Employment, Interest and Money.* New York: Harcourt, Brace.

Kiley, M. 2014. "The aggregate demand effects of short- and long-term interest rates". *International Journal of Central Banking* 10(4): 69–104.

King, M. 1997. "Changes in UK monetary policy: rules and discretion in practice". *Journal of Monetary Economics* 39: 81–97.

Kohn, D. 2009. "Central bank exit policies". Cato Institute's Shadow Open Market Committee meeting, Washington, DC.

Koijen, R. *et al.* 2019. "Inspecting the mechanism of quantitative easing in the euro area", Becker Friedman Institute For Economics At The University Of Chicago, Working Paper No. 2019–100.

Koo, R. 2009. *The Holy Grail of Macroeconomics: Lessons from Japan's Great Recession.* Chichester: Wiley.

Krishnamurthy, A. & A. Vissing-Jorgensen 2011. "The effects of quantitative easing on interest rates: channels and implications for policy". *Brookings Papers on Economic Activity* 42(2): 215–87.

Krishnamurthy, A. & A. Vissing-Jorgensen 2013. "The ins and outs of LSAPs". 16 September draft.

Krishnamurthy, A., S. Nagel & A. Vissing-Jorgensen 2017. "ECB policies involving government bond purchases: impact and channels". NBER Working Paper 23985.

Krugman, P. 1998. "It's baaack: Japan's slump and the return of the liquidity trap". *Brookings Papers on Economic Activity* 29(2), 137–206.

Krugman, P. 2012. "Earth to Ben Bernanke: Chairman Bernanke should listen to Professor Bernanke". *New York Times Magazine.* 29 April.

Krugman, P. 2012. *End This Depression Now!* New York: Norton.

Krugman, P. 2014. "Inflation targets reconsidered". ECB Forum on Central Banking, Portugal.

Krugman, P. 2015. "Economic forum: policy lessons and the future of unconventional monetary policy". Sixteenth Jacques Polak Annual Research Conference, Unconventional Monetary and Exchange Rate Policies, Washington, DC.

Krugman, P. 2019a. "After Draghi (Wonkish)". *New York Times.* 24 May.

Krugman, P. 2019b. "Running on MMT (Wonkish)". *New York Times.* 25 February.

Kuroda, H. 2013a. "Quantitative and qualitative monetary easing". Speech at a meeting of the Yomiuri International Economic Society, Tokyo.

Kuroda, H. 2013b. "Quantitative and qualitative monetary easing". Remarks at the International Council Meeting of the Bretton Woods Committee.

Kuroda, H. 2016a. "Introduction of quantitative and qualitative monetary easing with a negative interest rate". Speech at the Kisaragi-kai meeting, Tokyo.

Kuroda, H. 2016b. "Answers to frequently asked questions on 'Quantitative and qualitative monetary easing (QQE) with a negative interest rate'". Speech at meeting of the Yomiuri International Economic Society, Tokyo.

Kuroda, H. 2016c. "'Comprehensive assessment' of the monetary easing and 'QQE with yield curve control'". Speech at meeting with business leaders in Osaka.

Kuroda, H. 2016d. "Quantitative and qualitative monetary easing (QQE) with yield curve control". New Monetary Policy Framework for Overcoming Low Inflation. Speech at the Brookings Institution, Washington, DC.

Kuroda, H. 2017. "Quantitative and qualitative monetary easing and economic theory". Speech at the University of Zurich, Switzerland.

Kuttner, K. 2014. "Monetary policy during Japan's great recession: from self-induced paralysis to Rooseveltian resolve". Williams College, PIIE and NBER.

Kuttner, K. 2018. "Outside the box: unconventional monetary policy in the great recession and beyond", Hutchins Center Working Paper No. 47, Brookings Institute.

Kydland, F. & E. Prescott 1977. "Rules rather than discretion: the inconsistency of optimal plans". *Journal of Political Economy* 85(3), 473–91.

Lane, P. 2019. "The international transmission of monetary policy". Keynote speech at the CEPR International Macroeconomics and Finance Programme meeting.

Lavigne, R., S. Sarker & G. Vasishtha 2014. "Spillover effects of quantitative easing on emerging-market economies". Bank of Canada Review, Autumn.

Lenza, M. & J. Slacalek 2018. "How does monetary policy affect income and wealth inequality? Evidence from quantitative easing in the euro area". ECB Working Paper Series.

Liu, Z., M. Spiegel & J. Zhang 2019. "Optimal capital account liberalization in China". Federal Reserve Bank of San Francisco Working Paper Series.

Liu, L. 2016. "Home is where your cash flows are? UK-focused equities and the international exposure of the FTSE All-Share". Bank Underground.

Lo Duca, M., G. Nicoletti & A. Vidal Martinez 2014. "Global corporate bond issuance: what role for us quantitative easing?" ECB Working Paper No. 1649.

Malekan, O. 2018. "I created 'The Bernank' on YouTube. And I was mostly wrong". *New York Times*. 1 October.

Marshall, P. 2015. "Central banks have made the rich richer". *Financial Times*.

May, T. 2016. "The new centre ground". Keynote speech at Conservative Party conference in full. *Independent*.

McCauley, R. & K. Ueda 2009. "Government debt management at low interest rates". *BIS Quarterly Review*, June.

McCulley, P. & Z. Pozsar 2013. "Helicopter money: or how I stopped worrying and love fiscal-monetary cooperation", GIC Global Society of Fellows.

Mckinsey Global Institute 2013. "QE and ultra-low interest rates: distributional effects and risks". Discussion paper.

Merler, S. & J. Pisani-Ferry 2012. "Who's afraid of sovereign bonds?" *Bruegel Policy Contribution* (2012)2. www.bruegel.org/wp-content/uploads/imported/publications/pc_2012_02_debt_.pdf

Mersch, Y. 2016. "The ECB and the Federal Reserve – an ocean apart?" Speech at Harvard University, USA.

Meyer, L. 2001. "The global outlook and challenges facing central banks around the world". Edinburgh Finance and Investment Seminar.

Miles, D. 2012. "Winding and unwinding extraordinary monetary policy". Speech at RBS Scottish Economic Society Annual Lecture, Edinburgh.

Munchau, W. 2019. "The unbreakable, unsustainable eurozone". *Financial Times*. 28 April.

Neely, C. 2011. "The large-scale asset purchases had large international effects". Research Division Federal Reserve Bank of St. Louis Working Paper Series.

Ng, M., D. Wessel & L. Sheiner 2018. "The Hutchins Center explains: the Phillips Curve". Brookings Institution, 21 August.

Nicoletti, G., K. Wacker & D. Lodge 2014. "Measuring financial conditions in major non-euro area economies". Working Paper Series 1743, European Central Bank.

Nikkei Asian Review 2018. "It's official: Japan enjoys its second-longest postwar expansion".

OECD 2002. "Gini Index". *Glossary of Statistical Terms*. https://stats.oecd.org/glossary/detail.asp?ID=4842

OECD 2019. Household financial assets (indicator). doi: 10.1787/7519b9dc-en (accessed on 7 October 2019).

Office for National Statistics 2019. "UK private rented sector, 2018". London: ONS.

Orphanides, A. 2000. "The quest for prosperity without inflation". ECB Working Paper Series, WP No. 15.

Orphanides, A. 2001. "Monetary policy rules based on real time data". *American Economic Review* 91(4), 964–85.

Orphanides, A. 2002. "Monetary policy rules and the great inflation". Board of Governors of the Federal Reserve System.

Orphanides, A. 2003. "Historical monetary policy analysis and the Taylor rule". Board of Governors of the Federal Reserve System.

Packer, F., R. Stever and C. Upper 2007. "The covered bond market". *BIS Quarterly Review*, September.

Panizza, U. & C. Wyplosz 2016. "The folk theorem of decreasing effectiveness of monetary policy: what do the data say?" Paper prepared for the Seventeenth Jacques Polak Annual Research Conference, Washington, DC.

Pew Research Center 2017. "More U.S. households are renting than at any point in 50 years".

Phillips, A. 1958. "The relation between unemployment and the rate of change of money wage rates in the United Kingdom, 1861–1957". *Economica* 25(100): 283–99.

Piketty, T. 2014. *Capital in the Twenty-First Century*. Cambridge, MA: Harvard University Press.

Posen, A. 2015. "Policy lessons and the future of unconventional monetary policy". Economic Forum at the Sixteenth Jacques Polak Annual Research Conference, Unconventional Monetary and Exchange Rate Policies, Washington, DC.

Powell, J. 2013. "Advanced economy monetary policy and emerging market economies". At Federal Reserve Bank of San Francisco Asia Economic Policy Conference: Prospects for Asia and the Global Economy, San Francisco, CA.

Powell, J. 2017. "Prospects for emerging market economies in a normalizing global economy". At the 2017 Annual Membership Meeting of the Institute of International Finance, Washington, DC.

Powell, J. 2018a. "Monetary policy influences on global financial conditions and international capital flows". At "Challenges for Monetary Policy and the GFSN in an Evolving Global Economy", Eighth High-Level Conference on the International Monetary System sponsored by the IMF and Swiss National Bank, Zurich.

Powell, J. 2018b. "Monetary policy at a time of uncertainty and tight labor markets". Remarks at an ECB Forum on Central Banking, Sintra, Portugal.

Powell, J. 2019a. "Challenges for monetary policy". Speech at the Challenges for Monetary Policy symposium, sponsored by the Federal Reserve Bank of Kansas City, Jackson Hole, WY.

Powell, J. 2019b. "Monetary policy: normalization and the road ahead". Remarks at the 2019 SIEPR Economic Summit, California.

Powell, J. 2019c. "The economic outlook". Testimony before the Joint Economic Committee, US Congress, Washington, DC.

Praet, P. 2018. "Maintaining price stability with unconventional monetary policy". Speech at the Council of the European Union, Brussels.

Rachel, L. & T. Smith 2015. "Secular drivers of the global real interest rate". Bank of England Staff Working Paper No. 571.

Rajan, R. 2014. "'Competitive monetary easing – is it yesterday once more?" Brookings Institution, Washington, DC.

Reuters 2010. "Obama returns fire after China slams Fed's move". 8 November.

Reuters 2013. "Fed's Williams: MBS purchases give bigger 'bang for the buck'" 16 May.

Reuters 2015. "Bundesbank's Weidmann casts doubt on effectiveness of ECB's QE". 24 January.

Reuters 2019. "ECB hawk Lautenschlager resigns amid policy backlash". 25 September.

Rey, H. 2013. "Dilemma not trilemma: the global financial cycle and monetary policy independence". Jackson Hole Conference, Federal Reserve Bank of Kansas City.

Rey, H. 2014. "International channels of transmission of monetary policy and the Mundellian trilemma". Presentation at the Fifteenth Jacques Polak Annual Research Conference, Washington, DC.

Rivlin, A. 2015. "Thoughts about monetary and fiscal policy in a post-inflation world". Brookings Institution, Washington, DC.

Rogers, J., C. Scotti & J. Wright 2014. "Evaluating asset-market effects of unconventional monetary policy: a cross-country comparison". International Finance Discussion Papers, Board of Governors of the Federal Reserve System.

Rogoff, K. 1985. "The optimal degree of commitment to an intermediate monetary target". *Quarterly Journal of Economics* 100, 1169.

Rogoff, K. 2016. *The Curse of Cash*. Princeton, NJ: Princeton University Press.

Rogoff, K. 2019. "Modern monetary nonsense". Project Syndicate.

Rosengren, E. 2019. "Central bank balance sheets: misconceptions and realities". Speech at Credit Suisse Asian Investment Conference.

Roth, A. & G. Wolff 2017. "What has driven the votes for Germany's right-wing Alternative für Deutschland?" Bruegel blog.

Rudebusch, G. 2010. "The Fed's exit strategy for monetary policy", FRBSF Economic Letter.

Samuelson, P. & R. Solow 1960. "Analytical aspects of anti-inflation policy". *American Economic Review* 50(2), 177–94.

Schnabel, I. 2020. "Narratives about the ECB's monetary policy – reality or fiction?" Speech at the Juristische Studiengesellschaft.

Schuele, F. & D. Wessel 2019. "What is u*". Brookings Institution, 6 March.

Selgin, G. 2019. "Reflections on the repo-market imbroglio". Cato at Liberty.

Selgin, G. 2020. "The menace of fiscal QE", Cato Institute.

Sheard, P. 2014. "A QE Q&A: everything you ever wanted to know about quantitative easing". S&P Global Ratings.

Sheard, P. 2017. "QExit Q&A: everything you ever wanted to know about the exit from quantitative easing". S&P Global Ratings.

Shirai, S. 2018a. "Time for the BOJ to reconsider the 2 percent inflation target". *Japan Times.*

Shirai, S. 2018b. "The Bank of Japan's super-easy monetary policy from 2013–2018". ADBI Working Paper series.

Shiratsuka, S. 2005. "The asset price bubble in Japan in the 1980s: lessons for financial and macroeconomic stability". *BIS Papers*, No. 21.

Shiratsuka, M. 2009. "Way out of economic and financial crisis: lessons and policy actions". Speech at Japan Society in New York, 23 April.

Shirikawa, M. 2012. "The Bank of Japan's efforts toward overcoming deflation". Speech at the Japan National Press Club, Tokyo.

Stock, J. & M. Watson 2003. "Has the business cycle changed? Evidence and explanations". Federal Reserve Bank of Kansas City symposium "Monetary Policy and Uncertainty", Jackson Hole, WY.

Sudo, N., Y. Okazaki & Y. Takizuka 2018. "Determinants of the natural rate of interest in Japan: approaches based on a DSGE model and OG model". Bank of Japan Working Paper Series, Review Series, and Research Laboratory Series.

Summers, L. 2017. "Central bank independence". Address at "Bank of England Independence: 20 Years On".

Summers, L. 2019. "The left's embrace of modern monetary theory is a recipe for disaster". *Washington Post*. 4 March.

Summers, L. & A. Stansbury 2019. "Whither central banking?" Project Syndicate.

Swanson, E. 2011. "Let's twist again: a high-frequency event-study analysis of Operation Twist and its implications for QE2". *Brookings Papers on Economic Activity* 42(1): 151–207.

Taylor, J. 1993. "Discretion versus policy rules in practice". *Carnegie-Rochester Conference Series on Public Policy* 39(1), 195–214.

Taylor, J. 1999. "A historical analysis of monetary policy rules". In J. Taylor (ed.), *Monetary Policy Rules*, 319–48. Chicago, IL: University of Chicago Press.

Taylor, J. 2007, "Housing and Monetary Policy", NBER Working Paper 13682.

Thoma, M. 2017. "Federal Reserve independence: the never-ending story". *Milken Institute Review.*

Trichet, J. 2009a. "The ECB's enhanced credit support". Keynote address by Jean-Claude Trichet, University of Munich.

Trichet, J. 2009b. "What lessons can be learned from the economic and financial crisis?" Speech at the "5e Rencontres de l'Entreprise Européenne" organized by La Tribune, Roland Berger and HEC, Paris.

Tucker, P. 2018. "Are we asking too much of central banks? Conversation with William B. English". Yale Insights.

Tucker, P. 2019. *Unelected Power*. Princeton, NJ: Princeton University Press.

Turner, A. 2013. "Debt, money and mephistopheles: how do we get out of this mess?" Speech at Cass Business School, London.

Turner, A. 2015. *Between Debt and the Devil*. Princeton, NJ: Princeton University Press.

Turner, A. 2019. "Central banks have lost much of their clout". *Financial Times*. 23 August.

Ueda, K. 2000. "Causes of Japan's banking problems in the 1990s". In T. Hoshi & H. Patrick (eds), *Crisis and Change in the Japanese Financial System*, 59–81. Dortrecht: Kluwer.

Ueda, K. 2010. "The Bank of Japan's experience with non-traditional monetary policy". Policy panel at the 55th Economic Conference of the Federal Reserve Bank of Boston, Revisiting Monetary Policy in a Low Inflation Environment.

Ueda, K. 2012. "Deleveraging and monetary policy: Japan since the 1990s and the United States since 2007". CIRJE Discussion Paper, University of Tokyo.

Ugai, H. 2006. "Effects of the quantitative easing policy: a survey of empirical analyses". Bank of Japan Working Paper Series.

Vogel, E. 1979. *Japan as Number One: Lessons for America*. Cambridge, MA: Harvard University Press.

Wakatabe, M. 2012. "Turning Japanese? Lessons from Japan's lost decade to the current crisis". Columbia Business School, Center on Japanese Economy and Business, Working Paper Series No. 309.

Walsh, C. 2004. "October 6, 1979". FRBSF Economic Letter.

Warsh, K. 2018. "The knowledge problem". Remarks at Lessons Learned From 10 Years of Quantitative Easing, American Enterprise Institute.

Weber, A. 2010. "Monetary policy after the crisis – a European persepctive". Speech at the Shadow Open Market Committee (SOMC) symposium, New York City.

White, W. 2012. "Ultra easy monetary policy and the law of unintended consequences". Federal Reserve Bank of Dallas Globalization and Monetary Policy Institute, Working Paper No. 126.

White, W. 2016. "Ultra-easy money: digging the hole deeper?" Adam Smith Prize Lecture, National Association of Business Economists, Atlanta, GA.

Williams, J. 2003. "The natural rate of Interest". FRBSF Economic Letter.

Williams, J. 2019. "Money markets and the federal funds rate: the path forward". Remarks at the MFA Outlook 2019, New York.

Wilson, D. 2008. "Research on the effects of fiscal stimulus: symposium summary". FRBSF Economic Letter.

Woodford, M. 2012. "Methods of policy accommodation at the interest rate lower bound". Paper presented to the Jackson Hole Symposium, August/September.

Woodward, B. 2001. *Maestro: Greenspan's Fed and the American Boom*. New York: Simon & Schuster.

Yellen, J. 2009. "U.S. monetary policy objectives in the short and long run". Presentation to the Andrew Brimmer Policy Forum, San Francisco.

Yellen, J. 2012a. "Revolution and evolution in central bank communications". Haas School of Business, University of California, Berkeley, CA.

Yellen, J. 2012b. "The economic outlook and monetary policy". Remarks at the Money Marketeers of New York University, New York.

Yellen, J. 2017. "A challenging decade and a question for the future". Remarks at the Herbert Stein Memorial Lecture, National Economists Club, Washington, DC.

YouTube 2010. "Quantitative easing explained". 11 November. www.youtube.com/watch?v=PTUY16CkS-k.

Yu, E. 2016. "Did quantitative easing work?" Economic Insights, Federal Reserve Bank of Philadelphia Research Department, First Quarter.

INDEX